Advance praise for *Rocking the Ages*

"*Rocking the Ages* is a tour-de-force perspective on social change. Drawing upon decades of the richest source of empirical data on American consumer attitudes and habits, Smith and Clurman have created a profound anthology of the times—past, present, and future.

Successful consumer-need-focused marketing and proactive product development require a profound understanding of the motivation for, and direction of, change in consumer attitudes and habits. *Rocking the Ages* is the most concise and authoritative treatise on change yet to be published."

—Michael Goldblatt, Vice-President, Science and Technology, McDonald's Corporation

"Matures. Silents. Boomers. Trailing Boomers. Xers. These are the market segments you will be able to effectively target after you have read *Rocking the Ages,* the best and most comprehensive source of information on the difference between the generations. Well written, well researched, well worth your attention."

—Al Ries, author of *Focus* and coauthor of *The Twenty-two Immutable Laws of Marketing*

"More than a decade of global marketing has taught us the value of culturally sensitive marketing. If national/regional differences could be called 'cultural variations in space,' then generational differences are 'cultural variations in time.' Together they comprise a space-time geography all marketers need to learn to navigate. The effects of generational change always seem obvious in retrospect. The view forward is rarely so clear. *Rocking the Ages* helps us discern those factors, from among the many, that will *make the future* we hope to succeed in. Past is prologue, but identifying which aspects of the past presage the future becomes easier after reading this book."

—Jim Spaeth, President, Advertising Research Foundation

"A terrific book. I'm giving a copy to everyone in my marketing organization around the world."

—Hal Rosenbluth, founder and CEO, Rosenbluth Travel

"To really understand what's going on in the playing field of customer contact, you sometimes need an aerial view. *Rocking the Ages* gives each of us on the sidelines the benefit of a sage, insightful coach in the press box with a very specialized set of binoculars. I heartily recommend this book to all business 'coaches.'"

—Jim McCann, President, 1-800-FLOWERS

"It is obvious to all that successful marketing will, in the future, require increasing personalization. This is a daunting challenge, particularly for companies lacking a robust transactional data base tied to values and attitudes. J. Walker Smith and Ann Clurman have provided a privileged and personalized look into the heads of Boomers, Xers, and Matures, offering a unique understanding of what makes them buy."

—Bruce Schnitzer, Chairman, Wand Partners, Inc.

"There are hundreds of books by 'brains,' but *Rocking the Ages* is the first one that takes you to the heart of what makes consumers tick. Thanks to the Yankelovich MONITOR® our clients have been kept in touch—with *Rocking the Ages* they'll be enlightened."

—Roger Milks, Chief Operating Officer/Director of Global Strategies, Bright House Consulting

ROCKING THE AGES

ROCKING
THE
AGES

- - - - - - -

THE YANKELOVICH REPORT ON GENERATIONAL MARKETING

- - - - - - -

J. WALKER SMITH AND
ANN CLURMAN

HarperBusiness
A Division of HarperCollins*Publishers*

HarperCollins books may be purchased for educational, business, or sales promotional use. For information please write: Special Markets Department, HarperCollins Publishers, Inc., 10 East 53rd Street, New York, NY 10022.

FIRST EDITION

Designed by Logo Studios

Library of Congress Cataloging-in-Publication Data

Smith, J. Walker.
    Rocking the Ages : the Yankelovich report on generational marketing / by J. Walker Smith and Ann Clurman.—1st ed.
        p.   cm.
    "A Division of HarperCollins Publishers"
    Includes index.
    ISBN 0-88730-813-9
    1. Marketing—United States. I. Clurman, Ann. II. Yankelovich Partners. III. Title.
HF5415.1.S57   1997
658.8—dc21   96-52509

98 99 00 01 ❖/RRD 10 9 8 7 6 5 4

—·—·—·—·—·—

To Ari, the next generation
and
To Joy, together, for generations to come

—·—·—·—·—·—

CONTENTS

- - - - - - -

ACKNOWLEDGMENTS

Writing this book was an intellectual adventure that could never have been completed without the assistance and inspiration of many people. Our sincerest thanks go out to all of you.

A special thanks goes to Dan Yankelovich, Arthur White, and Florence Skelly, the founders of our firm and the pioneers of generational marketing. Their spirit of fearlessness, brilliance, and innovation lives on at Yankelovich Partners and continues to spark our imaginations.

We would also like to thank our many clients over the years, too numerous to name. Every project, no matter how big or small, has furthered our learning and professional development. To our clients, most of all, thank you.

Thanks also to the directors of Yankelovich, whose patience and support enabled us to spend the time it took to finish this project: David Callard, Richard M. Clarke, Tom Hill, Bruce Schnitzer, and John Struck.

Several of our colleagues at Yankelovich helped with many of the specific ideas that fill these pages: John Gilfeather, Doug Haley, Amy Schafrann, Jennifer Aaron, Christine Schneider Baskin, Barbara Caplan, and Dawn Coley. Many others kept us on track with facts and figures, documents and proofs: Maurice Barton, Michelle DeLamielleure, Charles D'Oyly, Margaret Gardner, Lisa Fret, Steve Makadok, Michelle O'Neill, Barbara Patrick, Sharon Romer, Sage Serricchio, Caroline Wilkerson, and, most especially, Karen Culp, without whom much would have tottered these past few years. Thank you. And to everyone at Yankelovich, thanks for making our working days so collegial and invigorating.

Sandy Deutsch and Arthur Shapiro, from the good ol' days of YSW, thanks. Tom Flynn, for making the arrangments that made this possible at all, thanks. Marc Kramer, for all those long hours in '91 and '92 and '93, not forgotten, thanks.

Special thanks to Gloria and Herman Clurman, Judy and Bruce Ruben, Delia DeLisser, Denise Larson, Babi Sommer, Bernice Stacy, Richard Derus, and Virginia Sadock. And also to Joy Smith, Jack and Marjorie Smith, Marjorie Campbell, and Dorothy Smith.

The final manuscript would never have taken shape without the assistance of Framji Minwalla at HarperBusiness, whose dedicated attention to style and structure was immensely helpful. Thanks to everyone on our team at HarperBusiness, especially Adrian Zackheim, our publisher, who kept us going with his unflagging enthusiasm and tireless encouragement.

We accept all responsibility for what's written here, but we can't take all the credit for some of the most interesting parts. These kinds of ideas have been bubbling up at Yankelovich for almost four decades now. We just hope that our small contribution in this book can help keep this kind of creativity going for many decades, and for many generations more.

PREFACE

IT ALL STARTED WITH A GIRDLE

Florence Skelly was sitting in her office at Daniel Yankelovich, Inc., one morning in 1968 when she picked up the telephone to take a call that would forever change the way marketers think about their customers and their markets.

Yankelovich was a small research and consulting firm, specializing in the analysis and forecasting of market and social trends that could help businesses better anticipate the needs of their customers. By the late sixties, the firm had begun to notice a distinct transformation in the marketplace. Ongoing strategic research into consumer motivations was turning up some unusual findings. And the firm's clients kept saying that something new was happening that they did not yet understand.

Marketers were aware of the winds of change. They were hearing about them from their children and from folk singers on the radio. They were seeing bright young adults dropping out of school to tune in and turn on. They were witnessing a declining interest in white collar careers, accompanied by the rising popularity of experimental lifestyles. They were watching as tradition and authority were flouted and new styles of fashion and homemaking and brand buying were flaunted.

At Yankelovich, we were seeing the first manifestations of these value changes and were learning more about the underlying dynamics as we talked in depth with consumers. New attitudes toward the marketplace were emerging. The traditional conformity and loyalty that had supported the creation of major consumer products brands no longer held. It wasn't clear yet what, if anything, was taking their place. The stage was set for that fateful telephone call.

On the other end of Florence's telephone line that day was the president of Playtex telling her that his own wife had thrown away her girdle. She remembers his concern and dismay, as she searched for an answer to the question he put to her: "What does this mean for my business?"

It wasn't just his wife. Women across the country were throwing away their girdles, and sales at Playtex, the industry's leading manufacturer of intimate wear for women, were, well, sagging. The forces transforming the marketplace for hundreds of products were also bringing change to Playtex.

Questions were being asked in corporate suites across the country as marketers, advertising executives, and operating officers tried to understand what was taking place. Who is out there buying? What are they thinking? Do I have to pay attention to them? How deep do these new attitudes run? Will they last or are they just part of a passing fad?

The initial research for Playtex completed by Florence and her Yankelovich colleagues yielded no easy answers. It started with a traditional look at Playtex's execution of the Four P's of marketing, but each looked okay. The Product was fine, sturdy with plenty of support. The Price was right, a good value for the money. The Promotion was substantial, with advertising targeting every mother and daughter in the country. And the Places where the product could be found were plentiful, accessible, and attractive. Clearly some other factor was eroding the market.

Then Skelly and her associates began to examine this marketing problem from a different angle. *From a generational angle.* A new generation of Americans was coming of age in the late sixties, and they were roiling the waters of the marketplace. Certainly there had been changes and reversals in consumer behavior before, but nothing as deep and perplexing as the kinds that were starting to occur in the sixties—changes that were rocking the very foundations of the loyalties consumers had for brands. Business leaders felt at sea, unsure of the course they should take.

At Yankelovich, our firm's senior consultants examined ways in which this sharp break in attitudes and values was affecting not only Playtex, but many of our other clients, from car manufacturers to travel businesses to spirits companies. They began to see an answer to Playtex's question of what these shifts meant to the bottom line. It had relevance to marketers across the country. The first clue had emerged and as they followed where it led, a whole new way of solving these kinds of marketing mysteries was created.

The new generation was casting old values aside and giving the old generation a fresh outlook on the marketplace. Playtex had built its marketing strategy by the book, focusing on its execution of the Four P's. But this textbook perspective on the marketplace was too restricted. It had missed something much more elemental: Under the influence of a new generation, traditional assumptions about fashion, appearance, and even virtue were undergoing radical transformation. This new generation of women had entered the marketplace with new opinions about what they wanted to wear. What had occurred was not a failure of marketing execution, but rather a shift in the underlying social values that determined how the new generation would respond to marketing efforts.

This new generation had some distinct ideas: Girdles were not comfortable. They were confining. Stodgy. Old-fashioned. Boomers just coming into their own as a power in the marketplace didn't want to wear them. When mothers tried to pass on esoteric girdle knowledge to their daughters, the daughters weren't listening. And in a seismic shift, the new freedoms demanded by the daughters were beginning to influence the buying habits of the mothers.

Skelly counseled Playtex on new strategies that would appeal to the needs and tastes of a new generation of women. For Playtex, this information translated into salvation, giving the company the direction it needed to modernize and better position its product. Stiff bone stays and rubber were abandoned. Softer, lighter, and more flexible fabrics were used. Playtex's sales snapped back.

UNDERSTANDING GENERATIONS

For other marketers the transformation was no less revolutionary. In examining the woes of girdle marketers, our firm had perfected a new tool for investigating and understanding consumer behavior, a tool based on generational marketing.

Generational marketing is a tool with powerful applications. Today, with multiple generations populating the marketplace— generations with vastly different values, motivations, and life experiences—smart marketers see that the Four P's alone are no longer sufficient. Understanding generational values and motivations has become essential because *each generation is driven by unique ideas about the lifestyle to which it aspires.* And it's these aspirations that determine the ways consumers spend and save their money. This is very different from the relatively homogeneous consumer marketplace of the immediate post–World War II era, a time when values and motivations were stable and centered around a shared vision of the American Dream.

The story about Playtex reminds us yet again of the first rule of marketing—know your customer. But in practice, this is hard advice to follow. The most difficult part is getting a handle on *exactly what it is about your customer that is the most important to know.*

This book is focused on one very important category of marketing knowledge—the mind-set of the generation to which your customers belong. By examining each of the generations active in the consumer marketplace today, this book will show you what you need to know about the generational experiences and values of your customers—how the experiences of a generation determine what they like and dislike, how they spend their money, and how they aspire to live their lives—in short, what their values are.

Only by knowing how the consuming motivations of your customers are tied to the underlying values of the generation to which they belong will you be able to tailor your products, services, and communications to their needs, interests, and desires. Applied knowledgeably, this will be a *key* source of competitive advantage for you.

Of course, understanding these generations will by no means answer every question about the marketplace. But it *will* answer core questions that have fundamental importance for your business. This perspective will give you the confidence it takes to avoid overreacting or underreacting to the forces buffeting the marketplace—in other words, confidence not to panic in the face of change.

For individual marketers, this will look like a broad picture, a view of the world from fifty thousand feet up. But it is still an informative perspective. The common experiences of a generation create a specific sensibility that touches each of its members in some way—that teaches its members what's funny, what's stylish, what's status, what's taboo, what works and what doesn't, what to aspire to and what to avoid. In statistical jargon, we say there is a "central tendency" within a generation that differentiates it from other generations. It is this tendency which has relevance for the marketing decisions that can make or break your business.

THE YANKELOVICH MONITOR

In the years since the Playtex call, Yankelovich has maintained a continuous study of the values and buying motivations of American consumers. We have come to understand them better than anyone else. And we have a unique method for doing so.

In 1971 we formalized our scrutiny and examination of values and buying motivations with the launch of the Yankelovich MONITOR®. This annual survey was the first, and remains the longest running and most complete, continuous tracking study of American values, lifestyles, and buying motivations. For over twenty-five years, we have been constantly probing the values and attitudes that make consumers tick. At the core of this research is an ongoing inquiry into the aspirations and expectations that make each American generation distinct—and the critical role that these factors play in shaping consumer trends.

To assemble the information, MONITOR surveys thousands of consumers sixteen years of age and older, in a nationally representative sample every year. Interviewers go to consumers' homes to conduct two-hour interviews face-to-face. And afterwards, consumers fill out another hour-long questionnaire that interviewers leave behind and return the next day to retrieve. Consumers are asked hundreds of questions across a broad range of subjects—advertising, government, books, education, food, appliances, technology, environment, finances, pets, charity, family, and travel, to name only a few. MONITOR gauges their confidence in themselves, their jobs and the economy, the control they feel they have over their lives, the things they associate with status and accomplishment, and the direction in which they feel they are going. And it tracks changes from year to year, now with a twenty-five-plus-year perspective on these trends.

This is an enormous amount of information, but it does not stop there. MONITOR is supplemented with other studies for which information is gathered in many other ways—in hundreds of telephone interviews, dozens of focus groups, and through on-line forums.

One special capability of MONITOR is something we call CnXn℠ (pronounced "connection"). This is a broad pool of thousands of respondents maintained in a separate panel. All have completed the MONITOR interview, and all have agreed to participate in further telephone surveys if and when we need to recontact them. Through CnXn we have the unique ability to go back to consumers about whom we already know a great deal, to ask them more detailed questions about narrower topics of particular interest to individual clients. We have done this often to delve more deeply into a wide range of business topics and marketing issues.

BLUEPRINT FOR SUCCESS

MONITOR itself, not to mention all of the supplementary work that builds off of it, is, quite simply, a blueprint for understanding the American consumer. It tracks our changing social climate and translates that data for marketers using many frameworks, but one in particular based on generational similarities and differences. This is a big part of exactly what you should know about your customers—*know the story of their generation(s)*.

Each generation bases its spending decisions on distinct values and attitudes. This book will give you the information you need to make your business decisions more closely tied to your customers' views of the marketplace. Our conclusion, based on years of research and analysis, is that generationally determined lifestyles and social values exercise as much or even more influence on buying and purchasing than do more commonly understood demographic factors like income, education, and gender.

Our track record is pretty good. By understanding generational transformations under way in America, we predicted early on the growth in natural foods and fibers, and the move toward less structured and more informal meals. A few years later, our generational analysis foretold the growth of catalog shopping and the drop in alcohol consumption. In the mid-1980's, we were prescient in understanding the generational changes creating new opportunities for premium products as well as those that later led to a decline in conspicuous consumption. Today, we foresee a renewed consumer enthusiasm for brands, retailers, and shopping, but with a totally new character and tone, one that we refer to as the "Possibility Agenda."

Technology, the economic climate, and competitive conditions are all vitally important in understanding the future direction of markets. But in today's rapidly changing environment, mastering each of those elements alone is not enough. New market trends wrought by generational differences are causing business upheavals, bringing new categories into being at warp speed, and causing old ones to shrink or disappear. Marketers who pay attention to generational marketing will thrive, just as Playtex did thirty years ago when it took the time to understand how generational factors were changing its customer base.

This book will provide you with the information you need to link each generation's values and motivations to the practical decisions you must make about products and advertising, about investments and strategies, about satisfying the needs and wants of your customers, and about fulfilling their future requirements. You will see how to find competitive advantage by *"rocking the ages"*— shaking up the marketplace through generational marketing.

SECTION 1

GENERATIONAL MARKERS

1

THE POWER OF GENERATIONS

There is an ancient proverb: "Men resemble the times more than they do their fathers." Within the wisdom of those words lie the seeds of generational marketing. Marketers who use the principles of generational marketing to understand the factors that influence the values and buying motivations of consumers stand a much better chance of spotting trends way ahead of the competition and reaching customers first in profitable new ways.

Members of a generation are linked through *the shared life experiences of their formative years*—things like pop culture, economic conditions, world events, natural disasters, heroes, villains, politics, and technology—experiences that create bonds tying the members of a generation together into what social scientists were the first to call "cohorts." Because of these shared experiences, cohorts develop and retain similar values and life skills as they learn what to hold dear and how to go about doing things. This affects everything from savings and sex to a good meal and a new car.

GENERATIONAL MARKETING

Generational marketing is a strategic business perspective that studies these cohort effects and highlights what's relevant for better business decision-making. Consider a couple of examples.

- When Betty Crocker introduced a line of completely ready-to-bake cake mixes in the 1950s, sales were disappointing. Those were the days of the stay-at-home mothers whom today we call the Matures. To Matures, who grew up in the Depression and sacrificed to achieve victory in World War II, hard work was a virtue. Anything too easy was suspect. Convenience seemed like cheating. Eventually, after applying this insight, Betty Crocker found success with a modified version that required adding an egg. This appealed to the Mature housewife's sense that a little work was a lot better.

- Seagram found sales of its whiskeys slipping in the early 1970s. The reason: Baby Boomers weren't drinking as much as their parents. Mainly, though, they were in a hurry. Boomers were too impatient to "learn" to enjoy liquor or to wait to develop a taste for scotch. After some trenchant marketing research determined that young people were looking for something easier to drink, Seagram responded by concentrating its marketing on a new line of white spirits, like vodka. These could be mixed with juices or sodas, and appealed to the Boomer demand for easy access to pleasure and enjoyment. Vodka did not demand an acquired taste.

As these examples illustrate, the marketplace always evolves in response to the different needs of each generation. The values, preferences, and behaviors of consumers can be understood—and shifts better predicted—by breaking down what accounts for them into three distinct elements: (1) Life stage, (2) Current social and economic conditions, and (3) Formative cohort experiences.

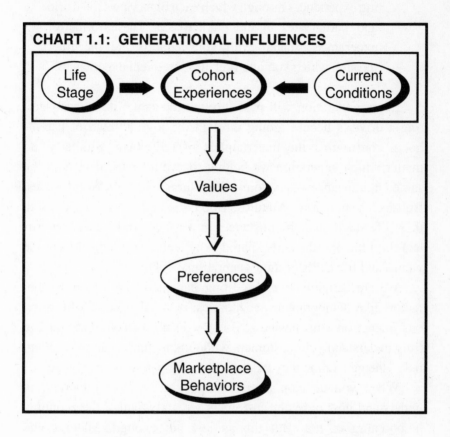

CHART 1.1: GENERATIONAL INFLUENCES

- *Life stage* is how old you are and, therefore, where you are in your life—physically or psychologically. We need different products and services as our responsibilities and requirements in life change.

- *Current conditions* are those events that affect what you can buy. Layoffs, recessions, import/export restrictions, political turmoil, technological innovations, taxes, and so forth, all set parameters within which consumers operate in the marketplace.

- Most influential, though, are the *formative cohort experiences* we all share as part of a generation. These create the habits that define and differentiate generations, the unifying experiences through which each of us views the world and participates in the marketplace. These formative experiences shared with your cohorts are the filter through which you interpret all subsequent experiences.

Every generation will pass through the same life stages—getting a driver's license, going through the joy and pain of parenthood, confronting the uncertainties of retirement. Similarly, no matter which generation we belong to, we all must deal with the same circumstances—economic downturns, wars, or World Series. But each generation—Matures, Boomers, and Xers—responds to these life stages and circumstances in ways determined by that critical third factor—the early shared experiences that helped form the values and life skills of their generational cohort.

We are certainly *not* suggesting that marketers ignore crucial factors like demographics, economics, or anything else with obvious impact on your business. But we do not believe that you can truly understand your customers without knowing what makes them tick—the generation they belong to is a big part of who they are.

When you develop a marketing strategy, it is important to understand how old your customers are and whether the economy is booming or not. But this is just not enough. Matures and Boomers have responded differently to economic recessions over the last two decades, recessions they have both faced at the same time. Same economic pressures, different consumption patterns. As we'll see, Boomers will look nothing like Matures when they reach retirement; Xers today look nothing like the Boomers of twenty or thirty years ago. Same life stages, different consumers. Generational marketing won't explain everything, but it will explain a lot, and help us better understand the ways in which different individuals will react very differently to the very same marketplace.

Borrowing loosely from social science terminology, we call the events that define a generation "markers." Think of markers as the key set of collective experiences that shape a generation's values and attitudes. These set the tone for a generation, give it direction, provide it with whatever sense of cohesion it has.

For the older generation, the Matures, some of the most significant markers are the Depression, the New Deal, World War II, and the GI Bill. For Boomers they include the Great Society, general economic prosperity and the expansion of suburbia, Nixon, color TV, and sex, drugs, and rock 'n' roll. For the current crop of young people, Generation X, they include divorce, AIDS, Sesame Street, MTV, crack cocaine, Game Boy, and the PC.

Markers help us see why past is not prologue. You make a mistake if you assume that just because your customers are turning a certain age they will behave in the same ways as those who turned that age before them. As obvious as this may seem, it is one of the most common mistakes made in marketing planning.

For instance, a marketer who bases sales and advertising strategy strictly on demographic data, like age, might assume that Baby Boomers will abandon the Rolling Stones and switch from Coca-Cola as they pass their fiftieth birthdays in the years ahead. This would have major implications for the music and beverage industries. However, a smart marketer who considers generational cohorts knows that these deeply implanted preferences are sticking with Boomers as they pass through each life stage.

Don't assume that Boomers will behave like Matures when they reach fifty. Life stage is not everything. When the Boomers began to turn thirty-five, predictions were rife that they would begin to save and become more conservative, politically and socially, just like their parents. It didn't happen. The Boomers rolled right on past thirty-five, remaining true to their free-spending, free-spirited ways. The habits acquired and formed early in life continued to shape their behavior. They did change their consuming, of course, but always in ways consistent with the core values characteristic of their generation. Yuppies, for example, were, deep down, driven by the same core values of fulfillment and self-enrichment as hippies.

Another common mistake is something we call "generational myopia," or the shortsighted application of the values and attitudes of your own generation to the development of strategies for marketing to another generation. We've seen this happen a lot—a marketer will misjudge events and motivations by applying the perspective of his or her generation without truly understanding the unique generational experience of a different target group of consumers. This is a recipe for failure. Each generation is shaped by different markers; you must walk with them in their shoes, not walk on them in your shoes.

MATURES, BOOMERS, AND XERS

Consumers active in today's marketplace can be divided, for all practical purposes, into three broad generations—Matures, Boomers, and Xers. Indeed, empirically, our MONITOR data verify that these are cohesive groups of consumers.

The Matures, born between 1909 and 1945, came of age under the shadows of the Great Depression, World War II, Korea, and the Cold War. Their attitudes toward life and work were formed in the crucible of economic upheaval, common enemies, and America's role as an emerging superpower. Matures grew up in tough times, so they had a more constrained set of expectations. As a result, their core values are what we think of today as traditional values—discipline, self-denial, hard work, obedience to authority, and financial and social conservatism.

These values still determine the way in which Matures relate to the marketplace. They have been slow to embrace new products. They saved their money and saw retirement and leisure time as rewards for hard work. Products that fit their basic values have succeeded—and will continue to succeed—because these values grew out of their shared experiences and still guide their consumption.

CHART 1.2: GENERATIONS AT A GLANCE

	MATURES	BOOMERS	Xers
Defining idea.........	DUTY	INDIVIDUALITY	DIVERSITY
Celebrating............	Victory	Youth	Savvy
Success because..	Fought hard and won	Were born, therefore should be a winner	Have two jobs
Style........................	Team player	Self-absorbed	Entrepreneur
Rewards because..	You've earned it	You deserve it	You need it
Work is...................	An inevitable obligation	An exciting adventure	A difficult challenge
Surprises in life......	Some good, some bad	All good	Avoid it— all bad
Leisure is...............	Reward for hard work	The point of life	Relief
Education is...........	A dream	A birthright	A way to get ahead
Future...................	Rainy day to work for	"Now" is more important	Uncertain but manageable
Managing money...	Save	Spend	Hedge
"Program" means..	Social program	Cult de-programmers	Software programs
Go watch...............	*The Best Years of Our Lives*	*The Big Chill*	*Reality Bites*

Born between 1946 and 1964, Baby Boomers are the most populous and influential generation in America. Born to prosperity in a time of booming postwar economic expansion, Boomers enjoyed unprecedented employment and educational opportunities. They took this for granted, and the shared assumption of affluence shaped their values and embroiled them in the tumult of events that filled the sixties and seventies. The value system of Boomers, the "Me Generation," was built on the sense of entitlement created by their presumption of continued economic growth. With little else to worry about, Boomers were able to be more self-absorbed, pursuing personal goals and instant gratification.

Indeed, while Matures came of age expecting little because of the sacrifices demanded by wars and the Depression, the overriding marker for Boomers was the economic prosperity of the postwar years, a prosperity that was so internalized that it has shaped all Boomer attitudes about the marketplace. Boomers could, for example, more easily embrace an inclusive social perspective because they assumed there was prosperity enough to make everybody a winner. Boomers believed there would always be plenty to go around—lots now and more and more in the future—so why not share with everyone.

Central to the story of Boomers over the last decade has been that their ingrained sense of entitlement has been overtaken by unmet expectations. This is particularly true for Boomers born in the last years of their cohort, the so-called Trailing Boomers. In general, though, all Boomers have had to learn to do with less, and the impact of this on the marketplace will be continue to be felt for the next twenty years.

The next group, Generation X, or Xers, could be dubbed the "Why Me?" generation. Born in the wake of the dominant Boomers, they have been buffeted by tumultuous political and economic conditions. They are wary and uncertain about America's position in the world and about their own place in America. Yet, contrary to the image portrayed by the popular media, this is a savvy generation, enthusiastically ready, willing, and able to take on the challenges they face.

For Xers, hard work is a pragmatic necessity and they tend to be careful in planning for the future. In many ways, Xers are embracing some of the values of Matures because they too have lived through uncertain formative years. For this reason, Xers seem better able to deal with economic downturns than their Boomer predecessors.

In the next three chapters, we will examine each of these generations, producing, in a sense, generational biographies that will establish a way to explore the specific marketing topics we will examine in the remainder of the book.

"AS CLOSE TO GOD AS WE GET"

Let's return to the proverb about men and their times. We know from social scientists that many early influences define how we think and behave. The key to understanding consumer behavior also lies in grasping the characteristics acquired when those consumers were young. Admittedly there are nuances within each generation—no individual person is their generation, lock, stock, and barrel. Some people change dramatically as they age, while others evolve less or remain the same. In addition, the interplay between generations can result in new needs that require new solutions. But the fundamental truth remains that marketers who recognize and seek to understand the impact of generationally based values on consumer habits will have an important competitive advantage over those who do not.

Indeed, it was a quest for understanding a new generation that contributed to the concept of generational marketing. Arthur White, one of the founders of Yankelovich Partners Inc., remembers the day in 1970 when he and Dan Yankelovich were summoned to Rockefeller Center by John D. Rockefeller III. Walking along the corridor on the fifty-sixth floor, he saw clouds swirling past the windows and, inside a grand office, one of the heirs to one of the greatest fortunes in American history. "This may be as close to God as we get," White whispered to Yankelovich.

But Rockefeller was not feeling very godlike that day. The previous summer he had seen a three-part documentary on CBS, called "Generations Apart." And it had disturbed him very much. Like millions of others, Rockefeller watched as the reporter talked, in a sonorous voice, of a "widening generation gap on attitudes toward sex, religion, drugs, and money." That term—the generation gap—over the years has become a permanent part of the nation's lexicon, a defining idea about those times.

"All through America," continued the reporter, "all around the world, there are young people who want to make things happen . . . To the older generation, it often seems the young lack a sense of history, lack a willingness or ability to recognize the great changes that have already taken place in our time. To the young, what has happened is irrelevant or inadequate. They see injustice remains; they're unsatisfied by justice gained . . . To attack the old invites repression. The old control the instruments of power. But to ignore or repress the young will not make them silent any more, nor docile, nor will it soften their hard view of the adult world. This is Walter Cronkite, CBS News."

This groundbreaking documentary was based on a nationwide survey for CBS conducted by our firm. So Rockefeller had summoned Messrs. White and Yankelovich to his office to discuss this new generation gap and the attitudes exhibited by the upcoming generation of Rockefellers and their peers. When they left the meeting, Arthur and Dan had a new assignment: Find ways in which business leaders could interact with this rebellious new generation of American youth.

The immediate result was a detailed and provocative three-hundred-page report. A more lasting result, however, was its impact on the way marketers think about marketing. The study marked another step in the evolution of generational marketing that began with the Playtex assignment. We had built a bridge between the esoteric world of social science and the commercial world of business. Marketers could now learn to make better strategic decisions about their brands by adding to their understanding of the marketplace knowledge of the generationally driven changes in values and lifestyles that shape the ways consumers spend and save. A new sophistication in marketing method had been born.

THE PAYOFF

Since the late sixties, and the Rockefeller study, this method has evolved and been refined. Over the years we have used generational marketing to help clients develop products and programs that are in tune with the present and poised for the future. In the early eighties, for example, we worked with a client, the publishers of a magazine called *Apartment Life*, to reposition the publication to catch the new wave of prosperous, independent Boomers. The country was emerging from the Reagan-era recession. Urban-oriented Boomers no longer wanted to live in cheap walk-ups, but neither were they ready to move to the suburbs. This had not been true of Matures before them, who had moved en masse into the newly created suburbs. To respond to this generationally driven shift, the magazine changed its name to *Metropolitan Home*, emphasizing a new luxuriousness and prestige in apartment living designed to appeal to this generation of newly prosperous Boomers.

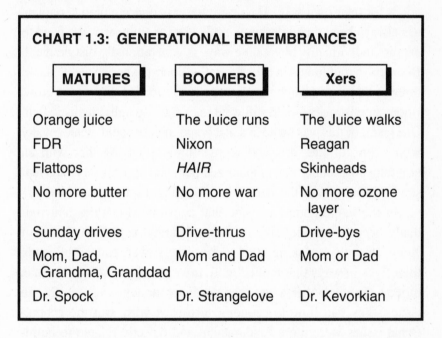

CHART 1.3: GENERATIONAL REMEMBRANCES

MATURES	BOOMERS	Xers
Orange juice	The Juice runs	The Juice walks
FDR	Nixon	Reagan
Flattops	*HAIR*	Skinheads
No more butter	No more war	No more ozone layer
Sunday drives	Drive-thrus	Drive-bys
Mom, Dad, Grandma, Granddad	Mom and Dad	Mom or Dad
Dr. Spock	Dr. Strangelove	Dr. Kevorkian

About the same time, we worked with another client to market do-it-yourself furniture to these same prospering Boomers, an assignment that also involved identifying the generational differences between Matures and Boomers. To Matures, do-it-yourself projects saved money and thus appealed to the value they placed on saving. This was not a Boomer value. So as these younger consumers became potential customers for our client, we searched for a new way to reach them. We identified an opportunity to link an interest in the home as a showplace to the generational priority Boomers have to show off their successes. Assembling and finishing your own furniture became, in this client's revised advertising campaign, a measure of status and accomplishment instead of a sign of thrift.

By the mid-eighties, we predicted that Boomers would move away from brand names as symbols of status and look instead for products that were more functional and utilitarian. This portended a shift away from the more traditional brand loyalty that had always characterized Matures. Boomers differed because, as a generation, they were never as single-mindedly focused as Matures on material goods for their own sake. The desire for experience, not materialism, has always been the underlying motivator for Boomers. The need to express individuality in creative ways is generationally distinctive to Boomers, a trait rooted in their formative cohort experiences. Thus we foresaw that even though the importance of functionality would grow, Boomer consumers would still want to express an individualistic flair. One result of this was the idea that a brand of beer could create loyalty with a line of lite, dry, and regular brews tied together with an umbrella positioning that emphasized personal expression as the reason for sticking with the same brand for all types of beer purchases.

In the late eighties, we saw that consumer lifestyles had suddenly become too cluttered and complicated, particularly those of Xers. Broadly speaking, these consumers were uncomplicating their lives in ways that looked more toward economizing time than money. From a life-stage perspective, money was hardly an issue—they had little to economize to start with. But the generational issues were more fundamental and directly related to building brand relationships with consumers at early ages.

From a generational marketing perspective, it is clear that Xers have a very different sense of the pace and intensity of life. This resonates with other generations too, but not in the same fundamental way. For Xers an accelerated pace is not just a fact, it is a given; not just a circumstance of the times, but a basic condition of life. The tools they use to deal with this are things like time-shifting technologies and protean fashions and styles. Back then we saw a

---

CHART 1.4: MORE GENERATIONAL REMEMBRANCES

MATURES	BOOMERS	Xers
The Golden Rule	Do bees and don't bees	Just say no
Red Square	Berlin Wall	Chernobyl
Bathtub gin	Acid	Crack
Pan Am Clipper Fleet	Pan Am Shuttle	Lockerbie
Electric chair	No death penalty	Lethal injections
How to Win Friends and Influence People	*I'm Okay, You're Okay*	*Men Are from Mars, Women Are from Venus*
"Are you now or have you ever been..."	"What's your sign?"	"Boxers or briefs?"

---

change coming in their definition of convenience—from the Matures' "do it quickly" and the Boomers' "do it efficiently" to their "eliminate the task." No longer, we forecasted, would consumers buy a different sneaker for every sport. Out of this shift in generationally driven values, cross-trainer athletic footwear was born.

REFUSE NOT TO KNOW

Your competition is already onto this. Yankelovich Partners was the pioneer of generational marketing, but others have used it over the years. Bill Backer, one of the greatest ad men of all time, was an early practitioner. Perhaps his greatest success was Coke's "Buy the World" ad campaign, featuring thousands of young people on a hillside in Italy singing, "I'd like to buy the world a Coke," an ad that the editors of *Advertising Age* recently voted as one of the fifty best TV spots in the history of advertising.

Many years later, Bill recalls that his goal in creating that ad was to improve Coke's approach to the market, which was at that time, in Bill's blunt opinion, simply "wrong." Its ads reflected "a view of the world held only by rich bottlers and stockholders," one that ignored the youth market because Coke's management felt it to be "a wasteland, degenerate and degrading." Moving the Coca-Cola Company into this market was a generational marketing undertaking that Bill says "nobody understood or wanted to learn." He recalls, though, with great satisfaction, how he undertook it, becoming in the process the "self-appointed Conrad who would take [Coke] into the heart of this jungle."

This perspective is still part of the practice at the agency that succeeded the shop Bill Backer helped launch years ago. Recently Bates USA restructured itself to match up its planning, creative, and account groups against consumer generational cohorts. A few savvy marketers got on top of this right away. As Bill Whitehead, the president and CEO, noted when announcing the completion of this restructuring, "We've seen it pay off in new business [for our agency] already." Indeed, Whitehead reminds us what his agency emphasizes to its clients—without an accurate view of generations, we are very likely to misinterpret what we see in the marketplace. "The popular view that the old are behaving younger is really mis-placed," says Bill. "It's rather that the young are becoming older, and those habits are sticking with them."

You need to know all about generations. The consumer market-place of today and tomorrow is no longer the homogeneous mar-ketplace of the fifties and early sixties that was dominated by Matures. Bill Backer started helping Coke when the Baby Boomer generation was coming of age and complicating the marketplace. Today's Xers have roiled the waters even further. The generational mix in the marketplace is greater now than ever before. And all of these generations are smarter, craftier shoppers than the shoppers of twenty or thirty years ago. In the next three chapters, we will profile each of these consumer generations, giving you the baseline information you will need to negotiate the challenges of the mar-ketplace and make your business succeed.

MATURES:
TRIUMPH AND CONFORMITY

They are Walt Disney and Bob Hope, Joe DiMaggio and John Steinbeck, Walter Cronkite and Ann Landers, Katharine Hepburn and Sidney Poitier. Matures were America's first Boy Scouts and Girl Scouts. Now they are the country's first "senior citizens."

On the journey from scout meetings to Sun City, this generation triumphed over the Great Depression, vanquished the Germans and the Japanese, and in the process built the suburbs and shopping malls of middle-class America. Under their stewardship, America developed miracle vaccines, instituted the New Deal, fueled an economic boom, dominated the Nobel prizes, built the interstate highway system. They cheered in 1927 when one of their own, twenty-five-year-old Charles Lindbergh, made the first transatlantic flight. And forty-two years later they were ecstatic when another, Neil Armstrong, became the first man to walk on the moon.

Matures accomplished their goals through hard work. They made sacrifices. They did it as a team. Indeed, by working together and then being amply rewarded for doing so, Matures created the most conformist culture of the twentieth century. As members of this generation came of age in the thirties, President Franklin Delano Roosevelt asked them to put aside "the dream of the golden ladder, each individual for himself" in favor of the vision of "a broad highway on which thousands of your fellow men and women are advancing with you."

It was the first president from the Matures, John Fitzgerald Kennedy, who defined his peers as "born of this century" in his inaugural speech of 1961. Since then, this generation has dominated politics and commerce as none before them. Indeed, the famous challenge JFK issued in that inaugural speech, "Ask not what your country can do for you, but what you can do for your country," aptly summed up the self-sacrificing commitment to bettering society that has always been a hallmark of Matures.

The members of the Mature generation were born between the turn of the century and the end of World War II. The years of their youth span the rise of the "American Century," a time enjoyed by them with their children, the Baby Boomers, as one of unprecedented wealth, power, and triumph. This generation includes two waves of consumers—the GIs, who came first and set the tone, and the Silents, who came next and flowed quietly, for the most part, into the mold. There are certainly some big differences between these two subsets, but because they largely shared the same generational experiences, the GIs and the Silents developed the same basic values and motivations. This is verified empirically—our MONITOR research shows them to be a cohesive, similarly motivated group of consumers.

The GIs were at the leading edge of the Matures. The Silents were the trailing edge, shaped mostly by the GIs before them but somewhat open to the influence of the next generation on the horizon. As we'll see, this boundary effect exists for all generational cohorts, as the power and influence of the group before fades and the next asserts itself.

CHART 2.1: VITAL STATISTICS OF MATURES

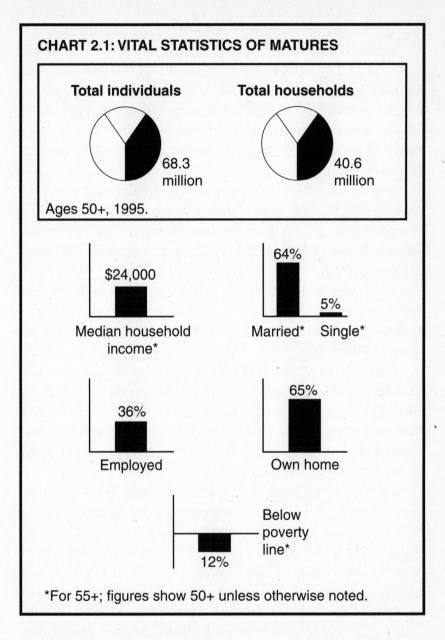

Total individuals

68.3 million

Total households

40.6 million

Ages 50+, 1995.

$24,000

Median household income*

64% 5%

Married*   Single*

36%

Employed

65%

Own home

Below poverty line*

12%

*For 55+; figures show 50+ unless otherwise noted.

The GIs take their name from the terms "general issue" and "government issue," describing uniforms provided to soldiers in World War II. More than half the GI men served in the armed forces. More important, this is a group that places a premium on being "general" or "regular" guys, team players who work within the system.

Similarly, the GI life cycle tracks the growth of government itself. When they returned from the war the GI Bill of Rights paid for their higher education and later helped them buy their first homes. As they came of age as civilians the government gave them jobs in unprecedented numbers. And today, as they age, they are receiving the most generous pensions and best subsidized medical care in the nation's history.

Small wonder this generation was so well taken care of by government—the GIs saw seven of their own in succession in the White House, beginning with Kennedy and extending through Lyndon Johnson, Richard Nixon, Gerald Ford, Jimmy Carter, Ronald Reagan, and George Bush.

The Silents bring up the rear. They tend to be more cautious and quietly assertive, serving in crucial back-room support roles as facilitators and bureaucrats. For leadership they have yielded to, and relied upon, the GIs.

Although the Silents have been on the edge of political power for three decades, they have never produced a president. And given current demographics, it appears that they might never do so. But they are not unsatisfied with having been indispensable presidential aides like Pierre Salinger, Bill Moyers, John Erlichman, Dick Cheney, and James Baker III.

Silents married young and had their children early. They outpaced the GIs in educational achievement. While they may not have produced a president, they did give America virtually every major figure in the twentieth century civil rights movement, from Martin Luther King, Jr., and Malcolm X to Cesar Chavez. They had the opportunity to fine-tune the America battled for by the GIs.

Despite the contrasts between these two subgroups, as consumers, GIs and Silents represent a single, cohesive generational cohort. They experienced economic upheaval during childhood. Discipline and self-sacrifice were cornerstones of their outlook as they came of age. At formative stages in their lives, the GIs and Silents were bound together—by common goals like overcoming

CHART 2.2: WHAT MATURES WANT MORE

IDENTIFY WITH:	MATURES	BOOMERS	Xers
Bill Gates over Michael Jordan	52%	35%	18%
Power over Glory	55%	46%	43%
Mustard over Ketchup	50%	43%	35%
Individual sports over Team sports	43%	30%	30%
A car over A truck	74%	60%	58%

Source: Yankelovich MONITOR® OmniPlus, 1996. TBWA Chiat/Day—Yankelovich Partners Collaborative Study on the New American Dream.

economic hardships and building suburban America, and also by the necessity to defeat common enemies, Germany and Japan, then the Soviet Union and China.

REBUILDING SOCIETY

As Matures came of age, they were faced with the daunting prospect of having to reestablish the basic social order itself. The national economy went from boom to bust just as the Great Plains dried up in a historic drought. Global economic prospects were no better. Armed, ideologically driven class struggles were springing up all over the world. Soon enough, the world went to war. Afterwards the devastation entailed in achieving that hard-won victory threatened to overwhelm and reverse the very triumph itself. Meanwhile, new threats had to be put down, while an atomic arms buildup gained increasing momentum.

The job of Matures was to rebuild. They shouldered the burden of ensuring that the foundations of a better life were put in place and subsequently protected. Matures found themselves called upon to assume an enormous social task—a formative experience that resulted in a sense of responsibility quite different from the easy-going assurance later felt by Boomers. Indeed, Boomers enjoyed the self-indulgent luxuries of stability and growth because Matures did what was necessary to provide them. In particular, the hard work and sacrifice of Matures built and shored up the modern consumer economy that we all now enjoy.

HARD WORK

Things weren't easy, but that was okay. Matures had to work hard to get things done, but that's how they wanted it. Growing up in the shadow of the Depression, they understood the necessity and virtue of hard work.

Matures set out to accomplish a big task, yet the rewards were big, too. They happily put their shoulders to the wheel and did it. Hard work was partly its own reward, in fact, because whatever got done felt earned, and thus was, by definition, better.

About fifteen years ago in our MONITOR research, we asked Matures to choose between learning a skill at a job or going to college for an education as the single best way to improve oneself. Overwhelmingly, Matures chose learning a skill, a choice reflecting the value they placed on blood, sweat, and tears. Today, when we ask this question of Boomers, who are now roughly the same age as those Matures we talked with years ago, they overwhelmingly choose college.

SELF-SACRIFICE

Matures believed that a lifetime of commitment was required to accomplish their goals. Duty came before pleasure. The job to be done required that they postpone their own gratification. Rationing in World War II, tax dollars sent overseas for the Marshall Plan, years given to military service, scrimping during hard times, all taught Matures self-sacrifice. Anything worthwhile meant giving up something else. Anything extra or left over had to be banked.

But this wasn't a problem. Indeed, self-sacrifice was seen as a virtue. It was good to dedicate one's efforts to some higher purpose. The nature of the ends they pursued—what they struggled against—lifted duty to a higher plane, and imbued Matures with a lasting belief in the inherent goodness of moderation and discipline.

There was a clear sense of purpose to what they were doing. World War II is remembered in retrospect, for example, as "The Good War." Because their aims were always unambiguously virtuous, Matures came to regard self-sacrifice itself as a virtue.

Much of this self-sacrifice by Matures, by the way, was on behalf of their children. Boomers were the beneficiaries of this indulgence, and thus, their formative experiences were different—they got all they wanted. This, as we'll see, has very different implications for the marketplace than the experiences of Matures, who had to defer getting much of what they wanted.

TEAMWORK

Matures learned the value of teamwork through their own individual struggles as well as those of the nation. They watched as government and business put aside their differences and teamed up to beat back the Depression. They watched as America and the Soviet Union joined together to defeat the Germans and the Japanese. They watched as, after the war, America teamed up in global alliances like the United Nations and NATO. Even individually, they each had the experience of conforming to the demands of a larger cooperative effort—as soldiers, as factory workers, as union members, as citizens.

Teamwork was the way things got done. The hard work and sacrifice were shared by all. An individual pursuing his or her own selfish ambitions and plans only detracted from the more important, broader purpose. It was better to sacrifice or suppress personal preferences, thereby finding a place on the team. This is the way really important goals were reached. Cooperation and mutual support made the sacrifice bearable, too.

AUTHORITY

Matures looked to the outside for direction and guidance. They certainly had confidence in their own abilities, but they used their talents to fulfill goals and priorities set by a broader authority. Loyalty and patriotism were an essential part of making a team work. Deference was essential.

This carried over to all domains. Experts were in demand for their advice and guidance. From Einstein to Dr. Spock, expert opinion was the determining authority. Matures developed a strong trust in institutions because it was these institutions, like government and big business, that solved the Depression and won World War II and the war in Korea. Political leaders like FDR and Eisenhower commanded huge popular followings, and between them and their vice presidents, Truman and Nixon, occupied the White House for all but eight years between 1933 and 1974. FDR's fireside radio chats were one of the comforts the GI Matures relied upon, and local authority figures like New York's mayor Fiorello La Guardia used radio in the same way to offer guidance and reassurance to constituents.

CONFORMITY

Teamwork and deference to authority meant putting a premium on fitting in. Matures prospered by thinking and doing together. Progress was assured as long as everyone followed the rules of the road and moved united in the same direction.

Matures developed this unity by conforming to a larger system of values that emphasized hard work as its own reward, financial security through savings, the good of the group before that of the individual, and a belief that the good life had to be earned. Though Matures have always had to sacrifice to meet the demands of this conformity, they also have always succeeded. For them, therefore, conformity and fitting in have been linked to success.

CELEBRATION OF VICTORY

Success after success, consistently achieved, reinforced for Matures the inherent correctness of their core values and provided the emotional satisfactions needed to defray the costs of the hardships they endured. Hard work and sacrifice never seemed to fail. Matures beat the Depression. They won wars. They rebuilt Europe and Japan. They staved off the spread of communism at home and abroad. They transformed America from a rural nation into a suburban one. They created a consumer market overflowing with affordable products that made life and work easier and more enjoyable.

Their standard of living improved because of what their victories brought them. The GI Bill of Rights gave Matures a chance to go to college and to buy homes. Rural America was electrified, and television offered a major new form of entertainment. The interstate highway system opened up the country. Suburbs filled with starter homes created affordable family communities that were clean, airy, and safe. And the government helped provide all of these things, either directly through grants and subsidies or indirectly through regulation and oversight.

The GI Bill of Rights, to take just one example, had enormous repercussions throughout America. The Serviceman's Readjustment Act of 1944 kicked in as GIs began returning home in 1946. Over the next ten years, $14.5 billion was spent by the federal government to put 7.5 million veterans through college or other schooling. In 1947 half of all college students were veterans. The veterans who took advantage of this immediately saw an impact in their wages—GI Bill veterans had incomes 40 percent higher than non–GI Bill vets in the four years after 1947. From 1944 to 1958, the Veterans Administration backed more than 2 million home loans.

Matures were the first to fully participate in the middle-class American Dream. They gave an enormous amount and reaped bountiful rewards. The values that guided them were vindicated by the boom in the consumer marketplace that began in the late fifties. Again, this was an experience fundamentally distinct from the way Boomers grew up. Boomers participated in the affluence created by the Matures without having to sacrifice and earn it.

Matures fared far better financially than their parents had. Home ownership rose from 46 percent in 1940 to 64 percent in 1960, a figure still unsurpassed today. To get a sense of the opportunity offered to Matures, look at the numbers that confronted the typical couple when they went to buy a first home in the fifties: Annual incomes averaged $3,000, mortgage interest rates were 4 percent, and new homes in Levittown, the archetypal suburban community, started at around $7,000. A far cry from the staggering prices and rocketing rates that Boomers and Xers would one day face.

The prosperity that Matures made for themselves, the respect they felt for institutions, and their desire to conform all translated into an enduring loyalty toward brand-name products. These patterns, despite years of attack, continue to rule the marketplace today. In nearly all consumer product categories, the number one brand today is the same as the number one brand fifty years ago. A colleague of ours in the consulting business once did an analysis of the position of major coffee brands across local markets nation-wide. He discovered that a coffee brand did best in the same markets where that brand had sponsored radio shows for the dominant station fifty and sixty years ago.

Madison Avenue was built on this brand loyalty. Matures responded to the advertising slogans of the day, and the most powerful slogans appealed to the ways Matures saw themselves and their world—as masters of the American Dream.

For instance, one of the most popular ad campaigns ever began its twenty-year run in the fifties. It succeeded because it aptly captured how Matures thought of themselves and their nation during those heady years following World War II. Timex would shows its watches going through various tortures—getting run over by an automobile, dropping over a waterfall, getting churned about strapped to the prop of a boat engine. Following each ordeal, the watch would be displayed, battered but still keeping time. "Timex—it takes a licking and keeps on ticking," John Cameron Swayze would intone. It was a slogan that spoke just as much to the sense of resiliency and constancy that Matures felt about themselves as it did to the indestructibility of the watch itself.

In a similar way, Gillette used a catchy jingle that spoke to this generation's self-confidence and clean-cut conformity. "Look sharp, feel sharp," said the ad. The virtue of hard work was enshrined in TV ads showing the singing "men from Texaco . . . who work from Maine to Mexico."

This vision of life was perfectly epitomized on the cover of *The Saturday Evening Post*, August 15, 1959. A young couple sit against a tree at night in each other's arms. They look up at the starry evening sky, picturing their hopes and dreams, seeing them floating in the stars. Instead of Orion or the Big Dipper, the universe they see is the American Dream—constellations outlining a split-level house in the suburbs, two cars, a TV, a stereo, appliances galore including a Hoover vacuum cleaner, two dogs, a girl at the piano, a boy playing ball.

Matures had postponed their material rewards, but when their hard work finally began to pay off, they became aggressive shoppers, obsessed with consumption and home ownership. In a sense, consumer goods came to represent the fulfillment of their spiritual values.

This was at the core of one of the most famous exchanges of that era—the so-called kitchen debate between Vice President Richard Nixon and Soviet Premier Nikita Khrushchev in July 1959. Nixon was escorting Khrushchev around the American Exhibition then showing in Moscow—a government-funded exposition of "science, technology and culture" designed to show off the consumer benefits of capitalism to Soviet citizens. As Nixon and Khrushchev wound around the various exhibits, they paused for a moment in the kitchen of a $14,000 model home put up by a Long Island builder and furnished by Macy's. Khrushchev used the opportunity to taunt Nixon about American consumer gimmicks and materialism. The Soviet leader fulminated about Americans having "the right to buy this house or to sleep on the pavement at night." Nixon responded with a ringing defense of free enterprise: "We hope to show our diversity and our right to choose . . . We do not want our decisions made at the top by one government official saying that all our houses should be the same." In Nixon's view, and the view of most Matures, consumer choice and political freedoms were one and the same: "Let the people choose the kind of house . . . the kind of ideas they want. We have many different manufacturers . . . so that housewives may have a choice."

It was a version of the American Dream that might well have been voiced by the couple on the cover of *The Saturday Evening Post*—or by any Mature. Success was measured in tangible, economic terms—homes, cars, appliances—all purchased, of course, at the right store. Value was a synonym for price.

Financial services were not complicated, either. People paid with cash. Mortgage interest rates were low; refinancing was unknown. Credit cards had not been invented. Instead, Christmas clubs thrived. Families would set aside funds in special accounts at their local banks. Housewives put special gifts on layaway plans and paid for these a little at a time. Only when all payments had been made could they actually take the merchandise home.

One of the clearest expressions of how Matures tied nearly all of their aspirations to material gain was the car-brand hierarchy established by General Motors. The entry-level GM car was a Chevrolet, marketed for mass appeal. "See the USA in your Chevrolet," sang Dinah Shore. A Chevrolet was the first step to the attainment of the American Dream. Its promise: the car that would start you on the drive from the bottom to the top.

As a family's income increased, they would move up to a Pontiac. Then came Oldsmobiles and Buicks. And the ultimate symbol of quality and success: the Cadillac. When new Cadillacs rolled across TV screens during the famed Master's golf tournament at Augusta National Country Club, the advertisements made a direct reference to the aspirations Matures harbored about the good life.

Matures, with their paid-off homes, retirement savings accounts, and secure jobs, were the stewards of American material life. They eagerly responded to marketing appeals that promised them a link to the American Dream, a shared vision of the good life to be lived in suburban homes surrounded by the material comforts they had worked so hard and sacrificed so much to get. This lifestyle was not only comfortable and secure, but also virtuous and morally correct.

Today many Matures have already retired, the earliest of any generation to date. They are richer than any previous generation of retirees, have better health benefits, better pension plans, more comfortable lives. In a reflection of their generational preference for conformity and material satisfaction, they created retirement centers, exemplified by Sun City in Arizona and the communities for senior citizens that dot the south Florida coastline.

But these retirement centers symbolize more than conformity and relative affluence. To some degree they also reflect the fears and concerns of Matures as they age. Across every survey we do, MONITOR included, Matures list crime and personal safety as their chief worries. Sun City and the gated communities in cities like St. Petersburg, Florida, offer refuge from a confusing and

CHART 2.3: GEN-O-GRAM—MEET A MATURE HOUSEWIFE

Born:	1935
Education:	High school graduate
Household:	Married; husband retired; two grown children; one grandson
On finances:	"We don't overspend. We watch our money. As long as we watch it, we are comfortable. We are able to enjoy the modest things of life."
On the times:	"For years, I felt left out as a housewife. But not anymore. I realize how important a housewife is. There should be more of us. Even now, my son is 39 and he reminds me, 'Mom, I am so glad you were home with us.' I am all for equal pay. I am very proud when I see women do well. But I did well, too."
On the generations:	"I think my generation was happier, calmer. The young people today, the age of my children today, they don't seem to have time to enjoy themselves. My grandson seems to be able to enjoy it more, although I think the people his age worry about their future. I think we need to bring back some manners in this world. If you haven't got the decency to be polite, everything flips off from that—you don't care about grades, ethics, work, honor. It is all interwoven."
Concerns:	"There is so much anxiety out there— shootings, crime, terrorism. Those militias disturb me. I never realized there was so much of that going on because I always had faith in my government to keep our country peaceful. I wish the world would calm down a bit, slow down."

increasingly threatening world. There they can live in seniors-only communities where they are safe among people with similar views and backgrounds, shut away from a world that is increasingly filled with difference and anger.

Matures, though, do not see these secure communities as isolating. In our MONITOR research, Matures describe themselves as happy and vivacious. Their advanced years are a proud, distinguished time for them, and they refuse to acknowledge loneliness or suffering.

Nowhere is this attitude reflected more clearly than in the American Association of Retired People (AARP), the most influential organization for Matures in the country. AARP and its 35 million members have played a major role in transforming aging into a badge of honor.

"You've already paid your dues," touts AARP in its membership pitch. "Now start collecting the benefits." So upbeat is the organization that its flagship magazine, *Modern Maturity*, is free of advertising that mentions pain, inflammation, or any of the stereotypical ailments of the elderly.

Smart marketers should take a lesson from the AARP—don't treat Matures as decrepit or broken down. The AARP has helped turn age into a badge of distinction and honor, but the celebration of age does not extend to reciting a long list of infirmities that your product or service can remedy. Marketers must avoid depicting older consumers in explicitly negative ways. Even Matures who are not as active and healthy as they would like to be dislike advertising assaults that remind them of their problems.

Marketers commonly err by emphasizing the biological age of their consumers. A few years ago, a major personal products company introduced a shampoo aimed at older women. The advertising explicitly mentioned that the product was designed for women over forty. There may be perfectly good reasons to switch to a different shampoo as you age. But the emphasis on age ensured that the product would be unpalatable to any self-respecting forty-plus-year-old.

A series of TV ads that Disney World aired are a prime example of how to appeal to Matures without pandering to them, while also poking a bit of fun at Boomers. In one ad, Boomer parents are pictured at home with their children, wondering aloud about what on earth their parents could be doing at Disney World. Then the camera shifts to the faces of two happy, healthy, older people in the Magic Kingdom. They are playing golf, swimming, dancing late into the night. For Matures, the ad makes a strong appeal to their conviction that they have earned a rich and full retirement—and are still young enough to enjoy it.

Marketers can reach this practical, hardworking generation as they enjoy their retirement, but not by selling products for "old people." They have to be smarter than that. Focus, instead, on themes that leverage the ways Matures are motivated to buy.

YOU EARNED IT

Play to the notion that this generation overcame daunting odds to achieve their successes. Don't be loud or brash; they already get the point. After working hard and sacrificing for so many years, they have reached their payoff point. This is even more so for GIs than Silents, but it is true for all Matures. They have reached a level of financial comfort and a time in their lives where they can feel freer to spend money on themselves ... because they've earned it. As John Houseman said in the Smith Barney ads many years ago, what Matures are enjoying today, they earned "[t]he old-fashioned way."

For most of their peak consuming years, Matures have forgone the extras. But this is not to say that Matures never spent money. Indeed, their spending built our contemporary consumer marketplace. Their style of spending, however, reflected the more cautious, disciplined values of their savings-focused outlook. Even as Matures spent, they actually saved a lot of money. And much of this spending was for others, especially their children.

All those rainy days they saved against have been weathered, though, and now is their time to finally enjoy a few fruits of their labors. This is the point to make to them—you can spend it on yourself now because you've earned it. That they have earned something through hard work speaks to their core values and gives them permission to open up their savings passbooks.

As they age, satisfied and secure, Matures will begin to spend more money on themselves. But they won't turn into profligate spendthrifts in the mold of their Boomer children. They resent the free spending of Boomers, an attitude most crudely reflected by the bumper sticker that boasts, "I'm Spending My Kids' Inheritance." Still, the innate frugality of Matures will ease up a bit as they put up their feet and enjoy themselves. The generation that did not indulge in immediate gratification is looking to get some now.

Our MONITOR research shows that consumers sixty-five years and older are the *least* likely to be cutting back on food purchases, shopping less, or adhering more strictly to a budget. They are also *less* likely to buy large, economy sizes or cut back on eating out. Part of this, of course, reflects older consumers with less flexibility in their lives. But it mostly shows that Matures have reached a level of financial comfort where they are less willing to deny themselves life's pleasures.

Nevertheless, the responses of Matures throughout our twenty-five-plus years of MONITOR research have consistently shown that their interest in pleasurable or exciting experiences for their own sake is low. They are not now and have never been as hedonistic as Boomers. They want to enjoy life, but they don't want to go overboard. The overriding attitude here is that they have enough money to enjoy their retirement, and they plan to do so—wisely and responsibly.

Some companies have begun to figure this out. Although this kind of advertising is new and its practitioners few, the financial services industry has been especially innovative in developing new products and strategies that are more appropriately focused. The motivating factor is simple—Matures have the money. Smart financial services advertising, such as recent print ads for Aetna, shows older couples reaping the rewards of their hard work, walking on a beach holding hands as the sun sets over the ocean.

Travel and leisure opportunities will grow as well. Lifelong, Matures have thought of leisure as a reward for hard work. After a lifetime of work, now is the time is now for these rewards. Consumers who restricted their vacations to two-week car trips every summer are now suddenly willing to pay $500 for a titanium golf club or $2,000 for a Caribbean cruise.

WISDOM

These are consumers who have seen it all—booms and busts, wars, sexual and cultural revolutions, political turmoil. Throughout it all, good times and bad, Matures have not just survived, they have thrived. And they have succeeded quietly, without a lot of braggadocio.

Their wide-ranging experiences and their abilities to persevere through it all have given them a strong sense of self-confidence as well as a quiet assurance that they do, in fact, know best. Our MONITOR data show that Matures are not intimidated by the knowledge and competence of younger people. They may feel that the nineties are passing them by, but they continue to believe that the wisdom of age, which lies only with them, is superior to the naiveté and inexperience of youth.

Advertising and marketing campaigns should emphasize the value of experience and wisdom. Turn a youth-oriented medium on its head by aiming for older customers and giving them recognition for the contributions their counsel can make. Tie your product or service to their ability to know the best value. Get your message into the unique channels that they rely upon to make a purchase decision. For example, while Xers rely on their peers for guidance about new products and Boomers use every bit of data they can get their hands on, Matures are more likely to turn to established institutions and authority figures. Celebrities like Jimmy Stewart and Katharine Hepburn have a strong influence among older consumers.

ASSURANCE

This is a generation that came of age respecting authority and institutions. Don't assume, however, that they will simply swallow anything they hear or read. Even Matures, the long-standing supporters of American business, are tired of being taken advantage of and have become more and more distrustful of big business.

You can leverage your brand name but you cannot live on heritage alone. Give Matures the respect they feel they have earned. And work to reestablish trust with a generation of consumers who learned at an early age that their personal goals were best served by big government and big institutions. The key here is to make sure that you design your message to fit the core values of this generation, especially values like frugality, responsibility, and caution.

VALUES CONSISTENCY

Do not forsake the basic values of this generation in an attempt to be contemporary or modern. *Financial discipline* will continue to be important to their style of participation in the marketplace. For instance, American Express introduced its senior membership program for cardholders who had retired or were about to do so. The program offered a reduced annual fee for consumers age sixty-two or older and other benefits, such as special offers from Hertz, Continental Airlines, Marriott, and Disney World. The message here is clear: You are retiring, you have plenty of money saved, but you will not betray a lifetime of sacrifice by becoming freer spenders now.

Doing something on behalf of others will also continue to be important. This is especially true as it ties into family. Matures are more than willing to spend money on their grandchildren. These are the healthiest, most active, and most available grandparents in history, and they are actively looking for new ways to spend time with their grandchildren. No older generation has ever shouldered such a burden for family extravagances. Twenty-five percent of toy sales are to Matures. For today's Boomers, as *Time* magazine says, the term "GI benefit" now stands for "Good In-Laws."

This generation wants opportunities to indulge their ingrained belief that they should make something better for someone else. They want to be able to say, "This is why I scrimped and saved."

CHART 2.4: THE "IN" CROWD

MATURES	BOOMERS	Xers
Rat Pack	"Leader of the Pack"	The Brat Pack
Nightclubs	Rock clubs	Rave clubs
Hep	Groovy	Edgy
Zoot suit	Bell-bottoms	Flannel
Vegas Flamingo	Vegas MGM Grand	Vegas Hard Rock
Kansas City	San Francisco	Seattle
Jazz	Rock 'n' Roll	Alternative

Take advantage of this. One novel strategy for servicing their needs was devised by Grandtravel. This travel agency in an upscale Maryland suburb of Washington, D.C., designed a series of vacation packages aimed at grandparents who want to take along their grandchildren on some of their jaunts. One of the most popular holidays is an African photo safari. Another itinerary offers an eight-day "Patriotic Panorama," sending grandparents and grandchildren on a grand tour of Washington, Alexandria, Arlington National Cemetery, Colonial Williamsburg, and Annapolis.

But you should balance any appeal for something new *against novelty for its own sake*. Our MONITOR surveys show that Matures are a lot less likely to want to try new products before anyone else. This is one of their key cohort characteristics. Launching a new product for Matures will require giving them the right kind of reassurance, so they will feel they are not just wastefully experimenting or splurging.

ALL-GENERATIONAL APPEAL

Some products and services won't make it even with a generationally appropriate message. Such products and services will need to have a broader appeal. Without it, Matures won't feel comfortable enough to buy them. So be on the lookout for ways to expand your focus and emphasize benefits that cross over all generations. This will let Matures respond to those benefits without feeling that they are stigmatizing themselves.

For example, large-type books have never been big sellers, because they carry the stigma of being for old people. Yet a growing number of Americans have difficulty reading regular print, especially on food packaging. Just put bigger letters on your packaging. Don't market it as packaging for old people. Matures will recognize the benefits without being told, and they can respond to your product without having to link themselves to an old person's product. Indeed, everyone in the marketplace stands to benefit if they can read labels more easily and from a greater distance.

Similarly, restaurants trying to attract Matures should invest in better lighting, inside and outside. Matures, the generational cohort most concerned about crime, will feel safer driving, and will be less likely to fall, in a bright parking lot. Besides, we all want a clean, well-lighted place. Car rental locations should also emphasize safety and security for all, knowing that this will have special appeal to Matures. Matures will find this sort of leveling out appealing in many, if not all, instances.

Over the years, we have worked with clients across a wide variety of product and service categories who automatically reject any consumer fifty years of age or older as a target for their brands. The rule-of-thumb is eighteen to forty-nine. We always have considered any general rule like this shortsighted, but this will be especially so in the future. Matures are starting to spend more aggressively than any older consumer group before them. And they will buy loyally from marketers who speak to their core values and motivations in generationally appealing ways.

Matures: Triumph and Conformity

1920
Women get the vote
Tommy gun invented
Band-aid invented
First rib-knit one-piece bathing suit by Jantzen
First radio stations, KDKA and WWJ, broadcast
Prohibition starts following ratification of 18th Amendment the year before
First Agatha Christie mystery published

1921
Chanel No. 5 introduced
First drive-in restaurant, Kirby's Pig Stand, opens in Dallas
First full-length feature film, *Dream Street*
First Miss America pageant

1922
T.S. Eliot's *The Wasteland* published
Sound effects first used on radio
First 3-D feature film, *Power of Love*
Reader's Digest begins publication

1923
Time magazine begins publication
Yankee Stadium opens in New York City

1924
Johnny Weissmuller first to swim 100m in under one minute
Lenin dies; Stalin assumes power
Teapot Dome scandal

1925
First national spelling bee
Grand Ole Opry begins
New Yorker begins publication
The Great Gatsby published
Scopes Trial
The Charleston dance craze

1930
Bobby Jones wins Grand Slam of Golf
Sliced bread introduced
First airline stewardesses on 12-seater Boeing 80
First soap opera on Chicago radio, "Painted Dreams"

1929
Clarence Birdseye succeeds with frozen foods
Color TV demonstrated at Bell Labs
Kodak introduced 16mm color movie film
American Austin (later, Jeep) introduced
Wall Street crash

1928
First practicable iron lung
Women's athletics included in Amsterdam Summer Olympics
First Mickey Mouse cartoon, "Steamboat Willie"
Amelia Earhart is first woman to pilot transatlantic flight
Harley Earl takes charge of GM's Art and Color Section
Bubble gum perfected

1927
Charles Lindbergh flies solo across Atlantic
The Jazz Singer, first widely seen talkie
Pez introduced
First Ryder Cup held in USA
Babe Ruth hits 60 home runs
First Academy Awards
First car radios

1926
NBC Radio started
Miniature golf started
Book-of-the Month Club started
Soundtrack for *Don Juan* produced on first 33⅓ rpm disk

1931
Alka-Seltzer introduced
Stereo sound recording patented
First regular TV broadcasts begin in
America
Inauguration of Empire State Build-
ing

1932
First Tarzan movie, with Johnny
Weissmuller
Lindbergh baby kidnapped

1933
Prohibition ends
Chicago World's Fair
King Kong released
FDR inaugurated
Chicago Bears win first NFL Cham-
pionship over New York Giants
Ecstasy with Hedy Lamarr is first
movie to depict sexual act
First drive-in movie theater

1934
First mass-produced streamlined car,
Chrysler Airflow
First Masters golf tournament
John Dillinger gunned down in
Chicago
First Laundromat
First quintuplets to survive past
infancy born in Canada

1935
Social Security Act passed
Penguin introduced paperback
books
Monopoly introduced
Two-piece bathing suits modeled in
Vogue
First full-length color film, *Becky
Sharp*

First blood bank opened in New
York
Nylon stockings introduced nation-
ally
First Varga girl pin-up calendar
1940

New York World's Fair opens
Little League baseball started
Gone with the Wind released
Goldfish-swallowing fad
The Wizard of Oz released
Start of WWII with German inva-
sion of Poland
1939

Don Budge first to win Grand Slam
of tennis
Teflon discovered
Frank Sinatra makes radio debut
Artificial bristles replace hog's hairs
in toothbrushes
The "War of the Worlds" broadcast
by Orson Welles
Hindenburg disaster
First issue of Action Comics with
Superman
1938

*Snow White and the Seven
Dwarfs* released
First worldwide radio broadcast of
the coronation of King George VI
1937

Life begins publication
Chaplin's *Modern Times* opens
Ferdinand Porsche designs VW
Baseball Hall of Fame opens
Dale Carnegie's *How to Win
Friends and Influence People*
published
Jesse Owens wins 4 gold medals at
Berlin Olympics
First *Billboard* popular music chart
Margaret Mitchell's *Gone with the
Wind* published
1936

1941 Lend-Lease Act passed
Citizen Kane released
The Maltese Falcon released
Pearl Harbor attacked by the
Japanese
First TV ad, for Bulova watches,
airs
United States enters World War II
Manhattan Project begins

1942 Tupperware introduced
Battle of Midway
"White Christmas" by Bing Crosby
released; biggest selling song
from a movie
Coty established American Fashion
Critics Award
Oklahoma! opens

1943 Pentagon completed
Frank Sinatra becomes first music
star to be screamed at by young
fans
Casablanca released
Jitterbug dance craze
First Lassie movie
Income tax withholding introduced

1944 GI Bill passed
D-Day invasion
Aaron Copland's *Appalachian
Spring* debuts
Harvard professor Howard Aiken
developed first digital computer
Bobby socks craze

ENIAC computer **1946**
Flamingo Hotel and Casino erected
in Las Vegas
Winston Churchill coins phrase *iron
curtain*
Bikini debuts at Paris fashion show
five days after US nuclear bomb
detonated on Bikini Atoll
Dr. Benjamin Spock's *Baby and
Child Care* published
First bank drive-thru in Chicago
The Best Years of Our Lives
released
Timex watches hit market for $6.95
First Cannes Film Festival
7-Eleven chain incorporated

A-bomb dropped on Hiroshima and **1945**
Nagasaki
Grand Rapids, Michigan, is first to
add fluoride to municipal water
system
World War II ends
Ebony begins publication
First bumper stickers
First ballpoint pens on sale at Gim-
bel's for $12.50 each
Penicillin introduced
First album chart published
United Nations chartered in San
Francisco

1947   Levittown, Long Island, built
Secretary of State Gen. George C.
   Marshall delivers Harvard speech
   that results in Marshall Plan of
   1948
Demand for power mowers surges
   due to move to suburbs
Term *cold war* enters lexicon
Kenneth Arnold of Boise, Idaho,
   first to sight "shining saucer-like
   objects," or UFOs
Jackie Robinson joins Dodgers roster
Charles Yaeger in Bell X-1 makes
   first supersonic flight
Polaroid Land Camera introduced
Bell Labs team invents transistor

1948   Hell's Angels formed
The *Ed Sullivan Show* first airs
Slinky introduced
First air-conditioning in Detroit-
   built cars
Baskin-Robbins created by merger
General Mills and Pillsbury intro-
   duce prepared cake mixes
GM and UAW agree to first auto-
   matic cost-of-living wage
   increases
Ray Kroc franchises McDonald
   brothers' hamburger stands
LPs from CBS; 45s from RCA
Lee Strasberg introduces method
   acting
Term *cybernetics* coined
Alger Hiss convicted of perjury

1949   Roller Derby started
Pillsbury bake-off started
Cortisone discovered
First cable TV systems go into
   homes
George Orwell's *1984* published
People's Republic of China formally
   declared by Chairman Mao

BOOMERS:
THE 78-MILLION-STRONG
GORILLA

"What do you want to be on your next vacation? How about a TV producer? Or a gourmet cook? How about an animator, or a comedian? An actor, or a landscape architect? If you've dreamed of trying new things, you can try them here at the Disney Institute."

In 1996, when marketers at Disney launched the Disney Institute, their new resort for adults in Orlando, Florida, they did it with the ultimate Boomer ad. The appeal to *be* something completely different on your next vacation, not just to *do* something different, was the equivalent of a full orchestra playing the Beatles—it struck every note in the Boomer songbook.

The ad is designed to appeal to Boomers' quest for *self*, what Boomer sociologist and former protest leader Todd Gitlin has termed the "voyage to the interior." It began with the earliest Boomers as a rebellion against their parents, grew into a rage against the government and the Vietnam War, and evolved into a sustained search for personal fulfillment. Tom Wolfe characterized the Boomers of the 1970s as the "Me Generation." Gitlin reminds us that this continues even today. Boomers, Gitlin said, haven't really changed, they've just gone from "J'accuse to Jacuzzi." As Boomers age and mellow, they remain focused on themselves.

The ad also reinforces Boomers' strong belief in their own individual capabilities. This generation was much better educated than its parents. Eighty-eight percent of Boomers are high school graduates, and more than 26 percent have college degrees. Boomers grew up being told they were special, and were given the advantages of education and training so they could be. Boomers continue to believe that if they want to do it—or be it—no matter what "it" is, they can. The Disney Institute promises "a vacation where every day is different—and every day is *yours* to design" (italics added).

Rather than harnessing their skills with the yoke of society as Matures did, Boomers have remained fixated on self-improvement and individual accomplishment. Matures and Boomers reflect two distinctly different value systems. For Matures, as we've seen, worth is measured in objective, external terms. Boomers look inward and evaluate their achievements in terms of personal fulfillment.

Boomers have reached a point where their desire to do things that improve themselves often extends even to their vacations, a fact this ad recognizes. The generation that spawned both hippies and yuppies doesn't just want to kick back on its holidays. Vacation time is time off to improve yourself and learn something new. Experiences that allow Boomers to have fun while rekindling their old quest for fulfillment—if only for a week or two—will be winners. Boomers want what the Disney Institute ad promises: "[O]ne unbelievable *experience* after another" (italics added).

The ad is aimed at Boomers who, entering midlife, are abruptly recognizing their own limitations. Unlike Matures years ago, Boomers have reached middle age worried they will not be able to

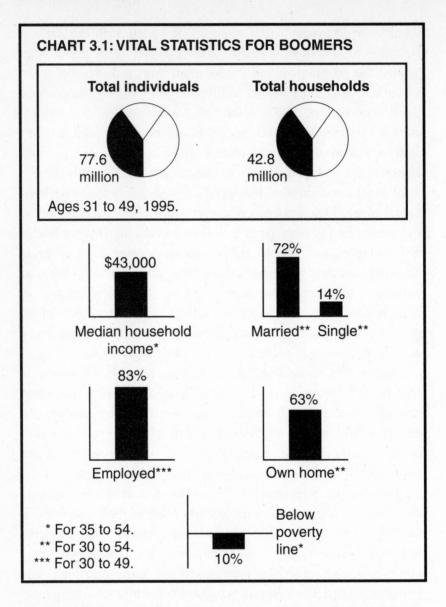

CHART 3.1: VITAL STATISTICS FOR BOOMERS

Total individuals — 77.6 million

Total households — 42.8 million

Ages 31 to 49, 1995.

$43,000 — Median household income*

72% Married** 14% Single**

83% Employed***

63% Own home**

10% Below poverty line*

* For 35 to 54.
** For 30 to 54.
*** For 30 to 49.

own the American Dream. But at a place like the Disney Institute, for a week at least, they can rent it.

The notion of fulfilling their dreams on a lifestyle lease reflects what has been the key quandary for Boomers over the last twenty years and will probably remain so over the next twenty. Boomers grew up with a strong sense of entitlement, and enormous expectations about the potential of life. But now the generation that thought it could fix the world finds itself beset by its own limitations and by seemingly intractable problems. The struggle to avoid this disappointment of expectations and still come out on top is a driving force behind much of what Boomers buy and consume. Come to Disney Institute, the ad seems to say, and beat the odds for a little while.

Small wonder that Disney got it right with this appeal. The huge entertainment conglomerate grew up with this generation. Most Boomers can still sing the theme from the Sunday night Disney show. They recall it, in fact, in association with one of the important markers of their generational experience—the spread of color television, a technological marvel that dazzled them as children with eye-catching shows like Disney's. As color TV took over American living rooms, the Disney program, on its new network, was rechristened "The Wonderful World of Color" and featured an opening in which Tinkerbell brought the screen into full-color focus with a magical touch of her wand.

Boomers expected that life would always unfold like this, ever encouraged in this belief by the indulgence of their parents and the apparently bright promise of the world around them. Author William Manchester predicted that Boomers would grow up "adorable as babies, cute as grade school pupils and striking as they entered their teens," after which, he said, "their parents would be very, very proud of them."

Boomers are the generational cohort active in the consumer marketplace today *that grew up with the expectations, life skills, and values created by the unbridled economic growth of their formative years.* It is this experience that binds Boomers together. The protests sometimes heard from the youngest Boomers—that Woodstock is irrelevant to them and Watergate a dim, adolescent memory—are valid, but these are not the markers that link Boomers. Rather, it is that consumers coming of age from the early fifties through the late seventies all shared a confidence that the progress and prosperity would never stop, which created the Boomer generational sense of expectation and entitlement.

More than any other experience, it was this idea of unending prosperity that shaped all members of the Boomer generation. With the belief that their future was secure, there were few economic worries to distract them, so Boomers felt free to focus instead on themselves, on experimentation, on fulfillment.

This Boomer focus on the self also was helped along by the ways they were reared. In traditional households across America, under the watchful eyes of doting mothers guided by Dr. Benjamin Spock, Boomers grew up spoiled and pampered. Spock helped create the most permissive parents in history.

The result of all this: Boomers grew up thinking they were special, destined for a special place in history. As they age, they still consider themselves special. After all, they have been the media's darlings all their lives. When the first Boomers hit thirty-five in the early eighties, the event was heralded everywhere. "Here Come the Baby-Boomers," said a cover story in *U.S. News and World Report*. "What the Baby Boomers Will Buy Next," chronicled *Fortune*. This media attention still goes on.

CHART 3.2: *KATHLEEN CASEY WILKENS*

America's first Baby Boomer, born in Philadelphia one second into the New Year, January 1, 1946. The first of almost 78 million more to come.

What sets Boomers apart from Matures and Xers is the sense of privilege. Aren't we fascinating, Boomers implore. As you might expect, this is also how they behave.

There are 78 million Boomers alive today, born between 1946 and 1964. Despite delayed marriages and a high divorce rate, Boomers these days are most likely to be part of a married-couple family. Even among the youngest Boomers, nearly two out of three are married.

Although most Boomers have not yet reached their peak earning years, more Boomers than ever are working today. Indeed, work itself is something that differentiates Boomers today from Matures or Xers. Matures are easing out, Xers are easing in, but Boomers are right in the middle of it all. Also, Boomers are tied to the workforce more strongly than Matures before them because of the presence of working women.

In one of America's most widely noticed birthdays, the first Boomers turned fifty on January 1, 1996. But despite the media hype, reaching the half-century mark is a Big Yawn to the Big Chill generation. Instead, what is important is that a few years ago the youngest Boomers passed thirty. All Boomers, whether they like it or not, are now the people Abbie Hoffman warned them never to trust.

But these aging Boomers will not be anything like the Matures they replace. Businesses that assume Boomers will take on the characteristics and values of Matures are in for trouble. Instead, as they have throughout their lives, Boomers will create a new marketplace. They will redefine the meaning of the "mature" market, and of what it means to be a grown-up. Their needs and wants will be similar to those of their parents, but their ways of satisfying them will be quite different. Smart marketers already understand the radical change to come in the character of midlife consumers.

WHAT I WANT

The first step in preparing for that change is to understand how Boomers got there. The postwar economic prosperity of the fifties, sixties, and seventies is the most critical generational marker for Boomers. As Boomers grew up, everywhere they looked, limitless horizons stretched out around them. They lived in affluent suburbs—if not in body then at least in spirit with the Nelsons and the Cleavers. College prep courses took many to SAT Saturday and then to campus. Robotics promised a twenty-hour workweek, and atomic power was going to generate all the energy ever needed— for pennies. Boomers didn't doubt it was coming; they'd seen models in action at places like GM's Futurama exhibit at the 1964 World's Fair.

Economic optimism freed them from worry about basic survival. They could live for today because they didn't have to worry about tomorrow. They could spend what they had because there was plenty more. They could share with everybody because there was lots to go around. They could, if they wanted, sign it all away or give it all up with the kind of casual indifference only possible for those who had not grown up under the constant threat of impending want and deprivation.

Boomers have always spent all of their money and even gone happily into debt, because they were confident that there was plenty more where it came from. Confronted with economic collapse and uncertainty, Matures learned to save. Boomers never faced that, and therefore learned to spend, and to spend for instant gratification—get it now, no lines, no waiting.

WHAT I DESERVE

Boomers feel that what they get is more than just something they have earned; it's what they deserve. Boomers presumed success, and expected nothing less. The largest impact of the economic prosperity of their formative years was the development of a strong sense of entitlement and expectation. Their idea that the future automatically would be better made this plausible to them.

While it was mostly the right moral reasons that motivated Boomers to take up causes like the civil rights movement and the women's movement, it was their rosy outlook, their certainty that there would be a slice of pie for everyone, that gave them the freedom to embrace a more inclusive society. Including others would not diminish what they felt they were entitled to.

WHAT I SAY

Boomers decided early that the old rules weren't meant for them. They were, after all, the best educated, most sophisticated Americans in history. Naturally they knew best when it came to running the country and managing its resources. Boomers always have broken the rules; they always have done things differently. The drugs, sex, and rock 'n' roll of the sixties and seventies only foreshadowed the really radical rule-breaking to come in the consumer marketplace of the eighties and nineties.

Above all, Boomers didn't want to be hemmed in by the conformity that rules demanded. Boomers were "individuals," so individuality was lionized while conformity was eschewed. Rules that interfered with this had to be broken, and breaking the rules was easy. There were no penalties. They were not ostracized by their peers. Instead, they were assured that a job and a paycheck would be waiting once they decided to settle down. Indeed, with plenty for all, rules could be broken with impunity. Something new could always be indulged because failure entailed no real loss. This is why Boomers have been rule breakers more so than rule-replacers.

WHAT IS RIGHT

Vietnam War protests and the environmental movement were markers of the moral certainty felt by these Boomers. They recognized that they were growing up in a pretty good system with a lot of exciting promise, but they believed it still needed fixing—not, however, the significant rebuilding from the ground up that Matures had faced during their formative years. Boomers felt the system was perfectible if they could just locate the evil within it and root it out. Their mission, as they chose to accept it, was to push the system closer to perfection.

Flaws stuck out to Boomers. These contrasted sharply with the promise of how things ought to be. Boomers believed they deserved better and they set out in battles, heavy with moral overtones, to oppose compromise, ignorance, greed, pork-barrel politics, and inefficiency.

Every fight was a clash of moral principles—good versus evil.

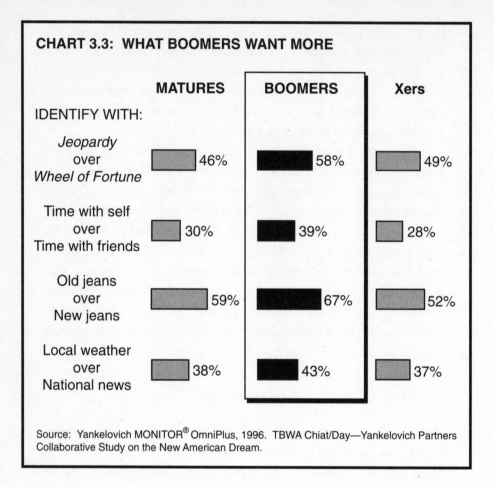

CHART 3.3: WHAT BOOMERS WANT MORE

Source: Yankelovich MONITOR® OmniPlus, 1996. TBWA Chiat/Day—Yankelovich Partners Collaborative Study on the New American Dream.

No surprise that a Boomer gave us Darth Vader and the Dark Side. Obstacles were seen as the ill-intentioned handiwork of evildoers, mucking up a system that otherwise would be just and good. The task was to find the bad guys and boot them out. Popular futurists of the sixties and seventies like Buckminster Fuller and Alvin Toffler preached liberation through enlightened technological engineering, encouraging people to work together to make sure this potential was not misappropriated by benighted interests.

This sense of purpose was captured in movies like the 1968 hit, *2001: A Space Odyssey*. Spiritual enlightenment is achieved after a courageous voyage to make contact with the alien "good" technology, but only after a desperate battle to shut down HAL, the "evil," misprogrammed computer technology that ran amok onboard ship.

WHAT I CONTROL

Boomers want to be on top and in charge. They believe they know best, and they act independently based on this self-confidence. They are unafraid to act as individuals abiding by none of the old rules, and they feel no lack of education or self-esteem to steer their own course.

The *Pentagon Papers* and Watergate showed them there was always a "real" story behind the scenes, which was within their control to uncover if they were dogged enough. Boomers expected the best, were sure that they were strong enough and smart enough to get it, and therefore fashioned themselves to be winners.

The struggle to remain in control, to get the meaningful rewards to which they have always felt entitled, has motivated much of the behavior we've seen from Boomers in the marketplace since the end of the seventies. This will continue to be true as Boomers move into the next millennium.

BOOMING ALONG

For early Boomers, things were simple and orderly. Life looked rich and satisfying. The Ricardos, Ozzie and Harriet, Donna Reed—these were the norm. In 1955 the first McDonald's appeared in Des Plaines, Illinois, and Disneyland, promoted as "The Happiest Place on Earth," opened in Anaheim, California. The Barbie doll showed up on retail shelves in 1959 as the epitome of contemporary female beauty.

It was the very success and affluence of the fifties that gave rise to the first significant change in postwar values. Economic prosperity freed Boomers to focus on themselves, leading to the revolt of the sixties and early seventies. Boomers began to challenge conventional values. They challenged authority, blurred gender roles, embraced the unconventional. They were young, free, and in control.

CHART 3.4: *Life* magazine's*
Top 10 Boomers

1. Steven Spielberg (b. 1947)
2. Steven Jobs (b. 1955)
3. Bill Clinton (b.1946)
4. Michael Milken (b. 1946)
5. Oprah Winfrey (b. 1954)
6. Edward Witten (b. 1951)
7. Bill Gates (b. 1955)
8. Bob Pittman (b. 1953)
9. Michael Jordan (b. 1963)
10. Roseanne (b. 1953)

* Special issue, July 15, 1996.

The conformity that had guided Matures broke down. Free of economic worries, Boomers saw no value in self-sacrifice for a common goal. They became more focused on self-reward and individuality. They didn't just want jobs and families and ranch houses. They wanted fulfillment and enlightenment. And traditional ways of doing things were obstacles.

The twin anthems for Boomers were Timothy Leary's "turn on, tune in, drop out" and Martin Luther King's "we shall overcome." In response, mainstream marketers strived to connect with these themes. Novelty, difference, adventure, these became marketing catchwords. Seven-Up, the "Uncola," turned thinking about soft drinks on its head, even promoting itself with upside-down glassware. Volkswagen, in one of the greatest print ads of all time, suspended a small, off-center photo of its VW "Bug" amidst a full page of empty white space and tagged it with a simple, provocative challenge: "Think Small."

Later, marketers connected with a growing interest in social issues. Virginia Slims reassured women that they too were players and reminded them, "You've come a long way, baby." Coca-Cola produced the first multicultural TV ad, assembling hundreds of young people of many nationalities on a hilltop in Italy to sing, "I'd like to teach the world to sing in perfect harmony."

It was tumultuous, but safe, adventure. There were, of course, unsettling things going on—missiles in Cuba, duck-and-cover drills, gas lines, DDT, the White House plumbers, cults—hints of a dark underside. But Boomers saw the world through fresh eyes. Though some of it seemed unsettling, nothing looked so awful that it could wind up actually destroying the promise of the future.

Before the seventies ended, however, the great expectations of Boomers bumped against some hard realities. The generation brought up to believe that everyone could be a winner began to see that there had to be both winners and losers. The generation brought up with the expectation of affluence began to understand that there wasn't enough to go around.

POST-1979

The year 1979 stands as *the* turning point for Boomers. Sirens at Three Mile Island were the first harbingers of trouble. This was a year of stagflation—soaring inflation and interest rates—and unemployment lines around every block. This was the year Islamic fundamentalists in Iran humiliated the "Great Satan" by taking sixty-three hostages at the American embassy in Teheran, and the year the cold war warmed up again with the Soviet invasion of Afghanistan. It was the year, too, that gas lines made their return, and the year that Lee Iaccoca, the ex-Ford manager who years before had introduced the enduring Boomer auto-icon, the '64 Mustang coupe, traveled to Washington to supplicate government for aid to keep Chrysler afloat.

For Boomers 1979 was when cracks began to appear in the facade of unending prosperity, and from then on they would never be quite as sure of themselves, never quite as assured of their prospects. To take that year's hit movie title literally, Boomers were in fact suddenly faced with *Apocalypse Now*.

Until 1979 Boomers believed any obstacles they encountered resulted from the manipulations of evil people, like Nixon, not from deep-seated, inherent problems in the system itself. They thought if they just got rid of the bad guys, everything would be okay. But the world didn't get rosy again when Nixon resigned. And in 1979 the frayed ends they had ignored really began to unravel. President Carter, with some prescience, foretold this in a nationally televised speech, much criticized at the time, about a national sense of malaise.

After the traumatic events of 1979, Boomers began to doubt the system itself. They felt they no longer could take their future for granted. In MONITOR, we saw this as the emergence of an approach to life that was much more hard-edged, which we called "The New Realism."

As the eighties dawned, the gap between expectations—always winning—and an unsettling reality—often losing—generated much Boomer angst. The desire for control now expressed itself as a single-minded focus on not losing. The Boomer goal became to win, indeed, to win at everything. Yuppies crept out from behind the long hair and tie-dye. If they couldn't perfect the system or change the world, they would simply enjoy it. The result was cutthroat competition through consumption, and a new philosophy emerged: "He who dies with the most toys wins."

This New Realism kicked into high gear in the mid-eighties with a burst of opportunities for affluence for the smartest and the shrewdest. The end of the so-called Reagan recession put more money into the hands of all these Boomers who had recently learned they had to aggressively take care of their own interests. The conspicuous consumption of the mid-eighties was, in fact, rooted as much in the complex psychology of control—to avoid the disappointment of adolescent expectations—as in the simple vice of greed.

BMW replaced VW as the car with cachet. Michelob said we could have it all, winning at everything at once. Lee Iaccoca, now running a resurgent, unapologetic Chrysler, stared us down on TV and dared us to play the game with him: "If you can find a better car, buy it." Brooke Shields wriggled into her Calvins and showed Boomers that thin was another way to win. Jane Fonda's workout tapes promised to make svelte winners out of us all. NutraSweet promised victory over sugar. The Home Shopping Network brought the game of consumption directly into our homes.

Trying to understand Boomer behavior after 1979, Florence Skelly named it the "strategic shopping" style of consumption, the practice of total control over participation in the marketplace. Boomers had become proficient at finding ways to prove they were still going to get all they had grown up to expect. Bumper stickers proclaimed, "Shop till you drop." Competing became finding the best product at the best price—in other words, strategic shopping.

Brands no longer dominated the marketplace. Boomers wanted control. Brand loyalty waned. Discount stores thrived. Boomers clipped coupons and used their smarts to ferret out the best deals. They wrested away so much control from marketers that by the mid-eighties, for consumer packaged goods marketers, spending on promotions exceeded spending on advertising for the first time ever. Marketers had capitulated to Boomers in this struggle for the control of transactional relationships.

Boomers declared themselves winners a bit too soon, though. As early as our 1985 MONITOR study, we saw clear signs that they were beginning to have doubts about their self-absorbed style of strategic shopping. But it took the shock of the '87 stock market crash to unleash this. Suddenly Boomers rejected the marketplace. "Shop till you drop" was replaced by "Drop shopping."

Boomers had tried doubly hard throughout the eighties. Yet, at the end of the decade, they found that their efforts to avoid disappointment had failed. Where Boomers thought they were winning, they were actually losing. Their trophy children were really latchkey kids, lost and aimless. They thought they were spending to win, but their debt was higher than ever. So was their weight. Diabetes due to obesity was at record highs. Their financial heroes were being hauled off to jail, forfeiting their Ferraris and leaving behind their trophy wives. Those who had done the laying off were now finding themselves laid off. Even fashion items like name-brand sneakers were coopted into gang garb.

Boomers turned bitter. They had played by the rules, worked extra hours, strived earnestly to realize their potential. But they kept coming up losers. We've done all we were supposed to do, Boomers reasoned, so it can't be our fault. They cast themselves as victims. And with this came the resentment and anger that dominated the late eighties and early nineties.

Boomers took out many of their frustrations in the marketplace. Relations with marketers and retailers strained. Tom Peters, the ex-McKinsey management guru, preached 100 percent customer satisfaction 100 percent of the time. This, of course, is an impossible, unaffordable goal, but the philosophy it embodies recognized the reality at the time that customers would be punitive for even a single mistake.

The era of the anti-brand blossomed. Boomer consumers focused on what they disliked rather than what they liked. Perrier, Audi, and Exxon were the most egregious offenders. IBM, GM, New Coke, and Intel all skated on thin ice. The last traces of brand loyalty disappeared completely from many product and service categories. Competitive shopping to win had given way to angry shopping avoidance.

Most recently, our MONITOR research shows that Boomers, and, indeed, all consumers, have finally begun to moderate their marketplace belligerence. In this, we see the third major manifestation of Boomer self-absorption and control emerging.

Boomers have regained their sense of possibility. They know their lives are filled with too much stress, much of it, unfortunately, of their own making. They now want to pick their battles more carefully, and are reorganizing their priorities to do so. This fresh perspective will guide Boomers through the middle-age years they now face—their peak earning years—and will create strong growth opportunities for marketers who understand the values driving Boomer consumption motivations in the years ahead. In particular, Boomers are likely to belie all recent prognostications of coming declines in their consumer spending. Boomers certainly have accumulated a lot and they certainly need to save, but it is their ingrained generational values that will motivate their fundamental consumer behaviors. Whether they need to or not, whether they can afford to or not, Boomers will keep spending.

NOT THE SAME

The most important thing to remember about Boomers is that they are rule breakers. Individuality over conformity is a consistent Boomer pattern. They always have done it differently than the way it was done before, and as they get older, they will continue to demand products that fit their individuality.

Developers of retirement and golf communities, for instance, are discovering that Boomer interest is far less than anticipated. Boomers are much less likely than Matures to retire to these kinds of cookie-cutter communities. Instead, they're looking for something with the kinds of sophistication and impertinence that has always appealed to them. At heart, Boomers remain nonconformists.

NOSTALGIA

Nostalgia is a strong Boomer hook. Their best moments were yesterday, when both they and their future were being heralded and celebrated. That's why you hear the rough, deep-throated voice of the late Janis Joplin pitching Mercedes-Benz, or why you hear well-chosen refrains from disco hits of the seventies being used as the soundtrack behind full-screen beauty shots of Burger King sandwiches. This is why Microsoft used the Rolling Stones; Nike and GTE, the Beatles; and Coopers & Lybrand, Bob Dylan. Rolling Rock has done it, too, though with more of a Trailing Boomer bent, using billboards depicting one of their icy-cold green bottles above the simple headline, borrowed from the Talking Heads, "same as it ever was." This also helps explain why Harley-Davidson motorcycles have enjoyed a resurgence. Many are being sold to Boomers pining to recapture old thrills.

There is a new yearning and nostalgia for traditional values among Boomers—the desire to re-create the carefree world in which they grew up, a time where life seemed simpler, more straightforward. For example, stay-at-home moms have become fashionable again. By the eighties, as the number of women in the workforce exploded, the role of the housewife fell into disrepute. But this has changed. Our current MONITOR data show a big jump in the percentage of consumers, especially women, who describe a housewife's job as interesting and challenging.

There is also a new yearning for calm. Boomers, the aging revolutionaries who once thrived on change, have always been more tolerant of living with a sense of chaos and disorder than Matures, and even Xers. Our trend data show that Xers today are less tolerant of chaos and disorder than Boomers were twenty years ago when they were roughly the same age. Now, Boomers too have tired of this.

Twenty years ago, a third of all Boomers said they were comfortable living with disorder, the highest of any generation ever. Today, only a quarter of them say this, a change reflecting a basic reordering of Boomer priorities.

FAMILY FOCUS

Our recent MONITOR data also show a rise in the priority of family and family activities. Compared with years past, Boomers want to spend more time with their children. They are more than twice as likely as Matures or Xers to report that raising their children is one of the ways they express personal creativity, and they are the most concerned about making sure their family eats healthful and nutritious foods. When asked in our MONITOR survey to select things they expected to do in the coming year, 39 percent of Boomers said they would "spend more time with my children."

When asked where they would like to see a return to traditional standards, three of the top four responses from Boomers were good manners, family life, and parental responsibility.

Although looking to spend more time with children and family, Boomers want to do this in innovative ways. After all, Boomers invented new forms of family through divorce, live-in lifestyles, and his-and-her children. Most important, though, is that the new focus on the family does not portend a retreat to the home. Rather, Boomers will be looking for enriching experiences that can be shared by the entire family in any setting, especially outside the home. And because Boomers will remain busy and time-starved, they will want to make sure that the time they get to spend with their children is a celebration, not merely an accommodation.

One market affected by this is food service. For years, restaurants attracted parents with children by offering informal, casual situations that were often noisy and messy. Good, accommodating kid settings, but not necessarily good, celebratory family settings. Boomer parents will be looking for something more special, perhaps a somewhat more formal setting with a calmer and quieter atmosphere.

Home building is another market that will be affected. It used to be that a builder couldn't sell an upscale home to Boomers without a Jacuzzi and double sinks in the bathroom. But Boomers have moved the center of home life from the self-indulgent bathroom to the family-friendly kitchen, a room that serves as a central headquarters for the whole family, and for guests too.

Realtors also tell us that front porches are one of the top priorities among Boomer buyers today. Even if their busy schedules prevent them from using that porch, Boomers seem to be soothed by its presence. After all, nothing better evokes the nostalgia for the traditional, family-focused times of their youth.

STRESS

Stress among Americans is at near-record highs, and Boomers are the most stressed generation in history. Not only do they face stress from the normal responsibilities of their middle age, they must also cope with the disappointment of their expectations and the disadvantages that these expectations created for them. In particular, Boomers expected plenty all their lives, so they learned to spend, not to save, and never concerned themselves with optimizing their finances during hard times. Their financial heyday in the mid-eighties showed only that Boomers knew how to spend during good times. The recent evidence about their abilities to manage during bad times is not good.

The major cause of Boomer stress is too many things to do, too many responsibilities to manage, too many decisions to make. The shift we've observed in our MONITOR tracking is away from the old strategic shopping style of consumption to a new style we've dubbed "strategic control." Strategic control is the practice of managing one's life through delegation and selection—consumers reprioritizing to recapture the possibilities of their lives. This is a

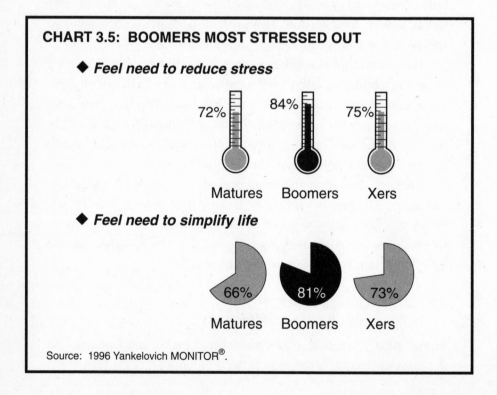

CHART 3.5: BOOMERS MOST STRESSED OUT

◆ *Feel need to reduce stress*

72%   84%   75%

Matures   Boomers   Xers

◆ *Feel need to simplify life*

66%   81%   73%

Matures   Boomers   Xers

Source: 1996 Yankelovich MONITOR®.

significant shift. Boomers today want to control only those things that are most important to them, and they are willing to accept some guidance even in those areas.

One whimsical manifestation of this is a service that picks up after pets, called "One Less Mess." The name, at the very least, captures the emerging Boomer search for less stress through simplification.

Honda has recently tried to capitalize on this. Honda TV ads emphasize their car as a mode of transport to a simpler, less stressful life. In one ad, a driver is trapped in the middle of a massive city traffic jam, complete with a screaming, bellicose cabbie. Suddenly a giant pencil eraser appears and wipes the screen clean of the surrounding noise and confusion, leaving the driver free to pursue a simpler course.

In another Honda TV ad, the camera follows a businessman as he arrives at work one morning and runs the gauntlet to his office. He stares straight ahead as various disasters affecting him are announced along the way—his credit cards are lost, his neighbor is suing him, his computer has crashed, he's stepped in something smelly. And then, when he opens the door to his office, it all fades away. There in front of him is his car, a Honda Accord, and nothing but his car, free of any other complexity. The announcer says to us, "Life gotten a little crazy? Try the simple simplicity of an Accord sedan." Only one word appears on the screen, set in relief against the white background: "Simplicity."

Along these lines, we expect a boom in personal services for Boomers eager to rid their lives of as much stress as possible. There will be a growing need for help in areas like money management.

The corollary to this, though, will be a recognition of what *not* to do. For example, many businesses are currently adding technology to replace people. From a financial standpoint, this is smart. But many of the technologies being added require that customers make more decisions. Boomers won't necessarily welcome being forced to do more for themselves—that's exactly what they're trying *not* to do.

This is something to pay special attention to in the growing cyberspace world of on-line services. There's the potential for enormous personal empowerment in accessing facts and sources on the Internet. But just because it's there doesn't mean Boomer consumers will want it. Thinking otherwise—the "if you build it, they will come" fantasy—is a continuing marketing mistake made by technology companies, and it's about to made again on-line. Boomers are not all that keen on having to decide among an infinite number of choices. One growing way that Boomers reduce stress is by selectively managing and delegating various priorities, so an on-line service that runs counter to this trend is likely to have a difficult time.

IN THE KNOW

There is a counterbalancing factor, though, to this Boomer desire to shed stress through simplification. Boomers do not want to be left feeling that by delegating more they have put themselves at a disadvantage, or have locked themselves out of being "in the know." Boomers always will remain control-oriented. They're just redefining exactly what that means.

This is a key idea. There are two major value trends at work— not only the growing need for simplification, but also the continuing need for control. Too much simplification leads to a loss of control, and is unpalatable. The marketing magic will come from providing simplicity along with control, not simplicity alone. If it's so simple that it's superficial, it will only add stress. Both needs must be satisfied simultaneously.

Automobile dealers found that no-haggle pricing is too simple. Consumers worry that the loss of control means they are not getting the best possible deal. It's the same problem with one-rate pricing for long distance services. And health maintenance organizations run the same risk. Managed care simplifies medical decision-making, but perhaps with too much loss of control. Finding innovative ways to strike this balance is one of the big, untapped opportunities in tomorrow's marketplace. So far, marketers have caught on only to the simplification side of this balance.

Boomers are demanding customers. They want the real story. They grew up seeing there was always a hidden truth accessible to people smart or determined enough to get at it. From the *Pentagon Papers* and Watergate to "Sixty Minutes" to Geraldo, Boomers have learned it takes intense, aggressive scrutiny to remain knowledgeable and in control.

They are as hungry as ever for information that tells them what's real and true about the products and services they evaluate. Ads should give them the kinds of information they can use to make detailed judgments. Far more than the other generational cohorts active in the marketplace today, Boomers are the most likely to want data before they buy—they are the most likely to seek the advice of someone who already owns a product or to consult consumer information services and reports.

Much of this is because Boomers are better educated than previous generations, and businesses have had to learn from scratch how to interact with these savvier consumers. Boomers have insisted upon a level of openness and access not available in the past. This is something Boomers will carry with them as they age, thus making the mature consumers of tomorrow more sophisticated than today's Matures.

Continuing education is one market with potential. Boomers will not lose their interest in acquiring knowledge, but more creative topics will be of special interest, like hands-on learning that combines an experience with a lecture—a weekend tending sea turtle eggs along with talks on ecology, or visits to historical sites along with books about the times. Additionally, business and financial information will be of growing interest as Boomers tackle new challenges in their careers and their finances.

Marketing strategies with the best chance of succeeding are those that reinforce the strong Boomer sense of self-reliance and individual superiority but don't require a lot of effort and participation. Our surveys find that Boomers have a lot of confidence in their own abilities and are apt to follow their own instincts.

"Mass customization" is a great way to balance these appeals—highly simplified while at the same time high in control and informative, precisely because it is customized. This strategy clearly works with luxury items and nonessentials, but it can be successfully applied to basic necessities as well. Although mass customization eventually may be extended to all consumers, right now the primary buyers for such goods are Boomers.

One of our favorite examples is the Custom Foot, a shoe store that opened in the affluent commuter suburb of Westport, Connecticut. Shoppers at Custom Foot have their feet scanned electronically to measure even the slightest size variations between their left and right feet. Then, with their feet measured mechanically, they use a computer to choose the style and material of their new shoes. The information is transmitted to Italy, where hand-crafted shoes are made and shipped two weeks later. The price averages $140 per pair, compared with $500 or more for regular custom-made shoes.

When Custom Foot opened, waiting lines were up to two hours long. Although customers come in all ages, the majority were Boomers, said Laura La Reddola, the store manager. "They are the people with jobs, who are on their feet all day," she added. "And they are the sort of demanding consumers for whom this sort of product would appeal. They are the quintessential Boomers."

The Custom Foot plans a nationwide chain of stores to capitalize on these Boomer consumers. Bigger companies are also using mass customization to find new niches. For instance, hotel chains are starting to record customer preferences in a central database. This helps them meet individual needs for particular customers no matter which of the hotels in their chain a customer stays at next. Mail-order computer companies now use software to translate buyer preferences into tailor-made computer components. Companies that maintain home pages on the Internet are starting to build in database systems that customize the screens seen by individual users based on personal choices made on previous visits.

NEVER SAY "SENIOR"

Even in the throes of nostalgia, Boomers still think of themselves as young. After all, they grew up in a time that celebrated youth. Boomers retain this belief in the superiority of their own fresh eyes over the wisdom of their elders even as they don bifocals. When asked to describe themselves in our annual MONITOR tracking, Boomers aligned more closely with the ways younger Xers described themselves than with the ways older Matures described themselves. Boomers, like Xers, say they are intelligent, ambitious, creative, romantic, impulsive, and sexy. In fact, as a median, Boomers give seventy-nine as the age they consider old. Boomers want to be, in the words of an old Dylan tune, "forever young."

Boomers, like Matures, will avoid products pitched to older consumers. A more subtle approach is required. Look at the way Dockers marketed its pants. They are stitched to accommodate middle-age spread, but that was never mentioned in the ads. Instead, the TV spots showed vibrant, healthy Boomers sitting around talking about their lives, in settings reminiscent of college dorms and frat houses, as the camera pans across the labels on their pants. It's a great way to drive home a point without turning off customers.

GAP has adopted a similar strategy with their multiple lines of jeans, sold with inoffensive size descriptions—"loose fit," "easy fit," and so forth. At GAP, you carry to the register a fashion that signals the comfort you prefer, not a generational label that announces your age.

One lasting effect of the youthful exuberance and self-indulgence of Boomers is their continued attraction to *romance and adventure* as antidotes to the dull routine of the everyday. For Boomers, this sentiment remains just as strong today as it was twenty years ago. Matures have simply *never* identified with this value. Boomers are still looking for youthful romance and adventure. This is why one of the full-page print ads for the Disney Institute shows an adventurous Boomer in an Institute T-shirt com-

---

CHART 3.6: MONITOR trend: _Romance and Adventure—_
"Antidote to Dull Routine"

% "strong" on Trend	Xers today*	Boomers then**	Boomers today*	Matures then**	Matures today*
	26	20	22	9	13

* Today: 1995.
** Then: 1973.
Source: Yankelovich MONITOR®.

---

pletely stretched out, reaching to find a handhold around the far edge of the rock outcropping on which he is climbing.

FIND NEW WAYS TO WIN

Boomers still want to be the winners they grew up expecting to be. They are responsive to products and services that help them find new ways to win, and to brands effectively positioned as choices for winners. This yen to win even as they age will create a new market for products like high-energy foods that give Boomers a youthful buzz. Think of it as the search for the next big tingle, for products with a burst of sparkle and fizz—skin creams and lotions that prickle, or drinks that bubble and effervesce, or are highly caffeinated. Powerful cars will be popular with Boomers trading in their vans as children leave home. Think of the Pontiac ad in which a Boomer driver slides behind the wheel and is transformed from businessman to race driver and back again. Go admire the new E-class Mercedes-Benz sedan. It's been restyled to replace the old boxy-looking front end with new curves that make the car sleeker and sportier.

But there are also areas where Boomers really don't want to try to win anymore. They now care less about style and are more concerned with comfort. Novelty for its own sake is out. So is gratuitous risk-taking. Brand names are no longer badges of success. And shopping is no longer entertainment. Functionality is what Boomers now want. In the future, this will be even truer—pizzazz will fizzle and function will flourish.

The trick is to let them know they are getting a good deal. It's a variation on appealing to Matures by telling them they have earned it. Boomers want to think of themselves as winning shoppers, so give them that reinforcement.

RETREAD, NOT RETIRE

Boomers will not retire, at least not in the way Matures retired. Instead, they will retread and keep on going. As they get older, they will be much more likely to start second careers than to leave the workforce entirely. This is a generation that does not view a leisurely retirement as their reward for years of hard work. Boomers will approach retirement as a work style, not as a lifestyle.

There are three reasons for this. First, Boomers won't have the financial wherewithal to retire. Second, Boomers are work-centered and will continue to focus on this. Third, Boomers are still looking for meaning and fulfillment. They always expected that work would provide this for them, so they will continue to work to find it rather than retire.

Money is going to be a problem for Boomers, so perhaps the biggest growth opportunity is in providing financial services. This is a generation about to face serious money problems. They were great yuppies, with all the skills it took to spend, spend, spend. Financial instruments and products that helped them spend went gangbusters. Home equity loans, credit cards, and mortgage refinancing thrived. Now, for many, things are about to change.

Boomers are beginning to get a glimpse of their future. When asked in our MONITOR research if they feel the need to reduce their debt level, 79 percent of Boomer respondents said they did. Even more, 86 percent, said they needed to plan for retirement.

These needs can translate into some real opportunities. Boomers learned early how to spend, but they never developed the attitudes, discipline, and skills required for financial hard times. Boomer savings rates have been quite low. They will increasingly delegate to experts and rely on those experts for advice and guidance.

There is tremendous marketing opportunity here for financial instruments designed to encourage Boomers to save. But Boomers can't simply be scared into saving. It will take an approach that leverages their yen to spend, one that establishes an equivalence between the need to save and the urge to spend.

Retreading goes beyond mere financial need, however. In our surveys, Boomers are by far the most likely to cite work as the primary way in which they express their personal creativity. They describe work as a career, not a job, and they reject boring jobs with good pay. While Matures have always put work and leisure in separate compartments—leisure as the reward for hard work—Boomers have not. Though this prioritization is now changing, work will always be important to them.

It will be hard for Boomers to let go of work for a retirement that completely indulges leisure activities. They will continue to want some connection to work. In a 1996 survey of people born in 1946, the oldest of the Boomers, fully two-thirds said they expected to continue working in some capacity after they reach retirement age.

While Boomers entered the workforce expecting that their careers would bring them fulfillment, for the last two decades, they have felt lucky just to have jobs. As they look towards the next twenty years, with financial responsibilities easing and life getting shorter and shorter, many Boomers will look to start over. They will choose brand new careers that can provide them with the self-fulfillment they sought and expected, keeping them in the workforce well past the traditional retirement age at which Matures moved to Florida and Sun City.

You don't have to wait until Boomers, who have just started turning fifty, reach their retirement years to capitalize on this trend.

You should aim products now at keeping them healthy and helping them sustain their energy and activity levels. They'll be looking to headhunters and career counselors to help them find the right second career, and they are not likely to want to wait until they're in their sixties to get started. They'll need more education and training, and especially entrepreneurial capital to start that frozen yogurt stand at the beach or the corner bookstore coffeehouse in their old college town.

Innovative work structures will abound as Boomers take on a grayer cast: more work at home, more informal workplaces, more casual clothes, and flexible hours to make time for rest and reenergizing.

Services designed for businesspeople will have to be reconfigured to accommodate these older workers and travelers. Take airlines. They'll need wider seats and more legroom to handle the coming wave of older business passengers who need more personal space in which to fit bigger bottoms and to stretch stiffer bodies. Take medical services. Older patients will need new devices and treatments as they leave the doctor's office to go back to work instead of back home. Take computers. Fuzzy gray backlit screens won't be popular with the trifocal business crowd, and there will be a demand for ultralight, hands-free hardware that can better conform to capabilities of older Boomer workers.

Boomers will remain the dominant consumer group in the marketplace for years to come. They will continue to expect to be the center of attention. But to get the satisfaction they expect, they will need help and support. Herein lies the opportunity for smart, generationally savvy marketers.

Boomers: The 78-million-strong Gorilla

1950
Diner's Club card introduced
"Peanuts" comic strip introduced
Korean War starts
FBI's Ten Most Wanted List first put
    out
Sen. Joseph McCarthy accuses 205
    in State Department of commu-
    nism
First human organ transplant

1951
Mickey Mantle joins New York
    Yankees
UNIVAC I begins operation for
    Census
Willie Mays joins New York Giants
CBS makes first commercial color
    TV broadcast
Lacoste tennis shirts first appear
Alan Freed coins the term
    rock'n'roll
First power steering offered on
    Chrysler Crown Imperial
I Love Lucy airs
Search for Tomorrow airs

1952
Today with Dave Garroway premieres
Kellogg's Sugar Frosted Flakes
    introduced
American Bandstand with Dick
    Clark premieres
H-bomb exploded in South Pacific
Dragnet first broadcast
Christine Jorgensen gets first pub-
    licly acknowledged sex change
    operation in Denmark
Art Linkletter starts TV variety
    show
Mad magazine first published
Scrabble introduced
National Enquirer first published
Tappan introduces first microwave
    oven for home use
Nixon gives Checkers speech
First Holiday Inn opens

1955
Thunderbird introduced
Gunsmoke first airs
Captain Kangaroo first broadcast
Lawrence Welk begins his TV
    musical shows
The Mickey Mouse Club first broad-
    cast
Disneyland opens
Montgomery bus boycott led by Dr.
    Martin Luther King, Jr., when
    Rosa Parks refuses to give up seat
    on bus
Play-Doh introduced
Ann Landers launches advice col-
    umn
Elvis signs with RCA

1954
First atomic sub, the Nautilus,
    launched
First mass inoculation against polio
Sports Illustrated first published
Swanson introduces TV dinners
Oral Roberts goes on TV
Willie Mays makes "the catch" in
    World Series
The Tonight Show debuts with Steve
    Allen as host
Brown v. Board of Education
The Wild One, first biker movie,
    released

1953
Corvette goes on sale
TV Guide first published
20th Century-Fox converts to Cine-
    mascope
Korean War armistice signed
Top-40 radio format established
Playboy published with nude photos
    of Marilyn Monroe
Coronation of Queen Elizabeth II

1956 Interstate highway construction
authorized
Wham-O Frisbee introduced
Don Larsen of New York Yankees
pitches perfect game in World
Series
Peyton Place published
Grace Kelly marries Prince Rainier III
Elvis releases "Hound Dog" / "Don't
be Cruel"; appears on *Ed Sullivan
Show*; stars in *Love Me Tender*

1957 Edsel introduced
Consumption of margarine sur-
passes consumption of butter
Racial unrest in Little Rock,
Arkansas, high school
Spandex invented
Leave it to Beaver debuts

1958 Permanent press introduced
First-class stamp rises for first time
since 1932, from 3 to 4 cents
Dodgers and Giants play for first
time on West Coast
Quiz show scandals
First American Express card
Grammy Awards launched
Hula Hoop craze
Elvis goes into Army for next two
years

1959 Beatnik craze
Barbie doll introduced
Ben-Hur in movie theaters
The Twilight Zone airs
Telephone booth stuffing is college
craze
Panti-legs, first pantyhose, intro-
duced
Alaska and Hawaii become 49th and
50th states
Berry Gordy, Jr., starts Motown
Records
Tang introduced

1961 Peace Corps started
Bay of Pigs debacle
Valium introduced
Wide World of Sports first airs
Catch-22 by Joseph Heller pub-
lished
Freedom riders travel through South
Roger Maris breaks Babe Ruth's
home-run record
Soviet cosmonaut, Yuri Gagarin,
first man to orbit earth
Bob Dylan's first performance in
Greenwich Village club
Mercury astronaut Alan B. Shepard,
Jr., first American in space
IBM Selectric typewriter introduced
Construction of Berlin Wall begun
Pampers introduced
First on-screen French kiss between
Natalie Wood and Warren Beatty
in *Splendor in the Grass*

1960 Eisenhower warns of "military-
industrial complex"
U-2 pilot, Gary Powers, shot down
over USSR
JFK elected President
First birth control pill, Enovid, goes
on sale
Xerox introduces first copier
Students for Democratic Society
(SDS) founded
Psycho in movie theaters
Häagen-Dazs ice cream invented
Teflon-coated cookware introduced
The Andy Griffith Show airs
The Flintstones airs
Chubby Checker starts Twist dance
craze

1962
Astronaut John Glenn orbits the earth three times
Freeze-dried foods introduced
Diet-Rite Cola introduced as first diet soft drink
Direct-dial long distance service started
Silent Spring by Rachel Carson published
Marilyn Monroe found dead in the nude
Johnny Carson takes over as host of *The Tonight Show*
Cuban Missile Crisis
First 007 movie, *Dr. No*, released

1963
JFK assassinated
Prayer in schools ruled unconstitutional
Trolls hit the market
General Hospital first broadcast
Martin Luther King, Jr., delivers his "I Have a Dream" speech
Instant replay first used for broadcast of Army-Navy game
Beach Party, first beach movie, released
Surfing craze takes off
The Feminine Mystique by Betty Friedan published

1965
First of LBJ's Great Society programs passed, including Medicare
Unsafe at Any Speed by Ralph Nader published
Malcom X assassinated
Skateboard craze
Bell-bottoms are fashionable
Bill Cosby is first African American TV Star on *I Spy*
Health warnings mandated for cigarette packs
The Sound of Music is released
Pop-top cans first used
Miniskirts introduced

1964
The Beatles arrive in America
Muhammad Ali wins first heavyweight title as Cassius Clay
Sidney Poitier is first African American actor to win Oscar
Berkeley free speech movement
Ford Mustang hits market
John Archibald Wheeler coins term *black hole*
First disco, Whiskey-a-Go-Go, opens in Los Angeles
Marshall McLuhan coins "the medium is the message"
Topless bathing suit shocks fashion world
Pop-Tarts introduced
First refrigerator magnets on market
The new math hits schools
Peyton Place first prime-time soap
New York World's Fair opens
GI Joe introduced

1966
AFL and NFL merge together

The Beatles release "Yesterday," the most-recorded popular song ever

Miranda rights mandated by Supreme Court

The Beatles perform their last concert in San Francisco's Candlestick Park

Charles Whitman kills 16 people, shooting from the University of Texas tower

Star Trek first broadcast

John Lennon utters "more popular than Jesus" remark

Chinese Cultural Revolution started

Watts riots in Los Angeles

Mission: Impossible first airs

1967
First Super Bowl played between Green Bay and Kansas City

Nehru jackets

Twiggy becomes popular in America

Muhammad Ali stripped of his title

Rolling Stone first published

First spaghetti western, *A Fistful of Dollars*, released

Sgt. Pepper's Lonely Hearts Club Band released by the Beatles

Thurgood Marshall joins Supreme Court as first African American justice

Race riots in Newark and Detroit

The Graduate released

1968
Navy ship *Pueblo* seized by North Korea

911 emergency number introduced in New York

Tet offensive

Laugh-in first airs; Nixon appears to say "Sock it to me!"

60 Minutes first airs

Martin Luther King, Jr., assassinated

Soviets crush Prague uprising

Robert Kennedy assassinated

Apollo 8 sends back images of "earthrise" on way to dark side of moon

My Lai massacre

Judge allows Karen Anne Quinlan to be taken off life-support

Violence mars Democratic National Convention in Chicago

2001: A Space Odyssey in movie theaters

Jackie Kennedy marries Aristotle Onassis

Cesar Chavez leads nationwide boycott of table grapes

Richard Nixon elected President

Judy Garland dies

Vietnam War peace talks begin in Paris

Mister Rodgers' Neighborhood first airs

Student takeover of Columbia University

Beatles form Apple Records

HAIR opens in New York

At Mexico City Summer Olympics, two African American athletes give Black Power salute on victory stand

1969
Apollo 11 astronaut Neil Armstrong
 walks on the moon
Easy Rider in movie theaters
Sesame Street first broadcast
Ted Kennedy involved in Chap-
 paquiddick scandal
First American teenager dies of
 AIDS in St. Louis, undiscovered
 until 1987
Tate murders committed by Manson
 associates
John Wayne wins Oscar for *True
 Grit*
First fern bar, Henry Africa, opens
 in San Francisco
*Butch Cassidy and the Sundance
 Kid* released
Bubble memory invented for com-
 puters
Premiere of *Monty Python's Flying
 Circus* on BBC
Woodstock
In Super Bowl III, New York Jets
 beat Baltimore Colts just as Joe
 Namath promised they would

1970
Monday Night Football first airs
Invasion of Cambodia leads to
 shooting of students at Kent State
First known interracial marriage in
 the state of Mississippi
Donahue show goes national
On a single day, four commercial
 jetliners hijacked by Arab terror-
 ists
Earth Shoes go on sale in New York
 on Earth Day
Women's Wear Daily coins term *hot-
 pants*
Nautilus equipment debuts at
 weightlifters' convention in LA
Waterbeds introduced

Ms. magazine launched **1972**
Nixon appoints first drug czar in
 war on drugs
Mark Spitz wins seven swimming
 gold medals at Munich Summer
 Olympics
Burt Reynolds nude in *Cosmopoli-
 tan* centerfold
At Munich Olympics, eleven Israeli
 athletes killed by Arab terrorists
The Godfather in movie theaters
Jonathan Livingstone Seagull pub-
 lished
UPC scanner codes introduced
Apollo 17 makes last lunar landing
Clifford Irving defrauds McGraw-
 Hill of advance on bogus autobi-
 ography of Howard Hughes
Deep Throat released
Nixon visits China
Supreme Court declares death
 penalty unconstitutional

Ban on TV advertising of cigarettes **1971**
All in the Family first broadcast
London Bridge moved to Arizona
Attica prison riots in New York State
Voting age lowered to 18
Term *workaholic* coined by psy-
 chologist Wayne E. Oates
First hand-held calculator intro-
 duced by Bowmar Instruments
 Corp. at a cost of $249
People's Republic of China joins
 United Nations
White House plumbers burglarize
 Daniel Ellsberg's psychiatrist's
 office
Walt Disney World opens
Pentagon Papers published
Wage and price controls imposed by
 Nixon
Ali's draft evasion conviction over-
 turned by Supreme Court

1973
Roe v. Wade decision legalizes abortion
Vietnam cease fire signed in Paris
Cuisinart introduced
Televised Senate hearings on Watergate begin
Billie Jean King defeats Bobby Riggs in Battle of Sexes
In Saturday Night Massacre, Nixon fires Watergate special prosecutor Archibald Cox and Deputy Attorney General William Ruckelshaus, and Attorney General Elliot Richardson resigns
Yom Kippur War starts, followed by an Arab oil embargo
18.5-minute gap discovered in a subpoenaed Watergate tape
In speech, Nixon says, "I am not a crook"
District of Columbia becomes self-governing
The Joy of Sex published
Free agency comes to baseball
American Psychiatric Association reverses itself and says homosexuality is not a mental illness

1975
Two assassination attempts made on President Ford
Fall of Saigon
Mood rings introduced
Jaws in movie theaters
New York City comes close to default
Jimmy Hoffa disappears
Advertising on T-shirts started
Pet Rock introduced
Federal government orders equal access to sports for women
Saturday Night Live first broadcast
Pie-killing craze
Martina Navratilova defects to United States

1974
Streaking craze
Digital watches introduced
Heimlich maneuver introduced
Hank Aaron breaks Babe Ruth's career home-run record
Frank Robinson is first African American manager in baseball for Cleveland Indians
Ali wins second title
Chris Chubbuck, TV commentator in Sarasota, Florida, shoots self in head live on air
Triathlon created
Nixon resigns
Ford pardons Nixon
Patty Hearst kidnapped by Symbionese Liberation Army
WIN buttons show up everywhere
People magazine launched

1976
Jimmy Carter makes "lust in my heart" comment in *Playboy* interview
Carter elected president
Rocky in movie theaters
First Apple computer created
Bicentennial celebration
Harlequin Romances started
VHS video recorders introduced
Personal ads take off
Supreme Court declares death penalty constitutional

1977
Jacqueline Means is first ordained female Episcopal priest
New York City blackout
Star Wars in movie theaters
Roots miniseries on TV
Son of Sam murders in New York City
Alaskan pipeline opens
Close Encounters of the Third Kind in movie theaters
Reggie Jackson hits 3 home runs on 3 first pitches by 3 different pitchers on 3 consecutive at-bats in the sixth and deciding game of World Series between New York Yankees and Los Angeles Dodgers
Elvis Presley dies

1978
Jim Jones and followers commit mass suicide in Guyana
City of Cleveland defaults, the first since Great Depression
Dallas first broadcast
First test-tube baby born in Oldham, England
Animal House in movie theaters
Saturday Night Fever in movie theaters
Love Canal evacuation
Proposition 13 passes in California
Ali wins third title
Camp David accords

Shah of Iran deposed and Ayatollah Khomeini assumes power in Iran
Hostages taken in US Embassy in Iran
Skylab comes crashing down
Soviets invade Afghanistan
Michelle Marvin wins palimony from Lee Marvin
Three Mile Island nuclear accident
Charlie Smith, last living former slave, dies at age 137
Susan B. Anthony dollar put in circulation
Sex Pistols' Sid Vicious dies of heroin overdose
Margaret Thatcher becomes prime minister of England
Stagflation rampant
Sebastian Coe becomes first man to hold 800m, 1500m, and mile world records
1979

GenX: The New
Pragmatists

Generation X, or GenX, is filled with twenty-somethings who are turned off and tuned out—to everything except MTV. It's a generation of slackers, whiners, and yuffies (young urban failures) with no expectations beyond "McJobs."

Not!

The Washington Post called them "crybabies," and ex-columnist for *The New Republic* Michael Kinsley, a Boomer who is now editor-in-chief of Microsoft's new cybermagazine, *Slate*, complained once, "These kids today. They're soft. They don't know how good they have it. Not only did they never have to fight in a war . . . they never even had to dodge one."

Get a life, Kinsley!

All this kvetching by Boomers—particularly in the Boomer-dominated media—comes from what GenX author Douglas Coupland described as "clique maintenance," the compulsion of one generation to bolster its own self-image by disparaging the next one.

But it was Coupland's book, *Generation X*, that fed the popular portrait of GenXers. In jacket copy, the book promoted itself as the story of "fanatically independent individuals, pathologically ambivalent about the future, and brimming with unsatisfied longings for permanence, for love, and for their own home." It was an unflattering picture of his generation, earning Coupland the title "Mr. X," a moniker he would like to leave behind. This portrayal of GenX is the one promoted by an older generation that judges the younger one by its own values, a classic example of generational myopia. Marketers who rely upon this portrait of GenXers will see their products and services fail.

As it comes of age, each generation complains about what it is inheriting. Boomers, especially, did it big time. There is much validity to the complaints of GenXers. Statistics clearly show that these young consumers face economic and social obstacles that did not exist for Boomers, obstacles that many see as even more intimidating than those faced by Matures. The important point here is that the conventional portrait of GenXers, wherever it comes from, is not the full picture.

To understand GenX, the place to start is just before GenX. Indeed, as with so many marketplace trends over the last twenty-five years, we need to go back to Boomers. Not all the way back. Just to the last wave of Boomers, a group variously known as busters or 'tweeners or, as we prefer, Trailing Boomers—"trailing" because the Boomer experiences of affluence and high expectations affected them too, although, in a different way. By looking at what Trailing Boomers experienced coming of age at the very end of the seventies and the beginning of the eighties, we can better understand the tougher marketplace realities that have shaped the Xer mind-set.

Trailing Boomers were born between 1960 and 1964. They turned eighteen between 1978 and 1982, the transition from the more carefree sixties and seventies to the more careworn eighties

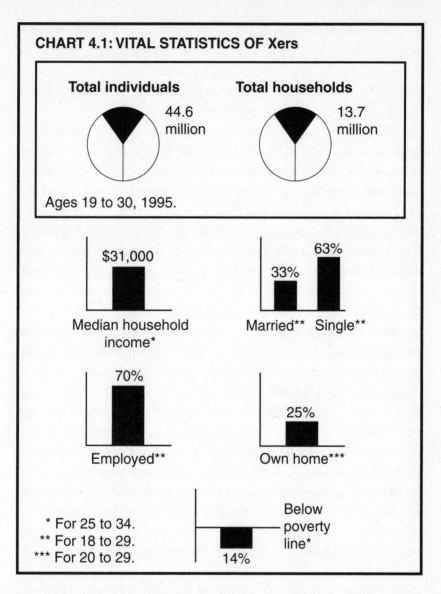

CHART 4.1: VITAL STATISTICS OF Xers

Total individuals

44.6 million

Total households

13.7 million

Ages 19 to 30, 1995.

$31,000

Median household income*

33% 63%

Married** Single**

70%

Employed**

25%

Own home***

* For 25 to 34.
** For 18 to 29.
*** For 20 to 29.

Below poverty line*

14%

and nineties. Trailing Boomers were, figuratively if not often liter-ally, the baby brothers and sisters of their older Boomer siblings. They ate from the same table, watched the same TV shows lying around the same family room, were regaled with tales of hippies and draft dodgers, came to know Vietnam as it wound down into the fall of Saigon, and heard about Nixon as Jimmy Carter vaulted from the governor's mansion to the White House. These very early experiences infused them with nascent Boomer expectations, in particular, the assumption that they too would be able to take prosperity for granted. The "system" automatically would give them the opportunity to do better than those before them.

What derailed Trailing Boomers was exactly what derailed all Boomers—the fallout from 1979. As they grew up, Trailing Boomers had every reason to expect the same easy teenage years their older brothers and sisters enjoyed. But while they were still in their teens, their expectations were fractured by the abrupt realities of gas lines and stagflation, of hostages in Iran and Soviets in Afghanistan, of nuclear meltdowns and corporate bailouts. This gap between adolescent expectations and adult realities has been present for all Boomers, but these experiences hit Trailing Boomers much earlier in their formative years.

Their values and life skills reflect this formative mix of high expectations and hard realities. Listen to Trailing Boomers talk and you'll find no connection with the pop-art, feel-good, tie-dyed psychedelic edge of the sixties and early seventies. Borrowing from other sources, they invented instead an alternative cutting edge: thrashing, angry, hard-core rock, a generational sensibility aptly compressed by one popular group into just two words—their aggressively unsentimental band name, the Dead Kennedys.

A contemporary expression of this sensibility is *George*, a new magazine of politics, culture, and commentary. *George* is the brainchild of its editor-in-chief, John F. Kennedy, Jr., a Trailing Boomer. Editorially it reflects the Trailing Boomer experience in its mix of Boomer values and Xer style. Its values are investigative, pointed, and serious, especially in regular features like the monthly interview conducted by Kennedy himself. But the content, put together under the motto "not just politics as usual," is droll, even sneering. The cover of early issues pictured entertainers with "attitude," like Howard Stern or Charles Barkley, posing in costumes caricaturing George Washington. "What's So Good About Virtue?" asks the title of one article. "Oprah or Uma?" is the headline question put to then-presidential candidate Steve Forbes in another.

This sensibility, behind its Bronx cheer, is all about *survival*. It says don't get your hopes up too high, too far beyond reasonable ambitions—advice born of hard personal experience. It says here's what it really takes to make it—a focus on pragmatics instead of ideology. It says lighten up, have some fun while doing something serious—reminding readers not to get too self-absorbed.

Trailing Boomers, like all Boomers, have been experimenters. But their experimentation has been more about self-preservation than self-exploration. They have had to reinvent how to live, how to play, how to work. They had no role models in this. They had no hint they'd be confronted with hard times, unlike Xers, who grew up with hard times. Trailing Boomers thus bridge generations—the last Boomers expecting perpetual abundance and the first Xers faced with breakdown and uncertainty.

Across this bridge, the generational experience motivating marketplace consumption fundamentally shifts. Early and middle Boomers felt they would flourish. Able to take survival for granted, they felt free to search for and experiment with anything new. Trailing Boomers were forced to confront the possibility that success, perhaps even survival, might not be guaranteed, but the brief economic boom of the mid-eighties bailed them out. *Xers are the generational cohort that's never been able to presume success.*

UNCERTAINTY

The eighties, full to bursting with excesses and failures, were a harsh tutor for Xers. The decade kicked off with the economic turmoil of the so-called Reagan recession, then moved into the conspicuous consumption and competition most commonly associated with the eighties, and finally concluded somewhat uncertainly after the unsettling stock market crash of 1987.

Much of the uncertainty experienced by Xers as they grew up, though, came from the generational debris Boomers left in their wake. Forget what the idealistic Boomers intended, Xers say, and look instead at what they actually did: Divorce. Latchkey kids. Homelessness. Soaring national debt. Bankrupt Social Security. Holes in the ozone layer. Crack. Downsizing and layoffs. Urban deterioration. Gangs. Junk bonds. Abscam, DeLorean, Barry . . . on videotape. Bakker, Boesky, Milken . . . off to jail. This is what Xers have: the Simpsons' neighborhood, not the Cleavers'; Roseanne's living room in Lanford, not Andy's front porch in Mayberry.

The world inherited by Boomers was one Matures had built up and filled with the (seemingly) certain promise of a better future. But, say Xers, Boomers overindulged, heedless of the consequences, bequeathing a world in tatters, a world with difficult, uncertain prospects for the future.

So the first lesson Xers learned was never to take anything for granted, especially if it's been handled first by a Boomer. You can never be sure of what to expect. The marketplace is unpredictable. Everything needs to be fixed. And because of this, you can't depend on any long-term plans. After all, Dad had planned on IBM—or on AT&T or on GM—and look what happened to him. Even a college degree has ambiguous value for Xers—it's a guarantee of nothing.

For Xers, the truth has been just as uncertain as their future. Television shows were often put together more in the style of David Copperfield than of Edward R. Murrow—truck explosions staged on news shows; audiences coached on infomercials. They saw that the memories of individual people can prove to be dangerously unreliable, recovered as they are, in many cases, with the help of overzealous therapists. Hidden epidemics of missing children and ritual satanic abuse failed to materialize after overwrought talk-show speculation. And unsavory gossip about the private lives of celebrities and public figures had a heyday in tabloid headlines and unauthorized biographies. No one, it seemed, was the person we had believed they were.

Boomers and Matures at least once knew a different world, but this was all Xers had ever known. Understandably, some Xers responded with devil-may-care detachment and even, for those most resentful of the legacy inherited from Boomers, hostility and anger.

It's an experience leading many Xers to conclude that, as the 1994 Winona Ryder movie was entitled, *Reality Bites*. The film opens with Ryder's character, Lelaina Pierce, making her valedictorian speech, which poses the challenge faced by her generation: "And they wonder why those of us in our twenties refuse to work an eighty-hour week just so we can afford to buy their BMWs. Why we aren't interested in the counter-culture that they invented as if we did not see them disembowel their revolution for a pair of running shoes. But the question remains, what are we going to do now? How can we repair all the damage we inherited? Fellow graduates, the answer is simple. The answer is . . . [She fumbles for the last page of her speech. But it's lost.] . . . I don't know."

The movie shows Lelaina and her friends forging a way to an answer. We hear them say that having your own place is the American Dream of the nineties. We watch them in anguish over an AIDS test, or over coming out. We observe them in their world of TV and malls and seventies trappings and convenience stores. Lelaina even remarks that a "Big Gulp" is all it takes to make her happy. We hear them reject the idea that they have some obligation to make the world a better place. We see their families, dysfunctional and overbearing. We see the jobs they are forced into, dead-end and deadening. Lelaina even loses one job because she can't define irony. Throughout, they deride and parody the media—commercials, MTV, the news, talk shows, all are jeered at constantly. One of the central story lines concerns Lelaina's struggle to make a documentary of her and her friends' lives, only to watch it get trivialized by a Boomer yuppie whose last name, appropriately enough, is Grates.

Through it all, though, the characters in *Reality Bites* find a way to move forward. They succeed through their own determination, their detachment from the farces around them, and their support of one another. GenXers certainly took a lot in the eighties, but they absorbed it and persevered. While the unease that permeates *Reality Bites* is indeed expressive of the anxiety and consternation felt by this generation—the sort of worry never felt by teenage Boomers— Xers have not given in to it. Like Lelaina, they hang tough.

The uncertainties of life experienced by Xers have made them wary and cautious; but only in rare cases, apathetic, profligate, or corrupt. Rob Lowe and Robert Downey, Jr., *do not* typify them. Xers are much more like Tabitha Soren, the serious, hardworking reporter for MTV, or Adam Werbach, the president of the Sierra Club, elected to office at age twenty-three.

Indeed, in many ways Xers have grown into consumers who are much savvier than Boomers or Matures, and therefore they represent a daunting challenge for marketers with only a surface understanding of their values and buying motivations. Xers are determined to be involved, to be responsible, to be in control—and to stop being victimized by life's uncertainties.

They're far better at living with uncertainty than Boomers. The Boomer focus on "live for today" was predicated on their certainty about the limitless future. Boomers were sure the future would take care of itself—that there always would be plenty more, so live for today. Xers are focused on living for today, too, but not because they feel assured about the future, but rather because they can't count on it. They do what they can today while the opportunity still exists. As the saying goes, "Life is uncertain. Eat dessert first." Uncertainty is a source of angst for Boomers, but a call to action for Xers.

The most frustrating thing about the future for Xers is their seeming inability to adequately prepare for it. They've heard all the warnings about Social Security and too much sun and exported jobs and declining biodiversity, but they are stymied by it. So rather than trying to fix everything, they focus on getting through today.

RISKS

One thing, though, is certain: the world is full of risks. And not just risks from bad things. There's a trade-off in everything. Matures

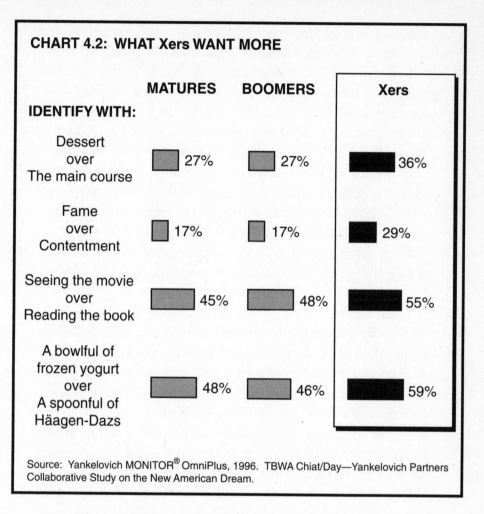

CHART 4.2: WHAT Xers WANT MORE

	MATURES	BOOMERS	Xers
IDENTIFY WITH:			
Dessert over The main course	27%	27%	36%
Fame over Contentment	17%	17%	29%
Seeing the movie over Reading the book	45%	48%	55%
A bowlful of frozen yogurt over A spoonful of Häagen-Dazs	48%	46%	59%

Source: Yankelovich MONITOR® OmniPlus, 1996. TBWA Chiat/Day—Yankelovich Partners Collaborative Study on the New American Dream.

and Boomers largely grew up in a black-and-white world—things were either good or bad. Xers, on the other hand, have grown up in a world where they see good and bad in all things. Everything is a mix of both, so every choice is a decision balancing rewards against risks. One important formative experience for Xers is that of having to weigh the trade-offs in everything.

Contemporary relationships require a balancing of the pleasures of sex and companionship against the possibilities of date rape and AIDS. Having a career means giving up a life, but just working a job means doing something boring. Drugs like cocaine are no longer the recreational pastime they were for hippies and, later, yuppie Boomers. Now they're balanced off against addiction, crack street crime, and international drug cartels. Science and technology have transformed life for the better, but sometimes a *Challenger* will explode, or a Hubble will have to be fixed at great cost and embarrassment, or a laptop will catch fire when booted up, or a super-virus will emerge as a result of pharmaceutical advances.

In making these choices, Xers have often found themselves picking between the lesser of two evils: McJobs or Microserfs; OJ or the LAPD; Mom or Dad; roommates or back home; a BA and no job or an MBA and no job; butter or margarine.

Some get paralyzed by the level of risk out there and cannot get their lives going. But many more accept these risks and trade-offs, even embracing them as a style for living.

When Mountain Dew TV ads show a bunch of Xer guys bored with the extremes of high-risk sports—been there, done that—they are appealing to a generational thirst for the next level of adventure and excitement, an adrenaline rush promised by the caffeine buzz of Mountain Dew. Risks are not to be feared, but rather to be overcome through total immersion. It's a generational chic, one as distinctive as the Boomer style based on prosperity or the Mature style based on sacrifice. Mountain Dew pokes fun at pop culture with an irreverence that makes sport of the extremes of physical adventure and the limits of cultural acceptability. The soft drink makes a statement about how life is to be understood and mastered.

Vigilance and adaptability are important. Since nothing lasts, and is certainly never unfailingly good, you must have the flexibility to change course or have backup plans. You need insurance against the bad consequences that always seem to happen. You must learn to hedge, know how to anticipate, know what to do, and be prepared to move fast.

Ask an Xer about the future and what you'll hear about is the here and now. Locking in plans for a future that is decades away makes little sense to young people who are struggling to manage their lives today. The feeling that wealth, resources, and opportunities are limited only confirms this for them. In our MONITOR research, 79 percent of Xers say they like to do things on the spur of the moment, far more than among Boomers and Matures. Similarly, 60 percent of Xers say they want to have fun now, letting the future take care of itself, compared with 38 percent of Boomers. Youthful consumers always have been more adventurous, but when we compare the attitudes of Xers today with those of Boomers twenty years ago, we see clearly that growing up in a risk-saturated world has had a great effect on the way Xers approach living.

Many Xers describe this as being "mature beyond their years." They feel that they have experienced middle-age pressures, choices, and responsibilities at an early age. They are used to making their own decisions and providing emotional stability for others. Xers see a price in Boomer lifestyles that they are unwilling to pay. There must be, Xers feel, something better out there.

And in searching for these better options, Xers have come to see there are many different alternatives, all equally valid. As a result, they have a less judgmental, more expansive opinion of the various ways people choose to be.

CHART 4.3: MONITOR Trend: *Social Pluralism—"There's No Single Right Way to Live"*

% "strong" on Trend	Xers today*	Boomers then**	Boomers today*	Matures then**	Matures today*
	28	15	21	4	14

* Today: 1995.
** Then: 1973.
Source: Yankelovich MONITOR®.

Our MONITOR research shows Xers to be, as a generation, the most socially pluralistic *ever*—that is, the least likely of any generational cohort to believe there is only one right way to live. This is a belief that grows stronger as people grow older. Our annual surveys tracking Boomers and Matures have shown each of these two generations steadily becoming more and more accepting of the alternative ways people choose to live (with, as you might expect, Boomers consistently more so than Matures). Xers, though, even as young as they are, show up in our data as more accepting of alternative lifestyles than today's Boomers and Matures. Xers are starting out today with pluralistic attitudes that are the strongest we have ever measured. As we look toward the next twenty-five years, it is clear that acceptance of alternative lifestyles will become even stronger and more widespread as Xers grow up and take over the reins of power, and become the dominant buying group in the consumer marketplace.

Diversity is a pivotal aspect of the Xer formative experience. No one thing is inherently good or bad—all things are potential options and the trade-offs have to be weighed and balanced. Each person must find an option that works for his or her own individual situation. If those choices work, then they're okay—respect and accept those choices, don't judge them or condemn them. *Diversity is the key fact of life for Xers, the core of the perspective they bring to the marketplace.*

DIVERSITY

Americans born after 1964 are already a powerful force in the marketplace, with $125 billion to spend each year on goods and services. This is partly because they get married later, partly because they are buying their homes later, and partly because an unprecedented number of them are still living at home with their parents. These are all factors with an impact on their buying power, but no one of them fully describes this generation. Indeed, beyond a few basic descriptors like these, Xers defy pigeonholing. While there *are* common themes and situations that apply to all Xers, which help us to understand them, the styles and inventions through which they express these common experiences and influences are much more diverse than those produced by prior generations.

Forget the pictures of alienated slackers hip-hopping through life in torn jeans. These one-dimensional media images are wrong. Diversity in all its forms—cultural, political, sexual, racial, social— is a hallmark of this generation, a diversity, accessible to everyone, that transcends even national borders. This generation shares in a greatly expanded global network of connections and influences. Further, this generation borrows even more freely from the cutting-edge influences of ethnic and cultural minorities in language, fashion, and music. The pace feels different for Xers, too—a whirling vortex of diverse images, messages, and chance opportunities.

Media are responsible for much of this. Every diverse thing that ever aired on TV is accessible to Xers, endlessly rerun on hundreds of channels and through countless video rentals. Computers, from CD-ROMs to the Internet, provide instant access to every kind of knowledge and trivia. Global information networks, from CNN to MTV, bring culture right into the bedroom.

Demographically this is the most diverse generation to date. They are 69 percent Caucasian, 13 percent African American, 13 percent Hispanic, 3 percent Asian American, and 1 percent Native American. Boomers, by comparison, are 75 percent Caucasian. Many predict that long before Xers reach middle age, non-Caucasian racial and ethnic groups will represent controlling pluralities in many states, including California, the symbol for many generations of the promise of the American Dream.

GO FIGURE

Marketers are faced with a multifaceted challenge. Along with Xers' diversity of opinions is an unprecedented sophistication about advertising that comes from a lifetime spent watching more of it than any other generation. GenXers are skeptical and irreverent, ready to buy but smart about marketing. Their attitudes about the marketplace demand several things of marketers.

First, *avoid slotting Xers*. They get quarrelsome when they think they are being narrowly classified. As one Xer put it in a posting on *alt.society.generation-x*, "There is a Generation X, but what it is isn't as important as what it ain't. Generation X is not 'alternative' music, 'grunge' fashion, post-modernism, urban/suburban living, advanced degrees or retarded literacy. Generation X is not unable to find a job or unwilling to hold onto one . . . In short, whatever 'picture' you've got, forget it . . . And if this bothers you . . . then you're taking the concept too seriously and need to get a life."

In a poll conducted for *Swing* magazine, a publication aimed at Xers, only 10 percent of the respondents chose "Generation X" as the name for their age group. Nearly half came up with labels so diverse they were lumped into the "Other" category. This is something to which Boomer marketers need to pay attention, especially since so much Xer pigeonholing comes from Boomers. This is generational myopia. Talk down to Xers and they will turn away. They don't want preachings from "baboos," as many of them refer to Boomers. They certainly don't want products baboos declare are good for them.

More crucially, Xers refuse to allow their lives to be stripped down to the stereotype of a marketing target group. A multipage Nike print ad that appeared in *Details*, another Xer magazine, taps into this sentiment. This ad announces, "Don't insult our intelligence. Tell us what it is, tell us what it does, and don't play the national anthem while you do it." In the lower right-hand corner of one of the many pages is the statement, turned graffiti-like on end, "I am not/A target market./I am an athlete." Nike, of course, is marketing by misdirection. What seems like a gibe at marketing is actually a very measured piece of marketing. But the point is, Nike understands the Xer aversion to labels and slots. Nike taps into this to reinforce an emotional connection.

Second, *facilitate eclecticism*. The generational diversity of Xers is a Boomer legacy. Boomers rejected the conformity that had guided Matures, and in its place championed individuality. Xers have had the opportunity to pursue the diversity that defines their generation because Boomers made it okay to be really different. In a very important sense, then, the "diversity" of Xers is nothing but the "individuality" of Boomers carried to an extreme. To borrow from a well-worn quotation, Xers stood on the shoulders of Boomers . . . and then bungee-jumped off.

It is with exactly this sense that marketing for Xer consumers should be approached. Xers aren't trying to foment cultural revolution. They believe that those kinds of morality plays are for Boomers, and that, besides, they never worked anyway. GenXers are just living and making choices within the bounds of the culture they've inherited. They'll make do. For Xers, "new" means finding the extreme edge of what's there already. And what's there is extensive and varied. Repackaged with the right attitude, they'll like it.

From diversity, then, comes the most emblematic cultural characteristic of GenXers: *retro-eclectic chic*. They don't have to fill up a blank canvas. New Xer styles sample and rearrange what's already around. They feed off of it and reconfigure it in innovative ways, much of which look back retrospectively, reworking old things into new fashion and styles. Nick at Nite is stylish because it's old TV done up in a novel way. Disco music and polyester platform fashions from the seventies are popular again. Conventional entertainments like bingo and bowling and board games and boxing are the hot new crazes. Rap and hip-hop artists have created modern megahits by sampling riffs and refrains from old R&B recordings. What's new are the eclectic combinations of old things.

Even lounge music is making a comeback. The Capitol and Rhino labels, to name two, have each put out lounge music reissues, with heavy point-of-sale promotion at CD retailers. It's old-time crooners like Dean Martin, Rosemary Clooney, Nancy Wilson, Jackie Gleason, Bobby Darin, Sammy Davis, Jr., Mel Tormé, Wayne Newton, and Nat King Cole. The appeal is retro, both the music and the jewel-case packaging. The sensibility is that of an offbeat eclecticism that reworks the old with a fresh look and a contemporary, brisk appeal.

Xers pick and choose from many places. They've seen it all. They have access to it all. And they use it all. This is a generation with a vastly greater variety of influences that come from all ethnic groups, all generations, both genders, all cultures. Mainstream is a mixed stream. Hence, we see Cindy Crawford in Charlie perfume ads shooting hoops with an ethnically diverse group of men.

This retro-eclecticism is frequently playful and mocking. The plots in hot, new Xer-oriented sitcoms like NBC's "Friends" often reenact scenes from old TV shows and movies, tongue-in-cheek, winking at the audience at home. Mountain Dew advertised its promotional giveaway of pagers with a voice-over that parodied the resonant, baritone voice used by TV game show announcers extolling the prizes awarded to contestants. Comfort Inns used Dennis Rodman, the antihero superstar of the Chicago Bulls, to showcase their service guarantees by spoofing the way questions are asked and answered on quiz shows. (Dennis gets the gong because he can only guarantee that he'll get all the pretty women, not every rebound too.)

Marketers tapped into the Boomer mania for novelty by flooding the market with anything that was new—styles, colors, flavors, line extensions, anything. Xers, though, want much less quantity and a lot more quality. Now, new is what's interesting. This, for example, is the style of the hot new Xer agency, Gyro Worldwide, founded by Steven Grasse, age 31. *The New York Times* described it in these terms: "[T]he agency's ads have a very specific voice and style . . . They tend toward varied sizes of type, vintage or retro photographs and, often, copy or images that do not really make sense . . . An ad for Reactor clothing is a riff on the 'Got milk?' campaign . . . It features a young man in Reactor clothes standing on a bunch of magnified cheese snacks with the tag line, 'Got cheese?'" It's the voice and style of retro-eclectic chic, and it's attracted clients like RJR Nabisco and Paddington.

Third, *learn to surf*. Within the diversity defining Xers, all choices are equally valid, so it's okay to put together any combination of building blocks. This is what happens on the Internet—sites linked together with hypertext enable the user to click at will to customize his or her on-line experience. It's mixing and patching, it's a quilt, a plaid, a personalized collage pasted together with various bits and pieces of the old and the new. Xers simply rearrange everything into a brand new aesthetic. Marketers must surf this diversity alongside them, with, of course, the proper attitude.

One Microsoft TV ad running during the 1996 NBA Finals showed this off. Opening to the clicking of a keyboard, a computer screen displays the declaration, "Microsoft Software lets you play on the Internet." The pointer clicks on the "start" icon, cueing the ad's soundtrack, Shonen Knife's rollicking rave-up of an old seventies Boomer ballad, the Carpenters' "Top of the World." Rocking along, the pointer clicks on the Internet Explorer icon, we hear dial tone, and we're off to "search the Internet." Flowers to sun to Sonny Bono to Mars and aliens and alien landing sites. Art classics and the Muppets. A plastic bathtub duckie. A hunting dog pointing, followed by a fire hydrant. An ocean liner sinking, followed by Queen Mary and more monarchs, butterflies included.

This is the new multimedia—music; still photos, text, icons, hypertext, drawings, full-motion video; both black-and-white and full-color; images sharpening as they download, others being reproduced and superimposed. It is involving and active—choices have to be made; the user keeps it all moving. And all the while images flash by, available on demand but undemanding. It's a surface aesthetic. Deep understanding is largely beside the point. It's about how it looks, about how it feels—its pace, its intensity, the way it grabs the user.

None of the images seen in this Microsoft ad are new. Some are very familiar. But all are done up in the way on-line users surf the Internet. It's things linked together, almost serendipitously, by theme, by alphabet, by visual puns. Choices instantly made, without risk and always reversible if they begin to bore or lead down a dead end.

It's not only fun, it's funny—the humor not in the things themselves, but in their combinations. It's like Nick at Nite's lineup on any given evening—"The Dick Van Dyke Show" to "The Munsters" to "Bewitched" to "That Girl" to "I Love Lucy" to "The Odd Couple" to "I Dream of Jeannie" to "The Mary Tyler Moore Show." In combination, individual items get reset in a new perspective, their self-importance mocked, even heckled. A popular show on the Comedy Channel directly illustrates this. Every episode of "Mystery Science Theater 3000" features some old B-movie being watched by two aliens and their human buddy. We see them in silhouette, as if we were sitting behind them in a movie theater. Their chatter throughout is nonstop wisecracking about the silly plots and gimmicks. It makes you wonder who could ever have taken these flicks so seriously. Certainly Xers have enough smarts to see through it all, and indeed, through all of the media tricks of the trade.

Fourth, *abandon the hard sell.* Because they've seen so much of everything, Xers feel as if they've seen it all. A hard sell falls on deaf ears. They've heard every pitch, they know every line, and they'll simply turn away from anything that smacks of marketing-ese. While all generations nowadays demand that marketers be more forthright and straightforward, Xers are a lot more hostile, and they have assumed this attitude towards marketing hype at a much earlier age. Xers want to be treated with more intelligence and respect than what they usually see.

No generation has grown up amidst more information and media than Xers. Boomers remember the appearance of the first color TV in their neighborhoods; Matures remember buying it. But Xers never remember a time without a color TV, indeed, without their own color TV. Even more important, while Boomers and Matures knew TV as a broadcast technology, Xers have known TV only as a cable technology, one that brings dozens of channels and sources of information to them at any hour of the day. Xers and CNN grew up together, so Xers take for granted the broader, more diverse global horizons immediately accessible on this all-news, all-day channel. The speed and convenience of information is different for Xers as well. Boomers grew up with IBM cards and mainframes, standing in line to submit and pick up jobs at the operator's window. Xers grew up with PCs and microprocessors, getting immediate feedback and dedicated attention from their machines. Boomers and Matures have learned computers as adults, on the job, as a tool for work; Xers learned as children, in school or at home, as a way to have fun.

Because Xers have been bombarded with such a great variety of information during their formative years, they have acquired an instinctive sense of what it's all about. They learned firsthand that much of it is simply to sell them something. Hence, their defensive antennae are always up. This is not, by the way, a defensiveness based on a demand for the facts, as it is with Boomers. Xers aren't put off so much by the lack of data as they are by the *lack of candor*. They want an honest approach, one that gets to the point and sticks to the subject. Dissembling will be instantly recognized and rejected.

Saturn knows this. Their ads emphasize low-key friendliness. Their pricing is a no-dicker sticker. They show their cars being made and delivered by down-to-earth, regular people who care about the people who buy them. They playfully spoof the diversity and loyalty of their buyers. Honesty on the lot and candor at the showroom are key elements, though, and are a major attraction to a generation cynical about marketing and retailing.

Nike knows this, too. The company rarely talks about its shoes with the superlatives used by pitchmen. Instead, Nike talks about sport and competition and striving to excel. Nike talks about what shoes are really all about—just getting the job done for your feet. TV ads spotlight athletes pushing through their limits, toiling and sweating as they exert themselves to put forth every last bit of effort.

In the multipage print ad from *Details* referred to before, Nike even lampoons marketing pitches that try to talk to Xers in any other way. The ad is filled with disparaging remarks about marketers and marketing: "If you put an officially licensed logo on a box of cupcakes in anticipation of world-class competition, you are

a marketer." "Notice: 'The spirit of competition' cannot be celebrated through customer discounts, manufacturer rebates, and fre-
quent flyer miles." "A list of alternative spokespersons for confused marketers: . . . If you sell snack foods—a pimple-faced adolescent . . . If you sell film—the guy who took that picture of the
Loch Ness monster . . . If you sell cigarettes—a dead guy . . . If
you sell aspirin—anyone who ever filled out an IRS long form."

So what about Nike, what does it do that's different? This ad tells
you: "We don't sell dreams. We sell shoes. We sell shoes to athletes."
And what about Nike spokespersons? Well, the ad explains: "A good
spokesperson always has a personal working knowledge of the product they are spokesperson-ing." Of course, Nike has fun, too. Not taking marketing seriously is not always serious work.

A few other marketers also understand this about Xers. Years
ago, MasterCard launched a campaign targeting Xers by sponsor-
ing seminars on how to manage credit responsibly. No hard sell,
just the bottom line on some useful facts and skills. Sprite, in its
TV ads, exhorts Xers to "obey your thirst." Drinking Sprite won't
raise the level of your basketball game, as we are reminded by the
fumbles of the all-thumbs teenage boys we see mishandling the
ball. What Sprite will do is quench your thirst, so obey it and drink
Sprite. This campaign adroitly combines the honesty and the irreverence it takes to break through to this media-saturated, marketing-
jaded generation.

Indeed, one of the Xer hooks in these Sprite ads is how they
are set up. The ads open with a look and feel suggesting another
one of those ads that talks about how its product will elevate the
user into doing great things. But the Sprite ads bring the curtain
down fast on that expectation, deriding any sort of self-important
message. Instead, the ads say, just focus on getting the job done:
"Image is Nothing. Thirst is Everything." Maybelline did the same
thing years ago with model Christy Turlington. Ads for Expert
Eyes Shadow opened with a larger-than-life setup that rapidly
changes into Christy on her couch laughing at the pompousness of
it all, saying, "Get over it!"

Fifth, *get some attitude*. Everything smells, so attitude sells. Especially if you can say it on an XXL Beefy-T. The T-shirts of shoe brands, for example, are emblazoned with smart, sassy remarks. Pithy is preferred. It's the attitude, not the brand, that makes the shirt.

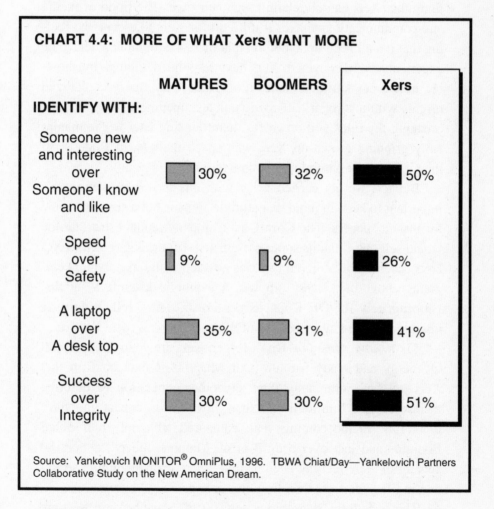

CHART 4.4: MORE OF WHAT Xers WANT MORE

IDENTIFY WITH:	MATURES	BOOMERS	Xers
Someone new and interesting over Someone I know and like	30%	32%	50%
Speed over Safety	9%	9%	26%
A laptop over A desk top	35%	31%	41%
Success over Integrity	30%	30%	51%

Source: Yankelovich MONITOR® OmniPlus, 1996. TBWA Chiat/Day—Yankelovich Partners Collaborative Study on the New American Dream.

"No Fear" is a shrewd business concept based strictly on attitude—that's all No Fear sells, attitude itself. It's just happenstance that the first place No Fear was able to sell attitude was on the back of T-shirts. Attitude can be executed or licensed in many ways, especially as Xers get older and their needs and tastes diversify even more—calendars, motivational tapes, pads, pens, auto air fresheners, watches, jewelry, you name it.

For a generation awash in the failures, excesses, disappointments, and uncertainties of the times, attitude is at least one sure thing that Xers can lay claim to as their own. The flood of media and communications makes it difficult for Xers to escape the feeling that it's all been done before, that there's nothing new left to be experienced or discovered. Xers have responded, though, by showing how a new attitude makes it all fresh again. Isuzu capitalized on this with ads for its off-road vehicles, opening with baby Xers breaking the rules laid down for them, leading later to the maniacally grinning grown-up Xers who speed their Isuzu Rodeos off the road and out onto more extreme terrain.

But lest we get carried away with this in our marketing, it's important to keep in mind that attitude alone is not a secret formula for instant success. The Coca-Cola Company thought that attitude would sell OK Cola, its super-caffeinated soft drink targeted to Xer boys. Each drably colored can was covered with terse, cynical epigrams about life. Every sip was a symbolic kiss-off to adults. Unfortunately for OK Cola, its pessimism didn't sell. What was missing was the key ingredient of fun.

Sixth, *have some fun.* Don't forget, Xers are young people, full of energy and ready for fun. Our MONITOR data confirm that Xers are far more likely than any other generation to describe themselves as "fun-loving." Nearly two-thirds expect to "have more fun" in the coming year, compared with only half of all Boomers and just over a third of all Matures. Indeed, almost 80 percent of Xers feel the need to find "more excitement and sensation in life," far more than Boomers or especially Matures.

This is both life stage and cohort. It's life stage because Xers are young. It's cohort because Xers are more committed to fun as a life value than Boomers or Matures ever were. Xers constantly tell Boomers to get a life. Lighten up. Have some fun. The bottom line—if life is awful, don't dwell on it; turn the tables, and make it awfully fun.

Xers keep life in perspective. Crusading is for Boomers; sacrificing for Matures. Our MONITOR surveys reflect this attitude in many ways, but perhaps no clearer than in our findings about cross-generational perceptions of work. Xers are the most likely to agree that they'd be willing to "work at a boring job as long as the pay was good," and they are the least likely of all generations to describe work as a career. It's not that they prefer boredom, rather, it's just that work is not an all-consuming passion for them. This is a distinctive balancing of priorities. Xers want a job *and* a life. Boomers, on the other hand—and this is something Xers see and explicitly reject—have largely seen their jobs as their lives, a generational pursuit of self-fulfillment in the workplace.

Indeed, fun itself, in clear contrast to Boomers, seems to be a purer passion for Xers. Remember Woodstock. This 1969 festival in the upstate New York countryside was the epitome of Boomer-style fun. But a lot of what made it fun for Boomers was the political and cultural statement that participation made about peace and music. Max Yasgur, on whose farm the festival was held, came on stage during one of the breaks and said to the gathered crowd, "This is the largest group of people ever assembled in one place. But I think you people have proven something to the world—that a half a million kids can get together and have three days of fun and music, and have nothing but fun and music." That's why the organizers had Max stop by and say hi—to have someone from the Matures generation remind the watching world that deep down in all that fun was a bigger social message about Boomer values— proving how responsible Boomers really were beneath it all.

In the follow-up work we do each year to add some depth to our statistics, we have listened as Xers watch and react to the Woodstock movie. They shake their heads and wonder out loud how Boomers were able to endure all that mud for three days, doing bad drugs and listening to such "bad music"—a reaction by Xers about how little fun it appears to have been. Contrast Woodstock with the Xer generation's Lollapalooza tours, their outdoor traveling equivalent. An annual event, Lollapalooza is about having fun again year after year, not about the politics of the moment. As the original organizer of this event, singer Perry Farrell, told *The New York Times*, his hopes were no more complicated than helping make the "tough situation" facing us "a little lighter or easier by giving people a tune to have in their head while they work." Nothing heavier than that.

In its TV ads, Taco Bell has consistently marketed fun to Xers. The constant elements here are fast-paced, high-energy scenes filled with party music and people having a good time. The desert is Taco Bell's playground, filled with young people at "the border," that extreme edge where all the fun is.

Seventh, *emphasize pragmatism*. Xers aren't out just to party. Rather, their emphasis on fun is part of a broader focus on pragmatism. The bottom line is about survival, not about ideology or mission. Instead of getting caught up in bigger causes and movements, Xers are focused on making sure they can get by. And they are prepared to do what it takes.

Indeed, with the lower expectations they've been forced to face, Xers tend to talk like a new Depression generation. Our MONITOR research finds they are a cautious and financially conservative cohort. As noted before, they are more willing to accept a boring job for the money, plus they are more apt to be thinking already about saving for retirement. They recognize all too well that the long gray wave of aging Boomers will have devoured the Social Security pie before any of them come anywhere near to drawing their first check.

Xer pragmatism thus means *hedging*—holding a little back; having a backup plan; betting like a short-seller. This element of their pragmatism is manifest, for example, in the later marriages of Xers compared with those of Boomers and Matures when they were younger. It's also manifested in Xers having to make do with such pragmatic alternatives as living with their parents—leading some Boomer wiseacres to fashion a new acronym for them, ILYAs, for Incompletely Launched Young Adults. According to one national survey, the portion of women in their twenties living with their parents rose to 24 percent in 1993 from 17 percent in 1977. Young men in the same age group are even more likely to live at home—35 percent in 1993, up from 30 percent in 1977.

One local newspaper reported the story of a Boomer mother who went so far as to sell her house in order to get her two perpetual live-in Xer sons out. While this is an extreme reaction, this pattern has affected home ownership, though mostly among Xers. Economics dictate that Xers are less likely to own homes than people their same age ten or fifteen years ago. Of course, this is true for every age group under sixty, but the point is that Xers are *starting off* in a much more restrictive market while Boomers and Matures have come to experience it only in the last ten years. Xers have learned pragmatism early, with the result that their spending reflects a more cautious, calculating, conservative approach, particularly as it relates to extravagance and indulgence.

Tide laundry detergent echoes this sentiment in one of its recent slice-of-life TV ads narrated by a young Xer girl. Her family situation reflects the realities of her generation—in this family, she says, "it's just me and Mom." She and her mom are shown doing things together, even sharing clothes. "Money's tight," she confesses, so things like clothes have to last. Tide does that for them. And when Tide makes their clothes fresh and clean, the girl concludes, it's like a whole new . . . yep, you guessed it, "attitude."

Xer pragmatism includes being *modular*. Xers live in a changeable world. You don't buy a home to live in for the rest of your life. You may buy; you may rent. But you will definitely be moving from place to place. You don't get a job right out of school and work there until you retire. You don't major in one thing and never master any other field over the course of your life. You stay flexible, continually adaptable.

There's a complicated emotional roller coaster that goes with this. Life is chameleonlike, but that doesn't mean that Xers never latch onto anything emotionally. They do, but they are forced by circumstances to be more cautious caretakers of their emotional commitments, hedging a bit and always prepared for change.

Xer pragmatism also means being *resourceful*. They have to be—they are graduating from college deeper in debt than their predecessors, and their salaries, adjusted for inflation, are lower than Boomers at the same life stage. Rather than being despondent, though, our MONITOR data show that Xers are confident they can deal with this situation. They are charged with a sense of purpose and capability, driven to succeed and confident of their own abilities. They are becoming a generation of entrepreneurs, getting things done on the strength of their own initiative.

Our MONITOR research also shows that Xers are far more likely than consumers in general to say they work hard at coming out on top. They are no less likely than Boomers to describe themselves as intelligent, self-confident, and well educated. And they put these skills to use. Over two-thirds of Xers agree that "I have to take whatever I can get in this world because no one is going to give me anything." Far fewer Boomers and Matures agree—only half and one-third, respectively.

When faced with challenges, Matures and Boomers have shouldered up by putting more muscle into it. Sweat was the measure of what it took to surmount a challenge. Xers will be more resourceful than that, working harder when it's required, but mostly working *smarter*, with more cunning and finesse. Matures and Boomers run off-tackle, straight into the line; Xers stutterstep in the backfield, waiting for a hole to develop. But Xers do run forward when they need to, unafraid of the hit.

It is no surprise, then, that we find Xers the most likely to say they depend on themselves and their own capabilities to get things done. They are willing to put in the effort it takes to get what they want out of life, and they accept that nothing comes easily. Unlike Boomers at their age, they don't expect anything on a silver platter. Resolved to do it themselves, not resigned, as many media portrayals make it seem, they rely on their own smarts to get things done. They look at life's challenges through the eyes of an entrepreneur.

They have to because they aren't sure who else to trust. Like Matures and Boomers, their confidence in all public institutions—

economic, political, religious, business, media, professional—has bottomed out. In this respect, they mirror everyone else, but while Matures lived most of their lives with confidence in these institutions and Boomers started out with confidence, Xers have lived their entire lives believing no institution can be trusted. Self-help is their only resource and their only protection.

When we look through our MONITOR surveys, we see a unique resourcefulness among Xers: groups of friends who have pooled their money to buy a building and rent it out for additional income. Individuals launching small record labels. Friends and cousins starting investment clubs to manage family finances. A designer creating new maternity outfits by retrofitting three pieces of existing clothing sold at Bloomingdale's. Individuals who met on vacation joining together to start a fashion export business. There are lots of diverse examples of Xers using whatever resources they find at hand to make a start. Xers are making lemonade out of the lemons left them.

Eighth, *provide prophylaxis*. Xers are the prophylactic generation. "Protect thyself" is their special commandment. Risks are everywhere, particularly things that can hurt that are not of their own making. Adolescence was much more innocent for Boomers. Experimentation was a risk-free plunge into something surprising and new. Even Matures, children of hard times themselves, recall their childhoods as safer, much less scary times. Not so today. Surprises are often bad—HIV-positive, date rape, computer viruses, exploding gas tanks, just-remembered childhood abuse, serial killers, a drunk driver running a red light, random acts of violence.

So protect yourself: Wear condoms. Stockpile your own blood. Designate a driver. Have safe sex. Just say no. As noted already, Xers live for today because they can't depend on tomorrow. But it's more. They live for today protecting themselves against tomorrow.

Of course, one extreme reaction to all this goading about being cautious is to chuck it all and do whatever, whenever, however. A backlash is emerging in some quarters—most notably, teen smoking is back on the rise. But the main trend *by far* is toward more responsible, diligent oversight of personal exposures and decisions. It is certainly the character and rhetoric of the times.

Ninth, *think in terms of enclaves*. Xers are the most peer-focused generation ever. Our MONITOR data show their overwhelming reliance upon friends for advice about what to buy and what to believe. This pattern is always true of younger consumers, but for Xers it will be an enduring, distinctive trend, not a youthful fancy for friends over family. After all, Xers are making stronger, more permanent cultural connections than any generation before them. Matures suited up and Boomers let their hair grow down, but these styles were easily changed when they got older. Xers are getting pierced and tattooed, making in the process a longer-term, more permanent commitment to their enclave identities.

From private families to public institutions, the traditional sources of emotional sustenance don't work for Xers. While Boomers largely grew up pampered and indulged in stable families, Xers were latchkey kids living through breakups and divorce. So, just as depicted in *Reality Bites*, Xers have turned to small enclaves of friends and peers for support to fill huge emotional holes in their lives.

Additionally, Xers have learned to be skeptical of third parties. Often these turn out to be dangerous, untrustworthy, or predatory, so Xers have developed built-in defenses to guard themselves. The closer personal bonds of their enclaves are relationships they can directly assess and, therefore, trust.

Our MONITOR data point to the importance of these kinds of relationships. In response to our question about which areas of life should see a return to more traditional standards, Xers are less likely than Boomers or Matures to cite any area, except two, sexual relationships and social relationships. Xers see these as different, in need of more conservative caretaking.

In their diversity, Xers aren't looking to be so different that they become hermits, isolated and unreachable. This, though, is one of their concerns. With more independence and more diversity, it's harder for any one person to find others "like me." While Xer diversity involves picking from a variety of sources to find one's unique and singular style, it is also about finding connection with others. Xers find this *connection amidst diversity* through their enclaves.

Xers populate small groups, all with distinctive ethics and characters, drawn and built from a variety of sources. In many ways these groups provide certainty and stability for a generation that has grown up with contrast, unrelenting uncertainties, and risks. Diversity and enclaving are a response to life not only as Xers find it, but also as they would prefer it.

But be a cautious marketer here. Xers are offended by any hint of stereotyping, especially based on their enclave identities. They turn away from advertising that labels them. Subaru found this out the hard way when a few years ago it used what *Newsweek* called "some moronic grungeboy" who tried to sell cars by comparing them to punk rock. It was, observed *New York Times* advertising columnist Stuart Elliott, "the Pearl Harbor Day of Generation X marketing" (an interesting cross-generational reference using a Mature marker). Done inoffensively, though, a marketing focus on Xer enclaves provides a strong opportunity to connect with this generation.

TECHNOLOGY

Through everything we've just examined, technology—computers and the Internet in particular—keeps weaving into the discussion. Indeed, for many observers what's most distinctive about Xers is their computer literacy and their facility and comfort with all forms of high technology. This is absolutely true, but its relevance to the experience of Xers is different than what is commonly understood.

Every generation becomes expert at the technologies commonplace to its times. The nature of those technologies, particularly the ways in which they enable consumers to control time and space, affects how each generation formulates its world view of possibilities and connections. Microprocessors are the distinctive technology for Xers. Indeed, Game Boys even more than PCs are their defining experience. And though they did not grow up with the Internet or the multimedia systems now overtaking us, this revolution will ultimately absorb Xers more fully than Matures or Boomers, simply because they are more comfortable with things like PC games, CD-ROMs, and joystick controls.

The biggest cohorting impact of technology on Xers, though, has been *the contribution it has made to their sense of uncertainty, risk, and diversity.* Technology has accelerated, and in some cases even helped trigger these things. It has created its own risks and trade-offs. It has made available a wider variety of choices and influences. And the look and lingo of technology, especially computers, is a ubiquitous element of Xer style.

That's why Xers are not only the most enthusiastic embracers of technologies, they are *also* the most skeptical and incredulous. As we've just discussed, this is the sort of attitude that Xers have about many things, and technology is *no* exception. Our MONITOR data show that, across the board, Xers are the most open to new technologies—they want them, they believe in them, they hope the future will be shaped by them. But at the same time, Xers are the most likely of any generation to agree that often the benefits of technology are outweighed by the problems. When asked about the credibility of information available on-line, GenXers are the least likely of any generation to say it is more credible than information available elsewhere.

As with everything else, there is, as Xers see it, no such thing as a purely good or a purely bad technology. Every technology is both good and bad, so trade-offs must be evaluated and weighed in each case.

Technology is just another of those things that show up everywhere, so Xers respond to it in the same ways they respond to other things. When Mountain Dew gave out pagers as a product promotion, Xers liked it. But when they realized that these very same pagers often will page them to deliver a Mountain Dew ad, Xers saw it as one of the trade-offs involved.

All of which is *not* to understate the role of technology in the lives of Xers. Information and electronic technologies have always been fundamental to how they live, work, and play. It is impossible to overemphasize its importance. Technology defines their *vocabulary*. It *ties together* their finances, their communications, their calendars, their entertainment. It creates the *bonds* and connections of their communities and families—particularly cell phones and beepers and voice mail. It *permeates* every nook and cranny—they've never driven a car without an on-board computer; they've never had a job without a PC on their desk; ads show the hippest of them atop slickrock desert mesas, having mountain-biked to the top, working away in the wilderness on a laptop; they've only ever fixed meals in the shadow of a microwave. These kinds of technologies provide the undisputed *guiding force* shaping their future. For Xers there is no unfolding of the future absent these technologies. And not just computers, by the way, because Xers understand that hardware evolves and changes, and often disappears completely. Specific technologies are a big deal while they're around, but it's technology in general that fashions and shapes the evolution of their world.

These technologies are part of the background—nothing special, just everyday. Using technology-speak and being technology-savvy *won't* distinguish one marketer from another, but in their absence a marketer will certainly stand out as generationally irrelevant. Xers will build their houses with technology, but marketers must be smart enough to recognize it won't be technology per se that drives their decision-making.

HOUSEHOLD BUILDING

Right now, Xers are important, even dominant, buyers of CDs, athletic shoes, movies and computer games, soft drinks, fast food, cosmetics, and outdoor equipment. Much of this buying, of course, is a reflection of their life stage. But it is nevertheless an active, interested purchasing that confirms their desire to participate in the marketplace, indeed, their desire to accumulate consumer goods as part of their lifestyle. As more and more Xers move into their early and mid-thirties, their needs will change. At this stage, they will have to face building their own households and supporting their own families. *This, indeed, is the next great opportunity with Xers.*

The marketing of shoes and CDs and such has already been pretty well staked out, but the marketing of furniture, appliances, financial services, family transportation, and the like has yet to be confronted. Still in the future is the struggle of Xers over the choice between a $50 pair of jeans and a $100 lamp for the family room. In these and in similar decisions, Xers will present a very different face to marketers, because they will create completely new types of households. Living at home and strapped by their finances, Xers will start off in new ways. Not only are their parents housing them longer, but many Xers still require support even after they've moved. This is a fact that people accept. Slightly over 80 percent of consumers of every age agree that life today is harder than it was in the seventies and eighties, and a third believe that parental obligations don't end when their children leave the nest. So when Xers begin building lives, marketers will have to understand the multiperson, shared decision-making that will operate in supplying these households.

The marketing challenge goes well beyond simply what to sell, but extends as well to how to sell. Xers will settle into households with a very different orientation toward traditional advertising, not to mention all the new media on the way. The most effective means of reaching this generation are visual. After all, *this* is the true TV generation. While Boomers gathered around the television set with their families to watch Ed Sullivan or Walt Disney, Xers spent much of their time in front of the tube alone or with young friends. They seldom watched with families because families had fragmented, and because millions of American households had more than one TV. While few homes had color television as Boomers grew up, just a few decades later nearly all did.

CHART 4.5: GEN-O-GRAM—MEET AN Xer DAD

Born:	1965
Education:	College graduate
Occupation:	White-collar manager
Household:	Married; two children; owns a Cape Cod with a big porch in a small subdivision
Technology:	1 phone line; 4 phones; 1 TV; 1 VCR; 1 answering machine; 1 computer with built-in fax
On shopping:	"When I buy something I check it out on the Internet. And I use word of mouth, friends. My grandfather has always been good at giving advice, without being a jerk about it."
On the family:	"I'm from a badly broken home. Granddad stepped in. A lot of values I have are directly from him."
On the generations:	"The older generation, the Matures, had a strong purpose. Society was so stable then. Today, things change so fast I think people my age are scared to jump in. I know a lot of people my age who are very close to their parents. Closer, I think than Boomers are with theirs. Not long ago, one of my uncles was really ragging on my granddad. My thing is, how badly could you have been raised and still turn out as well as you have? So often Boomers tend to demonize their parents."
Concerns:	"I worry most about what my children's future will be. I worry about whether my wife and I are raising them to be productive, positive people."

Add to this the growth of computers and the Internet, and the result is a generation with attitudes and values shaped much more by the visual image than by the written word. Xers are today the least likely of all generations to read or look at a newspaper. This has always been true of younger people, but it has become more pronounced. At the same time, the percentages of Xers going to movies, galleries, and museums are rising. Xer households will be built around this visual experience, and their family styles will reflect the independence they developed from the individual media interactions and self-directed entertainments of their childhood.

Last, remember that Xers are approaching homemaking with caution and concern. They have had to clear away the debris of Boomer households that lacked any enduring foundation. They do not want to repeat this, nor do they want to inflict it on another generation. Their desire to build households with more stability, though, will be challenged by the uncertainties facing them.

It is to these motivations and aspirations that marketers must direct their products. They need to help Xers overcome the barriers they face. These new pragmatists want households that work, filled with the products that will make that happen.

Xers: The New Pragmatists

1980

Jimmy Carter signs Chrysler bail-
out bill
CNN started
ABSCAM arrests
Reagan elected president
Yellow ribbons tied around trees for
Iranian hostages
Mount St. Helens erupts
Term *gridlock* coined during Man-
hattan summer traffic jams
United States boycotts Moscow
Summer Olympics
John Lennon shot dead outside
Dakota apartment building
"Who Shot J.R.?" episode of *Dallas*
airs
First 1-900 numbers used during
Carter-Reagan presidential debate
Post-it Notes introduced
Pop Rocks candy taken off market
after five years due to rumors that
it had killed Little Mikey
US EOC makes sexual harassment
in workplace illegal
US hockey team defeats Soviets for
gold medal at Lake Placid Winter
Olympics
The Official Preppy Handbook pub-
lished
Moral Majority started

1982

John Belushi dies of drug overdose
E.T. in movie theaters
Ground broken for Vietnam War
memorial
Princess Grace dies in auto accident
Smurfs introduced
Cats on Broadway
Tylenol tampering killings in Chicago
Thriller album released by Michael
Jackson
Dr. Barney Clark receives first arti-
ficial heart
Jane Fonda workout tapes hit the
market
Remote control is now standard
accessory for TV sets
USA Today begun

1981

Rubik's Cube introduced
IBM PC introduced
Reagan ignites jelly bean craze
Charles and Di wed
Pac-Man shows up in video arcades
Reagan shot
Carol Burnett awarded $1.6 million
in libel suit against *National
Enquirer*
Pope John Paul II shot in Rome
First space shuttle, *Columbia*,
launched
US air traffic controllers' strike
leads to firings by Reagan
CDC publishes first report on AIDS
epidemic
Dynasty first broadcast
Wayne Williams arrested in Atlanta
for child murders; trial is first to
use DNA evidence
MTV first airs
52 hostages held in Teheran since
1977
Sandra Day O'Connor is first
female justice on Supreme Court

1983

Last episode of *M*A*S*H*

Reagan proposes Strategic Defense Initiative

Martin Luther King, Jr., Day signed into law

Trivial Pursuit introduced in United States from Canada

Chrysler minivan introduced

PCP street drug epidemic

Vanessa Williams is first African American Miss America

Astronaut Sally K. Ride is first woman in space

National Council of Churches releases collection of Bible readings with no allusion to God as a male

Christine Craft awarded damages after being fired by TV station on basis of her age and appearance

Jesse Jackson announces run for presidency

The Day After airs on television

Lifestyles of the Rich and Famous first airs

Teenage Mutant Ninja Turtles introduced

Madonna's first album, *Madonna*, released

1984

Bell system broken up

First surrogate conception brought to term

Infomercials started

Federal government issues regulations to cut highway funds to any state with a drinking age of under 21

Supreme Court rules home videotaping of TV shows for personal use is not a copyright violation

Terrorist truck bomb kills Marines in Lebanon

Average cost of a new home is $100,000 for the first time

Reagan re-elected in 49-state landslide

The Cosby Show first airs

Bernhard Goetz shoots four on New York City subway

Los Angeles Summer Olympic Games

Geraldine Ferraro chosen as Walter Mondale's running mate

Yellow car window "Baby on Board" signs invented

Clara Peller does "Where's the beef?" TV ad for Wendy's

Newsweek declares this to be the year of the yuppie

1985
- Pete Rose breaks Ty Cobb's record for hits
- Federal study puts obesity in same category as smoking and high blood pressure
- CDs become popular
- New Coke introduced, then taken off market
- Halley's Comet passes by earth
- 39 remaining hostages freed in Beirut
- Live Aid and Farm Aid concerts
- For first time since World War I, United States is a debtor nation
- "We Are the World" nets $30 million for Africa famine relief
- Rock Hudson dies of AIDS
- Crack street drug first appears
- *Achille Lauro* hijacked by PLO

1986
- Space shuttle *Challenger* explodes
- *Oprah* goes into syndication
- Chernobyl nuclear accident in Soviet Union
- Start of Iran-Contra investigation
- Folding cardboard sun screens for car windshields introduced
- Imelda Marcos revealed to own 2,700 pairs of shoes
- Ivan Boesky fined $100 million for insider trading
- Three-point shot introduced in college basketball
- President Marcos flees Philippines
- Hands Across America
- Clint Eastwood elected mayor of Carmel, California

1988
- *Phantom of the Opera* on Broadway
- Jimmy Swaggart implicated in scandal over prostitutes, saying "I have sinned"
- Phillip Morris buys Kraft for $13.1 billion
- Last Playboy club, in Lansing, Michigan, closes
- Lights installed at Wrigley Field
- AIDS quilt
- Soviets withdraw from Afghanistan
- Pan Am flight 103 explodes from terrorist bomb over Lockerbie, Scotland
- NASA's James Hansen tells Senate panel that global warming already has started
- Computer virus, placed by Cornell graduate student Robert Morris, disrupts 6,000 computers
- KKR buys RJR for $25 billion
- Fanny packs named by *The New York Times* as summer hit

1987
- Reagan submits first trillion-dollar federal budget
- Cold fusion announced, later called into question
- Last broadcast of Garrison Keillor's "A Prairie Home Companion"
- Black Monday stock market crash
- Gary Hart and Jim Bakker implicated in sex scandals
- A. H. Robins company to pay $2.475 billion in damages for Dalkon Shield
- Charles and Di start living separately
- Spuds MacKenzie appears
- Geraldo starts talk show

1989
Exxon *Valdez* spills oil in Prince
William Sound, Alaska
Berlin Wall falls
Eastern Airlines files for bankruptcy
Menendez brothers kill their parents
Mazda Miata introduced
Arsenio Hall becomes first African
American late-night host
Batman movie in theaters
Pete Rose banned from baseball for
life in gambling scandal
Ayatollah Khomeini issues death
sentence against Salman Rushdie
for *The Satanic Verses*
San Francisco earthquake; World
Series game between San Fran-
cisco Giants and Los Angeles
Dodgers disrupted
Wilding attack on Central Park jog-
ger
Rob Lowe implicated in sex scandal
with underage girl at Democratic
National Convention in Atlanta
Field of Dreams in movie theaters
Virtual Reality invented
Invasion of Panama

1990
Perrier recalled in benzene scare
The Civil War by Ken Burns airs on
PBS
Saturn launched
The Simpsons airs on Fox
Nolan Ryan pitches no-hitter at age
43
Seinfeld airs first time
Three Northwest Airlines pilots sus-
pended for flying while under the
influence
President Bush raises taxes, break-
ing campaign pledge

1992
Arthur Ashe dies of AIDS
Mike Tyson convicted of rape
US forces in Somalia
Jay Leno takes over *The Tonight
Show* following retirement of
Johnny Carson
Murphy Brown segment in which
she gives birth as unmarried
mother gets attention of Vice
President Dan Quayle
Charles and Di formally separate
Los Angeles riots after acquittals of
police officers in Rodney King
case
Amy Fisher shoots Mary Jo Butta-
fucco
Clinton elected president

1991
Persian Gulf War
Rodney King beating videotaped
Anita Hill accuses Clarence Thomas
of sexual harassment in hearings
on his appointment to Supreme
Court
Dr. Jack Kevorkian's assisted sui-
cides get public notice
William Kennedy Smith acquitted
in rape trial
Magic Johnson announces he is
HIV-positive
Ted Turner marries Jane Fonda
Charles Keating convicted in S&L
scandal

1993
Rock and Roll Hall of Fame opens in Cleveland
Mississippi floods Midwest
Michael Jackson accused of fondling a boy in his Neverland Valley Ranch home
Snoop Doggy Dogg and Tupac Shakur both on trial for shootings
Evander Holyfield wins heavyweight title fight at Caesar's Palace, where parachutist dropped into ring during round seven
Branch Davidian cult building in Waco, Texas, burned to ground during siege, killing 72 people inside
"Clean-living" River Phoenix dies of multiple-drug overdose
World Trade Center bombing
Vincent Foster, White House aide, commits suicide
Space shuttle makes repairs to Hubble Telescope
Brady Bill signed into law

1994
Nancy Kerrigan attacked by associates of Tonya Harding
Menendez juries hung
Los Angeles earthquake
White House fired upon by gunman and plane crashes on lawn
On national TV, Roseanne kisses a lesbian character played by Mariel Hemingway
OJ arrested for killings of Nicole Brown Simpson and Ron Goldman; later acquitted
CIA operative Aldrich Ames arrested for spying for Soviet Union
Abortion workers killed at Florida and Massachusetts clinics
Heidi Fliess, "The Hollywood Madam," arrested
Baseball strike; World Series cancelled
Michael Jordan takes up baseball
1934 Loch Ness monster photo revealed by photographer on deathbed to be a hoax
Kurt Cobain commits suicide
Jackie O dies of cancer
Michael Jackson and Lisa Marie Presley wed

GENERATIONAL MARKETING

Technology, Pure and Simple

The Glen Canyon Dam on the Colorado River was dedicated September 22, 1966, twenty-three days shy of a decade after its construction was inaugurated by President Eisenhower—he ceremonially set off the first dynamite blast with a signal telegraphed from the White House. Capturing the drainage from a watershed covering 244,000 square miles, the Glen Canyon Dam rises 710 feet above bedrock and holds back a lake that stretches 186 miles upriver and encompasses 1,960 miles of shoreline. The dam is far more massive in virtually every way than its closest western rival, the Hoover Dam, finished thirty years earlier and located 400 miles downriver. Building it took 5 million barrels of cement, 10 million cubic yards of aggregate, 3 million board-feet of lumber, 130,000 tons of steel, 20,000 tons of aluminum, and 5,000 tons of copper. Its labor force put the town of Page, Arizona, on the map. And it was finished on budget, on schedule.

The Glen Canyon Dam is the technological capstone of the Matures. Virtually unrivaled in its complexity and the engineering prowess it took to build it, this great dam is a symbol of the can-do optimism that has always been a hallmark of the Matures. The program that put a man on the moon better captured the public imagination, but this dam fulfilled a core generational value to which NASA never gave a second thought. For most Matures, pride in the sacrifice and hard work it took to complete this dam was an expression of triumphant power—taming the Colorado River for the betterment of humankind.

But before it was even finished, the Glen Canyon Dam had become for some a symbol of America's industrial hubris, the hulking embodiment of a careless, destructive disregard for the consequences of technological advance. Boomers in particular began to feel that the spoils of technology were as likely to be ruin as riches. Indeed, the differences over the dam set off a debate that put the perspectives of distinct generations in sharp contrast.

The attitude of many Matures at the time was little different from that of Floyd Dominy, the irascible commissioner of the Bureau of Reclamation, who tirelessly championed dams during his quarter-century career at the Bureau. A hardscrabble child from central Nebraska during the teens and twenties, he grew to believe that letting any of nature's bounty get away unused was a wasteful failure to conserve precious resources. As Dominy once told writer John McPhee in an interview for a piece that appeared in *The New Yorker*, "Nature is a pretty cruel animal. I watched . . . people . . . compete with the rigors of nature against hopeless odds. They would ruin their health and still fail." For Dominy, using the muscle of our technology to dam western rivers was conservation in the highest sense—harnessing scarce water for productive use and consumption.

More than any other single event, though, Dominy's construction of the Glen Canyon Dam was responsible for creating the modern environmental movement that ultimately antiquated his views for the next generation. The inundation of Glen Canyon inflamed the passions of Matures like David Brower of the Sierra Club and writer Edward Abbey, galvanizing each toward more strident resistance to technological encroachments, offering an alternative to the prevailing view. Boomers, not Matures, responded. The moniker of "conservationist" was ultimately abandoned for that of "environmentalist," a rhetorical realignment that was accompanied by the creation of two of today's highest profile environmental groups—Brower formed Friends of the Earth after being voted out as head of the Sierra Club and Abbey was the intellectual inspiration and spiritual adviser for the more radical Earth First! The generations after Matures thought in terms of ecology, not economy; technology was often seen as a looming, ever-present danger to what they valued most.

One massive project. Two distinct views—and not just political ones, but views that carry over into the consumer marketplace. For those who understand the formative experiences of generations, the sharp divisions over the Glen Canyon Dam make perfect sense.

It's all in the markers.

- Matures saw technology as a savior, a symbol of progress and power. They used technology to overcome hardship and build their lives. The greater good to which technology was dedicated was worth the sacrifice. Perhaps even more important, Matures first experienced the power of technology as industrial might, as a force that required collective effort. This is a point of view many Matures find no longer relevant in the new information-driven marketplace.

- Boomers love technology but are suspicious of it. As with most things, Boomers have looked at technology as a character in a morality play. They see good and bad technologies, and they strive to avoid the bad and embrace the good. Growing up amidst abundance and prosperity, Boomers have felt less need to compromise. To a large extent, they see industrial technologies as bad, information technologies as good.

- Xers, who weren't around to debate Glen Canyon, also have a mixed view, but one that sees trade-offs in every technology. Nothing is entirely good or entirely bad. Xers weigh each situation individually. Further, they have experienced technological advance almost entirely as an information revolution, not as an industrial revolution, and this gives them a very different lens through which to view its risks and benefits.

Technology has meant many things over the years. In the consumer marketplace, people have encountered its changing face in the form of gadgets and labor-saving devices, especially household tools and appliances. From the durables and small electrical goods of the fifties and sixties to the miniaturized instrumentation and LED displays of the seventies to the computerized controllers and games of the eighties to the Internet of the nineties, products have changed dramatically.

Today, information and electronic systems, many of them digital, frame our interactions with technology—not only computers per se, but products run by computers and those that just look as if they're run by computers. While these are distinct, consumers and marketers react to them with similar values and motivations. They see them all as part of the same technological revolution. Generational marketing gives us a useful perspective on these values and motivations.

MIRACLES OF TECHNOLOGY

America was a rural nation when Matures came of age in the first half of this century. Only after World War II did Americans begin to move off farms and settle in large numbers in cities and suburbs.

The earliest life experiences of Matures took place in a far less technologically saturated society.

CHART 5.1: TECHNOLOGIES TO REMEMBER

MATURES	BOOMERS	Xers
Slide rules	Calculators	Spreadsheets
Mimeographing	Photocopying	Desktop publishing
Outer space	Inner space	Cyberspace
IBM	Apple	Netscape
Rotary phones	Touch-tone phones	Cell phones
Spirit of St. Louis	Concorde	*Columbia*
Party lines	Conference calls	Chat rooms

When Matures did come in contact with technology, they usually encountered it as something larger than life, and something that was making life better and easier: the building of railroads, the digging of canals, the clearing of intracoastal waterways. Franklin Roosevelt instituted a massive, multibillion-dollar, public works program based on the advantages of industrial and engineering technology, covering everything from hydroelectric dams and educational facilities to the modernization of the military and rural electrification.

Our easy access to all things electric makes it hard to visualize the impact of electricity and electric light on rural America in the thirties. Suddenly people everywhere could push back the night with a simple flick of a switch. Life assumed a new character as electricity brightened homes, city streets, and shops. Nature, through the cycles of the sun and the moon, no longer dictated the rhythms of life.

In the twenties and thirties, Matures watched in wonder, and sometimes in bemusement, as Buckminster Fuller, working from the premise that man's creative intelligence is limitless, developed design innovations in housing and transportation that continue to be studied today. Fuller's geodesic dome still is viewed by many as the single most significant structural innovation of the twentieth century.

For Matures, technology was even more than just the engine that raised the quality of their lives. In World War II it provided salvation for democracy. American techno-industrial power crushed fascism in Europe and Asia. Radar was first used in the forties. The atomic bomb, developed in secret by a team of the world's greatest scientists, ended the war with Japan. At the time the downsides went relatively unnoticed; no one seemed fully aware that when 100,000 people were killed in Hiroshima on August 6, 1945, technology had revealed a very different face.

In the postwar years, technology was synonymous with prosperity and progress. Agricultural technology led to hybrid corn and disease-resistant crops. Chemical fertilizers and pesticides were put into widespread use. Charles Birdseye had made life easier with quick-frozen vegetables. Antibiotics were first used late in World War II, and in the fifties a safe and effective vaccine against polio was developed.

The postwar consumer market was flooded with affordable refrigerators, freezers, cars, and TVs. By the middle fifties, most suburban homes had a television, a fitting illustration of technology tamed for the benefit of society—it kept children occupied and their parents entertained and informed.

Technology was a gigantic force of industrial might, larger than life, almost mythical. Ordinary people couldn't be expected to master it, but even if Matures didn't understand how it worked, its impact was positive and the trade-offs seemed pretty benign. So Matures went along, as they always did. If Einstein, FDR, and Ike said it was okay, well, Matures were content to believe them. And when they looked at the impact of technology on their own personal lives, they found plenty of proof that what they were told was right. Lots of good things were happening. Du Pont, the industrial giant, coined an advertising tag line that embodied this attitude: "Better living through chemistry."

There certainly were dangers associated with technology, but Matures ignored them because the benefits were just too great. After all, the emergence of America from its rural wilderness was linked directly to its awesome power. So when Matures in the Eisenhower administration looked at the benefits that flowed from the Hoover Dam, it seemed only natural to push for an even more massive project on the Colorado River thirty years later. But they failed to recognize, and really could not have seen from their generational perspective, that America was undergoing a sea change. A new generation had come of age, with new attitudes toward land, water, wild places, and ultimately, technology.

BOOM IN TECHNOLOGY

Boomers grew up surrounded by technology. Television had become ubiquitous. During their youth, scientific breakthroughs resulted in sweeping advances against childhood illnesses. In 1957 the Russians sent Sputnik aloft, launching an unprecedented focus on science education in the United States. President Kennedy's challenge to put a man on the moon captivated us and the rest of the world.

Boomers would seem the likeliest of generations to wholeheartedly embrace and revere technology. But Boomers were, as they came of age, rule breakers. And one of the rules that they broke was the blind acceptance of technology. They took for granted all the comforts that technology afforded. But they refused to consider every technology good; indeed, their experiences showed them otherwise. Their misgivings contributed to the Boomer turn towards trends like communal living and the back-to-nature movement, codified in alternative publications like the *Whole Earth Catalog*.

Boomers worried more about spiritual values, and technology was good only to the extent that it fulfilled these. If not, then it was suspect. Eventually the weight of Boomer suspicions, given momentum by such classics as Rachel Carson's *Silent Spring*, her eloquent recitation of the environmental degradations from DDT, and Ralph Nader's *Unsafe At Any Speed*, his businesslike exposé on the dangers of the Chevrolet Corvair, gave birth to the environmental and consumer movements.

Technology began to show an Achilles' heel. Smog choked our cities. Air and water pollution debates filled the halls of Congress. Academic studies of the effects of TV violence were front-page news. Occupational safety and health as well as consumer product safety were deemed in need of special federal oversight. Three *Apollo* astronauts died in a launchpad fire in 1967. Love Canal was pronounced a disaster area and evacuated in 1978, a precursor to the seemingly insoluble Superfund sites that still dot the nation. On March 28, 1979, an accident at the Three Mile Island nuclear facility near Harrisburg, Pennsylvania, caused a partial meltdown of the fuel core in one of the reactors. A small amount of radioactive gas was released into the air. Although the health effects were later determined to have been negligible, the psychological damage was immense.

To Boomers, it seemed obvious they needed to suppress and resist all of the bad, even evil, technologies. They were willing to accept only those they could tame. They focused instead on broad areas like robotics, computing, and telecommunications. They wanted progressive, value-sensitive technologies foretold by thinkers like Alvin Toffler and Buckminster Fuller, Theodore Rozak, and Charles Reich—technologies no worse than benign, and hopefully, ethically uplifting.

Marketers found opportunities in this value shift, most immediately for products that were natural or more environmentally friendly. By the seventies, some of the first so-called green products began to appear, in all product categories, from detergents to gasoline to shampoos to paint removers. Some marketing moves were subtler, though no less deliberate; for instance, appliance manufacturers switching to earth tones.

By the mid-eighties, with an emphasis on winning dominating their values, Boomers began to discover that good technologies were not only desirable for their own sake, but could also provide thrills and excitement. No longer warring against technological evils, they coveted items like BMWs and Volvos. They were fun and safe. PCs, personal organizers, microwaves, and cellular phones proliferated because they made people smarter and more effective. VCRs, Game Boys, videocams, and compact discs were just plain fun. And the best toys, of course, were the sorts of trophies, badges, and symbols that proved you were a winner.

From the middle of the sixties to the middle of the eighties, society's technological focus changed from the industrial—smokestacks, rockets, radio towers, concrete—to the information-related—silicon chips, microprocessors, software. Boomers liked this. Although reminded by Arthur C. Clarke's wordplay in the movie *2001* that just one step back of IBM is HAL, their more common experience with computers was liberating. They were wary of industrial technologies, but willingly embraced nearly all of the new information technologies. Indeed, it is this shift that divides the three generations—Matures shaped by industrial technologies, Xers by information technologies, and Boomers making the transition from one to the other.

Boomers, in fact, are the core customers for information technologies today. The popular media image of Xers surrounded by high-tech computer products and ensconced in digital lifestyles is inaccurate. It's the information-hungry Boomers who spend the most money on computers, faxes, cell phones, and related high-tech gear. They operate computers and other technological tools at work, and they use technology to bring their work home with them. Work remains extremely important to Boomers, so technology focused on work is likely to be most successful with this generation, though as we'll discuss later, technologies for the home are an emerging market opportunity.

MAKE MINE MICROPROCESSED

Xers share Boomers' comfort with and commitment to the new information order. But they handle the technology in more sophisticated ways because they grew up with it. So it's no surprise that our MONITOR data show Xers to be consistently more likely to deem a wider variety of household and information technologies as "making life better."

Xers know technology largely as microchips and information systems. Even mechanical products like automobiles are run now by these kinds of systems. And Xers are closer in spirit to the digital cutting edge. While massive projects for public works, basic infrastructure, and weapons for fighting wars represented technology for Matures, for Xers it's laptops, VCRs, cable TV, and the Internet.

Xers take a more pragmatic attitude, just as they do with everything else. They're faced with pros and cons everywhere they look. Video games are great fun, but smart bombs in the Gulf War and SDI graphics on news shows—the real-life equivalents—gave Xers a glimpse of technology's dark side. Television babysat their generation, but now Xers see that perhaps TV infused their world with too much violence. Personal computers are great, yet not without their own special problems. These perceptions also extend to non-information technologies. Product liability suits for flawed and negligent technologies are constantly in the news. Margarine turned out to be a processed food technology, as much a health risk as butter. As a result, of the three generations, GenXers are the most likely to agree that the problems created by science and technology will eventually outweigh the benefits. Xers embrace technologies, but they do so prudently, with caution and care.

TECHNOLOGY FUTURES

We certainly don't mean to draw distinctions among generations by characterizing any one as less technologically sophisticated than the others. Indeed, every generation is expert in the technologies and systems commonplace in their formative years. It's misleading, for example, to conclude from any disparity in computer skills that Matures have less technological savvy than Xers. Their savvy is just different. The key to future marketing success is to move forward in ways that match up the faculties and resourcefulness of consumers with the design and advertising of products.

Nine out of ten of all consumers affirm the inevitability of technology moving into all areas of life, like it or not. Consumers across generations will adapt—sometimes with ease, sometimes not—to technological developments. Recent ownership trends show this clearly. In 1990, 73 percent of American households had a microwave, compared with 86 percent in 1996. Universal remote controls, which did not even exist in 1990, are now found in over one-third of all homes. Interactive cable systems will regenerate demand for innovations in television sets and VCRs. Products like digital thermometers, commonplace today, were science fiction a few years ago. And there is a strong, continuing demand for technological enhancements across many other types of industries, ranging from health care to travel and leisure to financial services.

Technology is here to stay, but that basic fact doesn't tell us much about where to find competitive advantage in the future. For this we have to answer *how* technology will gain acceptance, and consequently *what* technologies consumers will adopt.

THE QUESTION OF HOW

The pace of technological change has dramatically accelerated, and along with it, the number and complexity of choices confronting consumers. Deregulation of the information, communications, and utility industries has had a huge effect on this. The single biggest challenge for technology marketers through the end of this century will be keeping pace with these changes as they affect the marketplace.

For consumers, irrespective of generation, too many choices are just as problematic as too few. Seventy-three percent of all consumers agree that "technology is so confusing these days that it's hard to know what to buy." And that sentiment does not reflect the impact of recent industry changes and realignments.

Too much high tech just overloads consumers—more decisions to make, extra tasks to do, arcane jargon to learn. Maintenance, compatibility, and performance all become new or more complicated worries. Until recently, all that consumers really had to decide were the specific features they wanted. But now, after deregulation, consumers will face a welter of risky decisions about relationships with service providers, decisions that will be unfamiliar and for which they will have less than optimal information. The face of the future is not simple, and certainly not friendly, for anyone, Matures, Boomers, or Xers.

The joke about VCRs always blinking on 12:00 A.M. tells on our collective technological ineptness. But this humor could turn deadly serious. It's a problem if you can't figure out in an emergency how to punch through to 911 on your new pocket-sized digital cell phone/pager/fax/organizer. It's also a problem if your home security/environmental control system goes down while you're on vacation because it's bundled with everything else through a single line that gets hit by freak lightning in a thunderstorm. Theoretically situations such as these should never happen, but then theoretically we should all be able to program our VCRs.

As technological complexity looms, consumers of all generations have actively retreated. Our MONITOR tracking clearly shows that stress due to overload is the single biggest issue facing consumers. They handle this overload by simplifying all aspects of their work and lives. Added complexity from technology runs counter to the effort to reduce stress, and thus is feared. The majority of consumers of every generational cohort agree that "technology sometimes intimidates me"—55 percent of Xers, 57 percent of Boomers, and 64 percent of Matures.

This complexity is even more problematic, given our growing dependence on it. Most consumers cast a critical eye on their dependence on something too complex to handle. In our tracking, 61 percent of all consumers agree that "society is so dependent on technology we don't know how to function without it."

New technologies will succeed through *simplicity*.

Few companies recognize this consumer need, a blind spot we see in interviews we've completed with business leaders. As part of our background work for our 1995 MONITOR survey, we queried CEOs about the overall trends they believe will have the most impact on tomorrow's marketplace. Virtually all mentioned, as one of the top three trends, technology's potential to create and enhance new products and services. Relatively few, however, had any concrete ideas about what shape these would take, or how they might be integrated effectively into the marketplace.

Simplicity has two aspects. First, focus on function. Forgo pizzazz; just get the job done. Don't obscure performance with other distractions. Cut through confusing, overblown hype, and simply deliver the bottom line consumers are looking for.

Second, put a high-touch face on the high tech. Make it friendly. Engineer in empathy. Don't overchallenge users. Minimize steps and components; consumers are put off by high tech hurdles. And don't be too serious. Build in some fun.

We aren't, by the way, recommending simplicity to the point of superficiality. Consumers still want control and sophistication. But they want it in a way that also provides simplicity, *not* in a way that trades off one for the other. This is the most common mistake marketers make in working on simplification. The big opportunity, as yet underexploited, is high simplicity that also provides high control. "Smart cards" do this—highly simple because everything's on one small chip, and high in control for exactly the same reason—but the uses of smart cards are as yet underdeveloped.

Nor are we recommending a slide down the design continuum from high tech to high touch. Unfortunately this has become a much too common way of thinking about the marketplace. These two concepts, in fact, do not stand at opposite ends of the spectrum. What we've seen is that all high tech and no high touch is not what consumers want.

Innovations that keep things simple have the strongest potential to create competitive advantage. But for each generation, simplicity entails a different application.

• For Matures, simplicity means *accessibility*. Matures are not put off by technology, they just never grew up with it at their fingertips, nor did they get the chance at an early age to become adept users of information systems. Hence, a lot of what they struggle with is the novelty of it all. In many ways it's just a matter of experience, not a matter of smarts.

Matures need more help, more explanation, on-the-spot training, better reference guides, proactive service and support. If you show them that everyone does it, you've appealed to their strong sense of generational conformity even while demonstrating accessibility, since so many others have figured it out. As they gain proficiency, reinforce that they've earned something special through their work and dedication. Mastery of these systems is proof of their skills and adaptability. The effort itself should be praised.

• For Boomers, simplicity means *efficiency*. Boomers struggle to find new ways to win, and to find better ways to balance their priorities. Getting things done faster and more systematically does both.

Technology, though, has been one of the things that has disappointed Boomer expectations. In particular, the efficiency promised early on by PCs never materialized and, in many cases, PCs have only added more tasks and responsibilities. Still, Boomers use PCs often, and remain open to improvements, looking with anticipation to the generation of hardware and software that will finally deliver fully what they want.

Work is central to Boomers, and concepts like personal productivity carry into all aspects of their lives. Life is simpler when it's more productive. When things get left to chance and go unmanaged, they get more complicated. Besides, they value efficiency at work in and of itself.

It's important to remember that while Boomers want simplicity, they do not want things to get so simple that they are kept from being in the know. Make more information and detail available to them when and as they want it. Reward Boomers with information, but don't penalize them if they don't seek out more.

• For Xers, simplicity means *practicality*. Technology is part of the fabric of their milieu. By itself, it doesn't make anything special—it should make things more practical, more useful, or more functional. Complicated, convoluted things aren't practical. Simpler things are.

Simple things focus on the bottom line. They don't come packaged with a lot of hard sell and they're easier to use. Xers want straightforward performance, not hype. In their evaluation of technology, they won't allow a reverence for scientific mystique to distract them from their focus on real-world effectiveness.

Technology as entertainment is more ingrained with Xers. They've grown up surrounded by rapidly evolving machines, and they've always found fun things to do with them, even when the machines weren't designed specifically for that purpose. The most pernicious, menacing hackers usually turn out to be motivated mostly by fun. Boomers developed the Internet for science and work, but Xers have always seen it, first and foremost, as fun. Technology adds an edge to things, makes them more interesting and enjoyable. And simple technologies are the most fun because they can be more creatively and eclectically repackaged.

For many Xers, the fun in technology only comes once they're totally immersed in all its convoluted and esoteric complexities. Needless to say, because of their exposure to contemporary technologies at a much earlier age, the definition of what's simple for Xers is different from what's simple for Matures. The diverse ways in which many Xers complicate technologies demonstrates their method of building from simplicity. Bottom line, they want technologies that focus on their needs.

The imperative for simplicity we see in our tracking is not a call for technological devolution. We don't mean less powerful technologies that force consumers to give up control and sophistication, but rather, simpler ways to understand, use, connect with, and benefit from them. A Kodak ad running late nights on TV, particularly during the 1996 Summer Olympics, serves as a good illustration of this.

The ad tells the story of a grunge-looking Xer who took some snapshots of his dad barbecuing in the backyard. He takes the film to Kodak for developing, and when he gets his pictures back, the clerk notices in one picture a speck, hanging in the sky above the guy's dad. So they blow it up. It looks like a UFO. No, says a black-suited mystery man who appears out of nowhere, it's just a hovering pie tin. The mystery man asks for and takes a CD with the picture on it. Meanwhile, the young guy goes home, pops his CD with the picture on it into his PC, and puts the picture out on the Internet for an upcoming UFO conference. The mystery man, unfortunately, discovers it on the net and calls from a secret hangar, where behind him white-coated scientists are poring over a UFO. He admonishes the young guy, who gets nervous and says good-bye so he can take another call clicking on call waiting. It's aliens! They're on-line, looking at his photo on their spaceship console, and they tell him, "Nice shot." Meanwhile the mystery man and two goons pull up at the young guy's house, march menacingly to the front door, and ring the bell. As the young guy gets to the door, the aliens save the day by zapping the three guys with a raybeam from their spaceship. When the Xer opens his front door, no one is there. Weird. And all because he took a picture of his dad and blew it up.

It's a crazy, fast-paced ad that pokes fun at popular opinions about UFOs and aliens and government conspiracies. More to the point, it introduces consumers to a plethora of high-tech stuff that focuses more on ease and fun than on the technology itself. A simple story with a simple message showing simple ways to do interesting things with Kodak products. The story relies on different kinds of technologies to move the plot along—cameras, film, developers, copiers, printers, CDs, PCs, the Internet, call waiting. Each technology is shown doing something beneficial. The ad focuses on how technology is used, not on the technology itself. So simple that even a regular guy who just wanted to take a picture of his dad has control over sophisticated uses of the technology.

This ad crosses over generations. The plot, filled with irreverent humor, includes people of all ages. Its tempo and tone appeal to Xers and Boomers. It exemplifies the sort of technological accessibility that interests Matures. Technology doesn't have to be overdone to be persuasively presented. A simpler approach is often the most effective.

THE QUESTION OF WHAT

The challenge for technology marketers is to find and replicate the lowest common denominator of technological simplicity. There are many ideas about what this might be. Airlines want ticketless check-in technologies that are as simple as ATMs. Financial service companies want telephone banking that makes managing money as simple as dialing a phone number. Cable TV providers want interactive technologies as convenient and efficient as point-and-click software.

These may indeed be the right models for each of these industries. Our MONITOR research suggests another, however. When we ask respondents about the technologies that make life better, only one gets mentioned by two-thirds or more of consumers in each generation: microwave ovens.

Of course, microwaves weren't always this popular. In their early years they were referred to as Radaranges—not particularly friendly. For many years microwave marketers had a product in search of a need. The technology itself was, as is so often the case, a serendipitous discovery. Dr. Perry Spenser was developing magnetrons for Raytheon when one day in 1946 he stood too close to one with a candy bar in his pocket. It melted, but Spenser saw possibilities in this mess. He tried popcorn next, and soon had it pinging off high-tech hardware all over his lab. He had discovered the cooker for the nineties.

But consumers didn't get it at first. Marketers tried convincing them that faster cooking and tabletop portability made it worth the price. But Mature mothers weren't interested in cutting corners on family meals. The hard work they put into mealtime was partially its own reward. So after research into generational priorities, the marketing emphasis in "fast family meals" shifted from fast to family. The benefits of microwaving for better serving your family gave this product the appeal it needed to get sales going. In turn, this meant that engineers had to drive down the complexity of microwave operations, otherwise mothers lacked the control they needed to use this sophisticated technology to better serve their families. Microwaves today have become the consumer standard for technological usefulness and simplicity— three-button operations that anyone can use, and that most households have.

The answer to the question "what," then, is *anything that's as simple as a microwave*. This is the lowest common denominator for technology in the consumer marketplace. In fact, microwaves are almost the only technological model that works for Matures. Other technologies like telephones or TV or clock radios are as widespread and as commonplace as microwaves. But no other technology is much cited by consumers as making life better.

As a model for technological simplicity, microwaves have a variety of appealing characteristics:

- Microwaves are familiar. You don't have to retrain consumers to use your system or machine.

- Microwaves are controlled by buttons for function and form. No programming. No multiuse controls requiring special steps or unusual protocol.

- Microwaves are compact.

- Microwaves do something elemental and basic—they cook food.

- Microwaves work fast and are forgiving of most misuses.

Perhaps most important, though, microwaves do not feature technology simply for the sake of featuring technology. They combine simplicity with control. They provide benefits while being consciously configured to mask the complicated inner workings of the technology that delivers those benefits. This is a crucial part of what consumers look for—the *features* that deliver the benefits, *not* the technology itself.

WHAT I GET, NOT WHAT IT'S GOT

Consumers want what technology has to offer—the features, the special effects, the conveniences. Across all generations, an overwhelming percentage of consumers, 86 percent, agree that "it doesn't matter if a product has the latest technology as long as it has the features I need." Features deliver the benefits, and it's the benefits on which consumers focus, not the knob or the dial or the chip. In our MONITOR tracking each year we ask consumers what factors influence their purchasing decisions. As recently as 1994, "many options and features" and "latest technology" were equally important. But in the last few years, across all generations, the factor of features has emerged as much more important than the technology itself.

We have characterized this in recent years as a consumer focus on "technology as a tool." The bloom is off the rose. Popular opinion has shifted greatly. From technology as savior, to technology as facilitator of spiritual fulfillment, to exciting toy, to just another tool. It if works, fine. If not, get rid of it.

Technologies no longer sell themselves—simply having a new technology no longer interests buyers. Consumers want benefits and if they can get those benefits from a product with little—or even older—technology, that's what they'll choose. For technology to make a difference, it has to deliver significant benefits.

Perceptions of benefits, though, are often tied up with price. Because technologies are commonplace, many have become commodities. This puts a ceiling on how much consumers will pay. This, in turn, makes it harder for marketers to build in more benefits to add the value that justifies something other than the cheapest price.

In our MONITOR research, nearly all consumers report they

are comfortable waiting for prices to come down before buying products—82 percent of Xers, 87 percent of Boomers, and 86 percent of Matures. The majority of consumers—about 60 percent in each cohort—agree that even though technology has made products easier to use, the hassle and costs of repair often make the benefits just not worth it.

In one of our more revealing MONITOR questions, we asked respondents to pick the one of two statements that better described their views: "When I buy a major appliance, I usually choose the model with nothing extra; most of those gadgets are just one more thing to go wrong," or "When I buy a major appliance, I usually choose the model with all the extras; they usually make the appliance better." Among Boomers and Matures, the majority picked the first statement—52 percent and 58 percent, respectively. Even among Xers, 41 percent picked the first statement.

Technology is inevitable and consumers are accumulating more and more of it, but the benefits of it all are often unclear. We suggest considering at least three areas for some value-enhancing marketing opportunities.

Build in fun for Xers and Matures. Xers look for this, and fun will help overcome some of the intimidation Matures often feel when confronted by new information technologies. Some built-in fun adds an intriguing edge to products.

After all, Xers and Matures feel a closer connection between technology and leisure. In responses to one of our MONITOR questions about whether technology has produced more leisure time—58 percent of Xers and 53 percent of Matures versus 49 percent of Boomers thought it had. Boomer focus on technology is much more connected with productivity and work.

Integrate technologies more holistically. A little over half, 54 percent, of all consumers feel that technology isolates people. In fact, many technologies are designed for single, isolated uses. This conflicts with the reemerging desire to connect more with other people. Hardware and software that resist isolation and create interactive opportunities will be well received.

CHART 5.2: GEN-O-GRAM—TECHNOLOGY WITH A MATURE

Born:	1944
Education:	College graduate; wrestling scholarship
Occupation:	High school teacher
Household:	Married; homeowner; two grown children; two grandchildren
On approach to life:	"I just started lifting weights. I belong to AARP. I believe you have to take care of yourself.
On technology:	"I am a techie. The information overload is real. I can't sleep anymore because there is so much to learn. When my son was stationed in Saudi Arabia, we talked by e-mail every day. I own 21 computers and four TVs, each with a VCR."
On the generations:	"I call American kids the garbage cans of the world. They feed them garbage food, garbage TV, and garbage consumerism. And older people—they are greedy. You don't tear down the old unless you have something better to put up. I worry that we are popularizing lifestyles that are not what I accept easily. "
Disappointments:	"At my old school, I developed a master plan and wrote 32 grants for $250,000 to bring technology into the school. I was happy in that job, but they closed the school and where I am now there is nothing. When I found out, I had to pull my car off the road, I was crying so hard. I want to die working. Maybe I can start a business to help lower-income people get a decent wage. Maybe I could start a coffee shop for people who do volunteer work. I worry that I haven't been as responsible a citizen as I could have been. I want a life that is meaningful."

Xers, of course, already make extensive use of technologies as part of their social networks. Still, 53 percent of Xers report isolation as a negative consequence of technology. Even the best users find it to be somewhat incompatible with community-building. *The New York Times* recently reported that many college campuses are struggling with exactly this problem. The report quoted Clifford Stoll, author and ex–Harvard researcher, who is a cyber-wary observer of the scene: "[W]e're turning colleges into a cubicle-directed electronics experience and denying . . . the develop[ment] of social adeptness."

One idea is to focus more on hands-free technologies. To the extent that a technology requires physical contact, it ties the user to a certain place at a certain time. This makes the focus of usage the technology itself rather than the lifestyle in which it's being used. That's isolating, so make it hands-free.

Take another look around the homes of Boomers and Matures. Technologies already permeate, but with today's returning focus on family, technologies that support and facilitate these kinds of values will tap into a key trend. Further, many tasks related to working and shopping that used to take place outside of the home are now conducted in the home, like home offices, home shopping, and banking.

But beyond all this, many aspects of the home environment have yet to be affected by technological enhancements. Opportunities associated with these untapped areas are showing up in our MONITOR data. Over the past decade we have seen a dramatic turnaround in attitudes about home care, especially among women. Today many more consumers think a home should be furnished so that it "is comfortable and easy to take care of" instead of being "gracious and attractive though it may mean more work to take care of." Technology can make a difference by making home care easier while also making it more attractive.

Boomers and Matures are more likely than Xers to favor ease over attractiveness in home furnishing and home care—80 percent and 83 percent, respectively, versus 73 percent for Xers. They are also more likely to renovate their homes, the ideal time to consider

building in technologies that upgrade the quality of their environment. On the other hand, Xers are likely to be looking at buying
their first homes. Given their greater facility with modern systems,
a totally wired, brand new starter home might be worth a small
premium to them.

There's nothing new about this in the modern era, by the way.
The 1939 New York World's Fair celebrated the dazzling and won-
drous improvements that technology was bringing right into people's homes. In his book about that era, Yale computer scientist
David Gelernter writes, "Housewives were the beneficiaries of the
most important technological revolution of the century, a revolution that made it possible for wives who couldn't afford servants to
devote themselves largely to a job or . . . to their children." This
revolution: the widespread availability of electrical appliances,
specifically vacuum cleaners, washing machines, and refrigerators.

We now stand poised to move forward again, this time to
"smart houses," houses that run themselves using internal computers, that can clean themselves, raise and lower their own lights,
adjust their own temperatures, manage communications and
finances, secure and protect themselves, bring entertainments to
their inhabitants, monitor the health of those who live there, and
call for emergency assistance when needed. No Hollywood FX,
this. It's here today. The only barrier, of course, will be consumer
resistance to technological complexity.

The marketing challenge is clear. Consumers are very concerned to see that the benefits of technology are not confounded by
its complexity. Only a simple solution will suffice.

CYBERCITIZENS ACROSS GENERATIONS

In unassuming East Village quarters, neighbor to the local Hell's Angels chapter, sits a gathering place for those who travel cyberspace. The deep, narrow space is lined on both sides with traditional cafe tables. There's a garden patio for warm-weather days. Books and magazines lie all around and original artwork hangs from the walls. Bills advertise concerts and performances. A small bar and a kitchen clank in the background. But this isn't just another drowsy downtown hangout. There's an energy about, an electric feeling that crackles the air, coming from the shiny white computers sitting on each table, whirring and humming.

The Internet Cafe, at 82 East Third Street in Manhattan, was the first of its kind when it opened in the spring of 1995. Along with sandwiches, salads, pastries, and tea, customers choose from a cybermenu that links them to the hottest sites on the Internet. Access charges are fairly modest—$8 an hour to surf alone, $25 an hour if you choose to have one of the cafe staff serve as your cyberguide.

This is the sort of bistro enjoying a boom all over the country—a place that's a part of, not apart from, patrons' lifestyles. You can find a cybercafe near you by checking out *globalcomputing.com/cafes.html*. And when you walk into one, who you find there, lost in cyberspace, will surprise you.

"We designed the cafe to welcome the new user to the Internet and to be an antidote to the sterile, intimidating environments that people often associate with new technology," said Arthur Perley, the founder of the Internet Cafe. Those who stop by are as likely to be learners as the learned, so the cafe offers instructional courses at all levels—"Internet Basics," "Computer Basics," "Advanced Internet," "Advanced HTML," or "Multimedia Web Publishing." An eclectic group comes here, not just a bunch of oddball, body-pierced East Village Xers with purple hair and tight black tops cruising the information superhighway. In our work we have dubbed these on-line pioneers "cybercitizens™"—members of the new commonwealth of cyberspace—to better signify the breadth of the population on-line.

On any given night, keyboards clicking, the cafe bustling and busy, the crowd of cybercitizens is an unmistakable mix of Boomers and Xers alongside a smattering of Matures. "We get people of all ages in here," said Grainne Keegan, who helps manage the cafe. "It's the sort of mix that reflects the neighborhood." But it also reflects the growing cross-generational appeal of, and participation in, cyberspace itself.

In our MONITOR-based scrutiny of this market, we find generational marketing issues to be at the forefront of those most important to cybermarketers. Since 1994 we have tracked the growth and development of cyberspace; our studies are published as *The Yankelovich Cybercitizen™ Report*. (If you're interested in surfing our way, more detail about these surveys is available on our web

site, *yankelovich.com,* or in the *Cyber-Insider* newsletter published
by our sister company, Cyber-Dialogue, at *cyberdialogue.com.*)

One thing is clear. Conventional wisdom about cyberspace is
far off the mark. The pop culture image of some overstimulated
GenX college dropout living with his parents, holed up at 3 A.M.
behind a bolted bedroom door, face awash in the dim glow from
his backlit computer screen, hacking his way into top secret government files, is wrong. Cyberspace is not like that at all, indeed, it
never was. In fact, this media-fed image doesn't even get the generation right.

FIRST ON-LINE

The early adopters of cyberspace were Boomers, specifically,
upscale male Boomers. This is exactly what the loose alliance of
Internet developers intended. The Internet was conceived as part of
a military strategy to protect crucial information and systems from
concentrated enemy attacks on central points, so the disaggrega-
tion achieved through an interconnected network of far-flung computers was vital. Scientists soon got on-line, and these uses eventually gave rise to the need for more powerful information intercon-
nections. Hence, the development of the World Wide Web.

Boomers got involved in the Internet after it was up and running because they had access to the hardware it took and the career
interests it serviced. For many years Boomer professionals, scientists in particular, nursed the Internet along. Only in the last few
years has this changed, largely because the Internet has opened up
to commercial businesses—a type of organization that was traditionally denied access.

As of early 1994 only 6 percent of U.S. adults had ever logged
on-line. Of that small group of early adopters, 54 percent were
Boomers. A year later the penetration of cyberspace had more than
doubled, to 14.5 percent of all adults. The bulk of these new
cybercitizens came from groups other than those that had spawned
the original Internet adopters. Now it was 46 percent Boomers. In

our tracking study most current at the time of this writing, we have seen a continuation of this. In data collected as of October 1996, penetration was up to 21.9 percent of all adults, a group made up of 52 percent Boomers. This is especially interesting because we can see in just a few data points the competing pressures affecting the commercial opportunities of the Internet—pressures that are generational in nature.

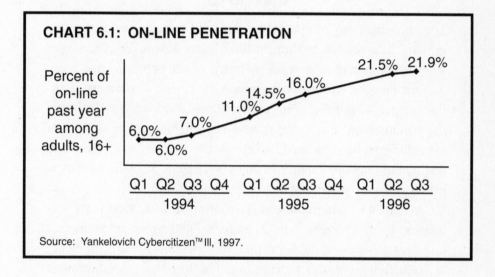

CHART 6.1: ON-LINE PENETRATION

Percent of on-line past year among adults, 16+

6.0%   6.0%   7.0%   11.0%   14.5%   16.0%   21.5%   21.9%

Q1 Q2 Q3 Q4   Q1 Q2 Q3 Q4   Q1 Q2 Q3
     1994   1995   1996

Source: Yankelovich Cybercitizen™ III, 1997.

On the one hand, cyberspace is broadening. On the other hand, Boomers remain the dominant group on-line. Despite the mainstreaming of cybercitizenry, the proportion of Boomers has not diminished, but in fact has rebounded.

This is not to downplay the importance of Xers in cyberspace. Indeed, when compared with their representation among the U.S. population as a whole, the percentage of Xer cybercitizens is pronounced. This is true for Boomers, too, though not nearly as much as for Xers. Matures, of course, are dramatically underrepresented in cyberspace relative to their size in the U.S. population.

Even accounting for this, however, the fact still remains that Boomers are the dominant generational group on-line. This is the framework for looking at on-line opportunities. While the total universe of cybercitizens is becoming noticeably more heterogeneous, the current commercial potential of cyberspace remains tied largely to the interests of the sizable number of Boomers on-line. Building cyberspace across generations will take place in this context—finding ways to make it more than just a Boomer boys' club without, at the same time, diminishing the appeal it has for Boomers.

WORK OR PLAY

The mainstreaming of cyberspace has already had an impact on the primary motivations behind on-line usage. Just a few years ago, when Boomers were a solid majority of all cybercitizens, work was the number one reason mentioned for using a commercial on-line service. One-third of all cybercitizens cited work as their primary motivation. But as the dominance of Boomers in the mix of cybercitizens has declined, work as the primary motivator has dropped to only one-quarter of all cybercitizens. It's still the reason mentioned most often, but its position has eroded.

Meanwhile, entertainment is mentioned with increasing frequency, from 11 percent to 21 percent, and more entertainment offerings are now available on-line. But something else is going on.

GenXers go on-line to have fun. They are the generation most likely to say they're surfing just to see what's out there. They are the most likely to participate in on-line games and social activities. Xers are not on-line to shop, nor are they on-line to seek out news and information.

Matures, on the other hand, go on-line to shop and to find news and information. Further, Matures do not venture onto the World Wide Web as much as other generations, preferring to enjoy their on-line experience through third-party services.

Boomers are the most likely to work on-line. They are also the most likely to access family-oriented services like on-line encyclopedias or children's services. However, Boomers share Xer interests in entertainment and surfing as well as Mature interests in shopping and news.

VIRTUAL SHOPPING

The growth we see for on-line entertainment does not carry over to all Internet business opportunities. On-line shopping, for example, has not expanded.

In our 1995 survey of on-line users, 22 percent of all cybercitizens reported an on-line purchase of some product or service in the previous twelve months. A year later, that percentage was down slightly, to 19 percent. The most popular types of products and services were purchased at the same rate from 1995 to 1996; the decline from year to year was in the average number of categories shopped by on-line purchasers.

Among those who did report an on-line purchase, half were Boomers and a fifth were Matures. Of course, there are more Boomers on-line, so we would expect to find more Boomers and fewer Matures making up the group of on-line shoppers. But given the interest of Matures in on-line shopping, there ought to be more purchasing by Matures than what we actually see. Even taking into account the smaller percentages of Mature cybercitizens, they just aren't shopping. In other words, while shopping is of strong interest to Matures, it is apparently not of sufficiently strong interest to get them to complete an actual transaction.

Matures are concerned mainly with on-line security. Matures, more than Xers or Boomers, strongly agree that better security is needed to protect their personal and financial information from unauthorized people. They also agree that it is too easy for someone to steal their credit card number if they use it on the Internet. In a special analysis we completed for a Conference Board meeting, we found that these concerns are directly linked to a diminished likelihood of making on-line purchases. On-line retailers need to address this.

Matures also are concerned about the value of what's available on-line. In a May 1996 survey, we asked respondents to compare shopping off-line in regular stores to shopping on-line. The majority of Matures felt on-line shopping was superior in areas related to product information and product comparison. But in all other aspects, including price, value, variety, returns, payment, and convenience, the majority of Matures felt on-line shopping was the same as or worse than shopping in regular stores.

The few on-line shopping advantages they see are not enough to motivate Matures to buy, especially when they also have concerns about on-line security. On-line shopping involves a new learned behavior, so something compelling must make it worth the effort it takes. In the minds of cybercitizens, that's missing.

VALUE

For our series of tracking reports on cyberspace, we developed a measure of the on-line commercial value represented by each cybercitizen. This measure is built from three broad components. *Access value* consists of the monthly charges incurred by a cybercitizen, *product* or *service value* consists of the past and potential on-line purchasing of a cybercitizen, and *efficiency* grades cybercitizens in terms of how easy it is to reach them with marketing.

The profile of cybercitizens with the highest economic value is familiar—predominantly men, Boomers, better educated, higher income. This isn't too unexpected, since Boomers spend the most time on-line, though less time per session, than Xers. They're just on-line more frequently.

Boomer cybercitizens subscribe to a greater number and variety of on-line services. They are more likely to have the kinds of computers and modems to enjoy fully what the Internet has to offer. They also have higher-than-average incomes and feel confident about their technological capabilities. All of these factors contribute to the above-average economic value of Boomer cybercitizens.

BOOM-PLUS

Boomers on-line are a lot like Boomers in general. What you know about marketing to Boomer consumers will stand you in good stead when marketing to Boomer cybercitizens. Their core generational values make them more receptive to cyberspace. The web is information-intensive and user-controlled, which satisfies their needs to be in the know and in control.

Among a variety of attitudes and values, however, we find a core set that is true for all on-line users, across all generations, distinguishing cybercitizens in general from consumers at large.

- Cybercitizens are self-assured. In our 1995 Cybercitizen Report, we looked at responses to one of our more telling MONITOR questions—whether they believe their IQs are above average. About two-thirds of the general adult population thinks this. But 80 percent of all cybercitizens consider their IQs above average! Cybercitizens think of themselves as "exceptional."

- Cybercitizens of all generations accept science and technology more readily than adults in general do. In the general population, Matures trail Xers and Boomers in their attitudes about technology, but among cybercitizens they are just about even.

- Cybercitizens focus more on work. The majority name work as one of the ways they express creativity. (But while Boomer cybercitizens are the most likely to report they go on-line more often at work, Xers are more likely to say they log on someplace other than home or work.)

- Cybercitizens focus less on the home. They are less likely to see home as a place to relax or to get most of their satisfactions in life.

- Cybercitizens are more optimistic about the future. They have more confidence that they will achieve the American Dream and they feel good about their prospects for the future.

- Cybercitizens are less focused on tangible goals and objectives. Compared with adults in general, they are less likely to see money as the only relevant measure of success, and are more likely to say they prefer to spend their money on experiences that will enrich their lives rather than on possessions. It's not that cybercitizens place less value on money; it's that they also want flexibility and authority—taking a day off when wanted, or being a manager at work.

- Cybercitizens more than other adults are enthralled by computers. Many more cybercitizens see the ability to use advanced technologies as a sign of status. Many more also report that working with computers is a way they express their creativity.

In these specific areas, cybercitizen generational cohorts differ from their counterparts in the general population. Apart from these differences, though, Boomers in cyberspace are like Boomers in general, and even some of the differences are just Boomer attitudes amplified a few decibels. That's not the case for the other two generations, however, Matures in particular.

MATURES ON-LINE

Matures on-line are a distinctive group of Matures. The differences just described, while important, do not touch on the most important characteristics distinguishing Mature cybercitizens from Matures in the population at large.

As a rule, Matures don't express much need for novel experiences and personal creativity. Not so for Mature cybercitizens! Our research shows only 47 percent of Matures in general expressing a hunger for new experiences, lowest among the three generational cohorts. But 70 percent of Mature cybercitizens express this need, second only to Xers. Similarly, just 55 percent of Matures in general desire more novelty and change, while 65 percent of Mature cybercitizens do. The bottom line is that 90 percent of Mature cybercitizens say they want more pleasure out of life.

The Matures who have flocked to the Internet are older consumers in search of new experiences. But not just any ol' new thing. They want to participate themselves. Among Mature cybercitizens, 82 percent report the need to fulfill themselves by being more creative—a percentage that almost ties them with Xer cybercitizens for the top spot, and a percentage far bigger than the 63 percent among Matures in general who say this. Similarly, only 54 percent of Matures in general say they want to know themselves better, compared with 73 percent of Mature cybercitizens.

The pattern of attitudes we see has two lessons. First, while the values of a generational cohort center around a distinctive point, there is always a range of opinions on both sides of that point. Under the right market conditions, it's often possible to isolate the subgroups within a cohort that hold some attitude closer to the average opinion of another cohort. That's true for cyberspace, and it has important marketing implications. Which leads to the second, more fundamental point.

Cybercitizens need novelty, fun, pleasure, and personal creativity. This is most apparent among Mature cybercitizens because it is so uncharacteristic of the vast majority of Matures. It's true among Xer and Boomer cybercitizens as well, but we don't notice it as readily because Xers and Boomers are oriented toward these values to start with. This explains why there are far fewer Matures online. And it shows us that many of the attractions cyberspace offers connect intrinsically with the idea of novelty, a point we'll return to at the close of this chapter.

Mature cybercitizens are not completely disconnected from their fellows, though. They share a common interest in local communities. Mature cybercitizens are the most likely to express an interest in becoming more involved in the life of their neighborhoods and communities—70 percent say so. And they are consistently more interested in local news and bulletin boards on-line. Still, these are not your typical Matures.

XERS ON-LINE

Xer cybercitizens don't stand out from their cohort as much as Matures stand out from theirs. But some things are worth noting. Xer cybercitizens see themselves outside the mainstream, and unlike others in their generational cohort, are more likely to feel that their personal values are not shared by most Americans. Perhaps this is why they go on-line—for the opportunity to find a like-minded community on the Internet. They appear much more interested in social connections on-line.

These differences, though, do not signal a broader alienation from society. Xer cybercitizens are, for nearly every public or private figure and institution we track, the most trusting among their generation. This is particularly true when we look at certain individuals and institutions, like older people, doctors, TV news, news in magazines, and religious leaders. But make no mistake. This higher trust is not uncritical. Our MONITOR research also shows Xer cybercitizens just as acutely concerned about protecting their privacy from abuse by the institutions they trust.

Perhaps most important, the high skepticism about science and technology true of the majority of Xers is undiminished among Xer cybercitizens. This is noteworthy because it is not true of Boomer and Mature cybercitizens, who are less likely than their counterparts in the general population to believe that the problems created by science and technology will eventually outweigh the benefits.

One other notable thing distinguishes Xer cybercitizens from their Boomer and Mature counterparts. Boomers and Matures first accessed the Internet at home, 54 percent and 52 percent, respectively. Work is second, 30 percent and 25 percent, respectively. Only 38 percent of Xers mention first logging on at home and only 20 percent mention work. On the other hand, one-quarter mention school and 16 percent mention a friend's house.

Xer cybercitizens learn the Internet in a completely different environment and under completely different circumstances. This certainly affects their perspectives about the web. Irrespective of their total numbers on-line relative to Boomers, cyberspace deco-rates all parts of Xers' lives and shapes their perceptions about what they can do, how they can do it, and what they can look for-ward to. Boomers and Matures have found ways to squeeze the Internet into their lifestyles, mainly as a home-based experience, but for Xers the Internet doesn't stand apart, looking to be accom-modated and given a place. It already is woven into the fabric of their daily lives.

GENERATIONAL PRIORITIES ON-LINE

The first priority for cybermarketers is obvious: Boomers. They provide the easiest path to success on the Internet. If you target Boomers, marketing on-line is worth considering. This is particu-larly true if your product or service involves information-intensive decision-making. Pharmaceuticals, automobiles, insurance, invest-ments, and real estate are all good candidates.

Pharmaceuticals serve as an especially good illustration because the Internet has a close fit with the business model cur-rently driving success in that category. Much of the opportunity today for pharmaceutical companies is tied up in finding ways to directly communicate with patients, the end users of their products. Pharmaceutical companies want to build awareness for a product, not by bypassing doctors, but by reaching more people who can benefit from their message. While physician detailing has been the traditional method, direct-to-patient advertising on TV and in mag-azines adds to that.

The Internet provides another vehicle for direct-to-patient communications. A web site devoted to a pharmaceutical product can provide information upon request and give recommendations for follow-through. Moreover, such a web site can create support networks by facilitating contact among people who have the same condition or with physicians who specialize in treating that condi-tion. Reference materials can be hot-linked and notices of thera-peutic breakthroughs posted.

In many cases, of course, Matures will take greater interest, particularly for chronic illnesses. Xers may prefer using the web for sports-related medicines. But Boomers will take a strong interest in many different medical topics, particularly those related to children, and to the new health risks they now face as they age, like heart disease and cancer.

Making Mature cybercitizens a priority is a more complicated decision. Matures interested in cyberspace are not like others in their cohort. The example of one well-known Mature, the late Timothy Leary, while admittedly a bit over the edge, illustrates the point. During the sixties, Leary was an outspoken proponent of LSD, a position that cost him his professorship at Harvard. Late in life he took up surfing the net as his new form of tripping. It became his new cause, and he preached enthusiastically everywhere he could about the marvels of cyberspace. He lauded cyberspace as the ultimate form of consciousness expansion. Then, after he was diagnosed with terminal cancer, Leary painstakingly documented the progress of his disease on his personal web site. He said he wanted to live forever in cyberspace.

Timothy Leary by no means typifies Mature cybercitizens. But his lifelong search for novelty and personal creativity does illustrate how the values that distinguish Mature cybercitizens are connected to the opportunities they see in cyberspace. This is the place where they can satisfy desires and interests that distinguish them from others their age.

From a marketing standpoint, on-line offerings for older cybercitizens based on the values and desires of older people in general will not succeed. While an on-line offering for Mature cybercitizens cannot ignore their life-stage needs, it must do so in a way that looks and sounds like something designed for Xers. And it must simultaneously reassure them about Internet security.

Xer cybercitizens are easier to figure out. They're on-line for fun, but this will change over the next few years. It's not that they won't want fun, but that their use of cyberspace for other things will increase with new life-stage priorities.

BUILDING AND SUSTAINING AN ON-LINE MARKET

Broadly speaking, the tenor and tone of the Internet fit the kinds of people who already have chosen to go on-line. This will evolve, though. Soon cyberspace will mature into a fast-moving, highly competitive, and even more demanding medium. And it will take generational marketing savvy to succeed there—smarts enough to keep Boomers happy, to build bridges for Matures, and to blaze a trail to the future so Xers can settle and civilize cyberspace.

Think about the future of cyberspace in terms of the four steps it takes to build a sustainable on-line market.

- First, marketers must *interest* consumers. Without interest, cyberspace stalls. This means creating both a basic openness to technology and a sustained interest in cyberspace itself.

- Second, consumers must have the *capabilities* to go on-line. Right now this means having access to a com-

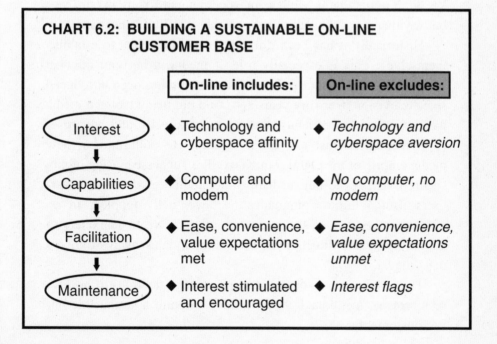

CHART 6.2: BUILDING A SUSTAINABLE ON-LINE CUSTOMER BASE

	On-line includes:	On-line excludes:
Interest	◆ Technology and cyberspace affinity	◆ *Technology and cyberspace aversion*
Capabilities	◆ Computer and modem	◆ *No computer, no modem*
Facilitation	◆ Ease, convenience, value expectations met	◆ *Ease, convenience, value expectations unmet*
Maintenance	◆ Interest stimulated and encouraged	◆ *Interest flags*

puter and a pretty fast modem. All cybercitizens are not created equal—those with faster modems are guaranteed a better on-line experience; those with slower modems are denied access to many offerings. This presents a marketing challenge: whether to give up features and sophistication to accommodate people with slower modems, or to concentrate efforts on a smaller, narrower market.

- Third, access to cyberspace must be *facilitated*. Even with high interest and powerful capabilities, if it's too hard to get on-line, people won't go.

- Finally, consumer participation must be *maintained* over time. Marketers must continually stimulate and reinforce interest. Interactivity is crucial to this.

Cyberspace is approaching a critical juncture. Most observers take it for granted that the on-line market will continue to explode. We don't doubt that it will become a permanent fixture in our lives, but whether it has the legs to become the next TV is uncertain.

Historically it has been difficult for new markets to establish themselves. This is especially true of media, a big part of what cyberspace is all about. No new mass medium has been introduced since television over fifty years ago. And not many targeted media have survived more than a few years of novelty and advertiser experimentation. Just ask Chris Whittle. He built the hot new media empire of the eighties in Knoxville, Tennessee, using highly targeted vehicles to deliver hard-to-get audiences to major advertisers. But Whittle Communications eventually toppled, in no small part because of the resistance of mainstream marketers to any substantial redirection of marketing monies away from the mass media.

That's why we recommend step-by-step attention to the four requirements mentioned above, needed to build a sustainable on-line customer base.

Interest

Today's cybercitizens like technology for its own sake. As cyberspace expands, we need to remember that the users attracted to it purely because of the technology are on-line now. The next wave of new users will demand better features and more benefits, and will be less impressed by technology per se. They won't be as caught up with computers, but will have other priorities they will expect technologies to serve. They will be more cautious, concerned about security and decency on the Internet. Cyberjargon and net-wit will nettle them. The avalanche of connections and options and information will overwhelm them.

To attract the next wave of users, cyberspace must become as effortless as possible—easy to get onto, easy to use. Too many choices and too much self-direction will tax consumers already overloaded and looking for shortcuts. The next wave of users, even more than the first, will want the Internet to simplify their lives, not add complexity and stress.

Capability

To be a cybercitizen you need to have certain skills: You must be reasonably literate; be able to peck at a keyboard; know at least the minimum amount about modems, telephone lines, and downloads; know how to enter a web address; and know how to work with Internet access software.

The current hardware requirements of the Internet demand all these skills. More sophisticated hardware won't diminish these needs; indeed, the more powerful the hardware, the more complicated the skills.

Now, these may not seem like much, but don't forget, most companies put significant resources into computer training and support for applications much less demanding than the Internet. Add to this the fact that cyberspace is a home-based experience for most, and so lacks the convenience of help desks and in-house consultants. Consumers will have to learn and maintain their cyberspace skills themselves. This will keep most Matures out of the market.

As long as cyberspace is tied to the computers we use today, it will bump up against a relatively low ceiling of opportunity. Computer hardware is a governor restricting its growth. Having to own a computer makes the cost of entry pretty pricey—expensive enough, at least, to keep many Xers out, notwithstanding their receptiveness to it otherwise.

Technology will eventually free cyberspace from the computer as we know it today. Network computers may do it, or hands-free systems like voice-activated technologies, or interactive cable TV modems that bring cyberspace to your television screen. The issue for cybermarketers is not whether, but how quickly. Until these improvements happen, the pursuit of business opportunities on-line will be limited.

Facilitation

As part of our 1995 cybercitizen work, we conducted an in-depth analysis of the kinds of performance attributes users want most in an on-line service. We were surprised by the results. At the top of their list were not things like high-end graphics or fancy games or high-resolution video services, but rather the basics—ease, convenience, and value. This held across generations.

To facilitate access to cyberspace, cybercitizens want services that make it easy and convenient, with good value for the time and money they're spending. It almost sounds as if we're talking about soap, and in a way that's exactly what we are talking about. In every category, consumers want the basics first. No matter how much glitz you've got on your web site, if it's hard to get to or expensive to access, people won't go there.

This is something often forgotten about cyberspace marketing, and indeed, about the marketing of all products. If we focus too much on the pizzazz and forget the nuts and bolts, consumers won't buy it. Cyberspace still needs work on the basics.

In theory, facilitating access to cyberspace should be easy. After all, the Internet is all about interactivity, making things as easy as possible for individual users. Interactivity just means listening and then doing what people ask for; not just once, but all the time. Tom Hill, a private consultant who pioneered the notion of interactive marketing nearly three decades ago, gives a more formal definition: An interactive marketing system is one that (a) actively solicits feedback in a two-way exchange of information, (b) analyzes the feedback, and (c) takes action based on the feedback (either in real time or delayed).

Hill was an early pioneer. In 1968 he founded Newmedia Marketing Companies, a firm that applied database marketing and computer automation to execute interactive marketing programs for major packaged goods companies, automobile manufacturers, and TV networks. Lately he's been busy developing web sites that build in a high level of interactivity. Compared with what he's worked with in the past, Hill sees cyberspace as light-years ahead in its potential to facilitate a more satisfying consumer experience.

"The power of cyberspace," says Hill, "is that the right sort of on-line system can learn. On its home page, it can watch exactly what you do there, visit after visit, and soon come to know you so well that everything you subsequently see and do in cyberspace can be personalized, and then continuously updated to always be exactly what you want." He likens the highest level of interactivity to a "Saville Row tailor," a person devoted to your complete satisfaction and enhancement, who first listens to you and then customizes according to your desires.

Use interactivity to facilitate participation, but don't push the highest level on everyone. The type and degree of interactivity that's sought varies by generation. In our 1995 research we investigated exactly what types of on-line interactivity cybercitizens prefer. We included a range of interactive options, from less involving things like "actively scans for relevant information" and "provides relevant information for purchases you are considering" to more highly involving things like "makes recommendations based on your interests and preferences" and "interacts with you based on how you've used it," even "feels just like you're interacting with another human being."

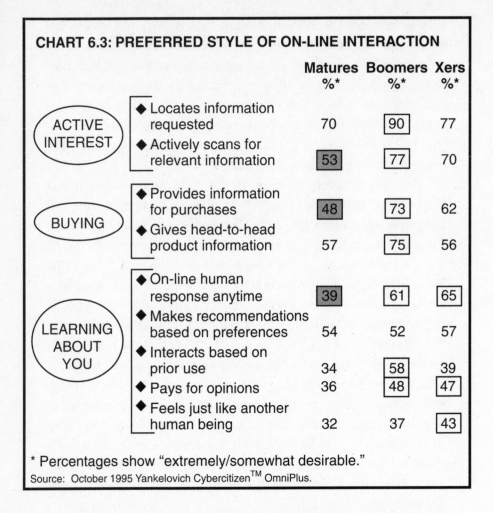

CHART 6.3: PREFERRED STYLE OF ON-LINE INTERACTION

		Matures %*	Boomers %*	Xers %*
ACTIVE INTEREST	◆ Locates information requested	70	90	77
	◆ Actively scans for relevant information	53	77	70
BUYING	◆ Provides information for purchases	48	73	62
	◆ Gives head-to-head product information	57	75	56
LEARNING ABOUT YOU	◆ On-line human response anytime	39	61	65
	◆ Makes recommendations based on preferences	54	52	57
	◆ Interacts based on prior use	34	58	39
	◆ Pays for opinions	36	48	47
	◆ Feels just like another human being	32	37	43

* Percentages show "extremely/somewhat desirable."
Source: October 1995 Yankelovich Cybercitizen™ OmniPlus.

The one sort of interactivity most preferred by every generation was "locates specific information you request." Seventy-seven percent of Xers, 90 percent of Boomers, and 70 percent of Matures cited this as "highly desirable." Beyond this, however, some important differences exist among generations.

Boomers want interactive support for things in which they have an active interest. They also want a system that learns, so that it can be customized based on how it was used in previous sessions.

Like Boomers, Xers have a strong interest in all types of on-line interactivity, though not nearly to the same degree. Xers show a distinctive interest, though, in interactive support that is more humanlike.

Matures are the least likely to cite any form of on-line interactivity as highly desirable. They want information, though, so their preferences more closely resemble those of Boomers than those of Xers.

Maintenance

Cyberspace is a novelty right now. As we saw before, much of the current interest in the Internet is associated with the search for creative new experiences. Unfortunately this novelty of cyberspace will not maintain interest over time. When it wears off and there's nothing else compelling to be found, cyberspace will experience a tailspin. Special effects and gadgetry do not, in and of themselves, deliver the benefits it will take for the Internet to sustain itself. Cybermarketers must work to ensure that the Internet satisfies interests beyond faddish curiosity.

The best way to do this is to develop the Internet as a new and creative medium—a format for delivering information and creative content. Cybercitizens are heavy media consumers. Reading, going to the movies, watching a video or TV are the things they are likely to do in their free time. They also actively look for new TV programs, new cable channels, and new magazines. The Internet could be just the new media experience they seek.

We track the activities cybercitizens say they give up in order to go on-line. Most, 76 percent, say they give up nothing. Among those who do give up something, media activities bear the brunt. TV takes the biggest hit—nearly 80 percent say they watch less television to go on-line. Next is reading books and magazines, then reading the newspaper. Sleeping follows, then listening to the radio. Of the top five activities affected by on-line participation, four are media-related. Shopping, socializing, and playing sports are far down the list.

Both in the interests of its users and the cannibalization of other activities, cyberspace looks and feels like another medium. If they think of it this way, cybermarketers can answer the question of what benefits to provide in cyberspace. Apply media ideas, not technology product ideas or leisure activity ideas.

The Internet soon will stretch our thinking about the very definition of media and leisure. Right now high-tech media and high-tech leisure products remain distinct. The closest overlap is the video game, a leisure activity played on a TV screen. But consumers still experience watching TV and playing a video game as different activities. Cyberspace will change that.

On-line systems will soon absorb these into a high-tech media environment. Leisure will become just another media offering. Indeed, other media may simply meld with cyberspace, particularly if cable TV brings on-line offerings into the home.

The history of media shows that a successful new medium does not displace others as it is introduced. Instead, the new one gets accommodated as all the old ones readjust. Radio didn't displace newspapers. TV didn't displace radio. Cable TV didn't displace broadcast TV. But in every case, the practice and purpose of the old media changed as each new one established itself.

This pattern will most likely hold true with the Internet. Over the long haul, however, the impact of cyberspace could be very different. It will not only compete with the old media, forcing them to readjust yet again to survive, it will, for many, be the very platform used to make the needed adjustments. Cyberspace could become the carrier common to all, competing in all arenas—format, content, and distribution.

This is a long way from happening, though. It will require much more infrastructure before it is even realistically conceivable. Still, this is a vision of the future guiding many cyberspace developers and investors.

Among cybercitizens, Xers sense this the most. Seventy-two percent believe that some significant event will occur before the millennium is out—by far the highest across generations, and much higher, too, than the 55 percent of Xers in general who think so. Perhaps their connection to the Internet has heightened their sense of foreboding. Perhaps they're connected to the Internet because they naturally are more sensitive to the future. Or perhaps it's because something portentous really is emerging out there, especially on the Internet, and Xer cybercitizens just know better than anyone else that theirs is the generation that will surf the breaking edge of this coming wave.

THE MODERN MEDIA BABYLON

The towering infrastructure of modern media—the antennas, satellite dishes, cells, and such—spire towards the heavens, monuments to our engineering prowess. More and more of these monoliths go up every day, their foundations laid down pell-mell in the consumer marketplace. In our MONITOR tracking of consumer reactions we see an underside to this profusion of media. And this is where the opportunities for competitive marketing advantage lie.

Consumers face ever-growing choices. They have avidly given them all a try, encouraging media marketers to bring out even more. But unchecked, this growth is in danger of accelerating out of control.

Indeed, the range of choices is already mind-boggling. Consumers, while intrigued and willing to spend money, are showing signs of frustration. Without some help and consideration from marketers, consumers will have a hard time dealing with much more. The reasons aren't hard to see.

- It's clutter—too much of the same. Fifty channels and nothing's on.

- It's confusing—too much to figure out. *Time*. Time Warner. Time Warner Cable. Time Inc. *Time for Kids*. Time Online. Time Life. *Time Digital*. Time out!

- It's out of control—too much to handle. Urban sprawl in the global village.

One reaction is just to stonewall it. We see, for example, more than 60 percent of consumers in every age group agreeing that "in the past I paid closer attention to the TV when it was on; now I put the set on out of habit and don't really watch it." All through the nineties we have tracked this as a constant expression of dissatisfaction.

Too much has become very little. The enthusiasm for media invention and innovation should not be mistaken for uncritical infatuation. Get a handle on the difference, and your marketing will be on the inside track.

There's a ring of technology to all of this. Indeed, the two are connected—technology drives much of what goes on in media, and media are central to how people experience technology. The issues in the media marketplace, though, are about information proliferation, not system complexity. The challenge to marketers is therefore more about *personalization*.

ALL THAT STUFF

This burst of media has built for decades, but seems especially pronounced of late. You've heard all about it—facts and figures fill the popular press. Here are a few of our favorites about television.

- By 1990 every household in the U.S. had a TV set. Practically every household with a TV set had a color set. Less than fifty years ago, there were fewer TV sets than movie theaters.

- Depending on how you count, there are now six or seven major television networks, up from three just a few years ago.

- Between 1980 and 1990 the percentage of all U.S. TV households with a VCR went from 1 percent to about 80 percent.

- Subscription to cable TV has skyrocketed since 1980, with about two-thirds of all households now wired for cable.

- Television's complements—videodisks, camcorders, universal remotes, home entertainment systems, video game players, interactive cable modems, home satellite systems, high-definition television—are all new in the last several years.

- Television is now breaking through traditional barriers. CNN, for example, recently announced plans to deliver headline news via personal pagers. This presumably will come with hooks back to the channel itself, and to advertisers.

Then there are all the other media. Magazines and books are having a heyday. Radio formats blister the airwaves competing for listeners. Movies have rediscovered younger consumers and find more and more secondary distribution channels. Sales of CDs, CD-ROMs, video games, and computer games are stronger than ever. New media are the rage, and while most won't succeed, trials and test markets have flooded the country. And the Internet, as we know, will carry much of this off in directions we haven't even contemplated yet.

Advertising adds another level of complexity because it trans-forms everything else into another new medium. T-shirts and caps. Shopping bags. Floor tiles. Watches. Store receipts. Beach towels. Car and bus paint jobs. Menus. Coffee cups. Golf tournaments. Ticket stubs. Stadium seats. College bowl games. The Olympics. One venture group even developed plans to launch into orbit a huge billboard that would have been visible worldwide. That, at least, got nixed, but other types of ads keep coming at us. If you live in a metro area, you see about one thousand advertising mes-sages every day.

The same kind of thing is happening with media industry play-ers. Government deregulation is opening up every media market to any monied concern. Even utility companies, one of those few businesses with an actual wire already running into consumers' homes (the others being phone and cable TV companies), are look-ing hard at how to provide information and entertainment to sub-scribers.

Corporate mergers and joint ventures have consolidated some of these efforts at the top, only to unsettle them more at the bottom. Time Warner and Turner, Microsoft and NBC—these are brilliant strategic coups, but they obscure even more the face of the future, mainly because these corporate combinations scale everything up by a big multiplier, further complicating an already chaotic market-place.

To the ordinary consumer, all this proceeds at a breathless pace, producing a media market that has fast become, ironically, inaccessible through too much accessibility—all conceivable combinations of every possible piece of information and enter-tainment in a media market so vast it is threatening and over-whelming. Getting swamped, though, is not the worst of it. What's even worse is the responsibility of it all—so many deci-sions fraught with so many potential mistakes, and thus more stress, even as we try to get information and entertainment to manage and relieve stress.

Media marketers seem content to go along with things as they are, competing for a viable position that can thrive past future shakeouts or further technological advances. Meanwhile, consumers are heading toward an impasse. While they eagerly continue to take up all new media offerings—and to enjoy them—they feel less and less good about where, ultimately, this all will take them.

FINDING A HAPPY MEDIUM

Consumer views are mixed. On the one hand, in our MONITOR tracking they report increasing satisfaction with what's available. A growing percentage agree that the quality of magazines, newspapers, television programming, and cable TV programming has increased over the last few years. Xers are most likely to report improvements; Matures, the least likely.

On the other hand, they are concerned about the sheer bulk of available media. Sixty percent or more of every generational cohort report they feel overwhelmed by all of the sources of information available today. And they remain doubtful about its veracity. Matures report this skepticism about the accuracy of what's in the media more than Xers, 81 percent to 72 percent, but it is high in every cohort.

The message is clear. To consumers, good quality is still no good if there's just too much of it. People agree that it's all getting better, but at the same time they feel that it's all getting to be too much, a problem compounded by distrust. Media companies have done a good job raising the quality of their offerings. The next challenge is to figure out how to put these offerings within easier reach of consumers by giving them a closer personal connection to what's available.

Everything depends on this. As it stands today, the majority of consumers are so put off by the media that they are willing to support increased government regulation of things like advertising on TV, violence on TV, or advertising to kids. These are as high priorities for government oversight as concerns over things that can kill you, like toxic waste, air and water pollution, or nuclear accidents. Marketing intrusions through the media are regarded as more serious invasions of privacy than government wiretapping or polygraph screening for employment. Increased quality notwithstanding, consumers don't feel a deep personal connection to the media. They use it—indeed, they use it more and more—but they aren't completely comfortable or happy with it.

CHART 7.1: MEDIA ICONS

MATURES	BOOMERS	Xers
Walter Winchell	Casey Kasem	Howard Stern
Edward R. Murrow	Walter Cronkite	CNN
The Velvet Fog	Elvis	Madonna
The Duke	Butch & Sundance	Billy Crystal
Steve Allen	Carson	Leno
John Huston	Robert Altman	Oliver Stone

Public television has been forced to deal with this trend lately. Its funding threatened by congressional actions that enjoy support among constituents, the Corporation for Public Broadcasting has started airing reminders of the value of public TV. Ads rely on the testimonials of ordinary people about how public TV shows uniquely fit their values and cater to their personal needs and interests. If public TV doesn't do it, they wonder aloud, who will? The purpose is to rebuild a personal connection with viewers, one that will invigorate them enough to make their opinions known to their elected representatives.

Each generation requires a different approach. We recently completed a MONITOR-based study for the Magazine Publishers Association (MPA), assessing the new ways consumers want to receive and use media and information. The MPA undertook this to understand the role for magazines in the media marketplace of the next millennium. Not surprisingly we found that the personal connections most sought differed from generation to generation.

MATURES: SUMMARIZE IT

Matures are the analog generation. They grew up with newspapers, and with the rise of radio; they played the piano or a 78-player at home. Books became even more accessible after Penguin introduced the first paperbacks in 1936. When TV came along, Matures were its first buyers; early TV stars were old radio favorites like Sid Caesar, Ed Sullivan, and Milton Berle. Berle, in fact, was known as "Mr. Television" because many consumers bought their first TV to be able to see him perform.

Radio brought World War II into homes across America. Edward R. Murrow's voice reported the Battle of Britain. FDR reassured us with his Fireside Chats. Serials and variety shows were our common entertainments. But radio was only a brief way station on the road to modern media.

For Matures, computers had nothing to do with media. Indeed, the computers Matures knew were pretty primitive. Massive collections of tubes and wires, the earliest models could do little more than solve simple math problems. A bug was really a bug, in fact. The term was coined in 1954 by Grace Hopper, a computer pioneer in the Navy, when a two-inch moth got stuck in one of the relays on the computer she was working with. During World War II, computers were used to break German and Japanese codes, but they were still a long way from being used to power or embellish any medium. When computers finally did make their first big media appearance—election night in 1952—they were treated ignominiously. CBS had arranged to use a UNIVAC computer to forecast the election; but the computer's initial prediction of a landslide, which later turned out to be correct, was disbelieved and quickly changed by its operators to give a different result.

After World War II, television changed everything. By the end of 1950 there were 10 million TV sets in American homes, up from just 1 million the year before. Three years later the majority of all Americans had one. Other milestones were passed in rapid succession. In 1963, for the first time ever, Americans spent over $1 billion on TV sets. In 1965, almost all of NBC's and one-half of CBS's and ABC's programs were broadcast in color. And on July 20, 1969, at 10:56 P.M. EST, the world watched TV as Neil Armstrong set foot on the moon.

TV became the new way of life. It provided a broader connection that made the new suburban lifestyle more livable. Living rooms were centered around the TV. Morning habits were changed by Dave Garroway and NBC's "Today Show." Evening habits also changed, and to feed them, TV dinners came onto the market. Companies designed furniture to hold TV sets and to cradle TV viewers. We soon had TV tables, TV trays, and *TV Guide*.

Every other medium had to make room. Other mass audience media, like magazines and radio, changed to survive the onslaught of TV, replacing old programming with specialized formats targeted to niche interests. Afternoon newspapers couldn't compete because they weren't as timely as the evening TV news. But newspapers found, too, that TV listings and TV entertainment news were good draws for subscribers. Movie stars sought out the exposure TV could give them, as did rock 'n' rollers. The first prime time TV rock music special was broadcast in 1957. Even movies had to reinvent their style and their distribution because of competition. Gimmicks like 3-D, used first in 1951, couldn't sustain movies against the onrush of TV.

Matures adopted TV and adapted to the changes it brought. But since then the accelerating pace of the media marketplace, along with its increasing computerization, has bypassed them. In our work for the MPA, we found Matures much more likely than any of the other generations to feel there is too much information out there to digest—78 percent, versus 64 percent of Boomers and 58 percent of Xers. Today's media marketplace is not friendly to Matures. It presents them with an array of choices and decisions they find unwieldy.

The sort of personal connection Matures want from the media

marketplace is one built around *summarization*. They prefer a good summary to a good selection. Choice in today's media marketplace requires a whole new set of skills and activities. Matures feel that they know what they want. They would rather just get that and not be forced by the media to do more.

Matures are the least likely to say they use as many different sources of information as possible and the least likely to feel a need to be part of the "information age." They would rather know a lot about a few specific topics, and are the most likely to agree that, in an ideal world, they wouldn't have to deal with any more information than is absolutely necessary.

Matures prefer their information summarized—a preference expressed by 75 percent of Matures versus only 59 percent of Boomers and 56 percent of GenXers. Of course, nobody wants extraneous detail, but combined with their other attitudes about the information they want, it's clear that Matures prefer a more synoptic delivery of information. We see this in our MONITOR tracking of their media behaviors as well.

In general, the attitudes of Matures about TV reflect concerns about language and content. Matures espouse a more condensed set of interests and preferences while expressing much concern about what's showing up in the media today.

- Don't throw the gauntlet down over values. The TV shows that Matures like best entertain without controversy. Shows like *Matlock*, *Dr. Quinn, Medicine Woman*, and *Murder, She Wrote* rely on linear narratives where the conclusion of each episode summarizes and resolves the plot. If this defines your marketing strength, don't give it up. CBS learned this lesson when it made a brief foray into NBC-style programming. Its older audience objected and so CBS quickly returned to its core strengths with this audience.

- Offer everything in a single source. Present advertising as information. Make it what consumers want to know, not what you want them to know. If it's less pushy and more forthright, consumers will trust it more. *Rx Remedy*, a magazine published by a company of the same name located in Westport, Connecticut, is a good example of this. They have a circulation of more than 2 million consumers over the age of fifty. They maintain a database with the various medical needs of each of their subscribers. This is a marketer's gold mine. It's a boon to subscribers too, because they can keep up with the latest news through the magazine, and can also be assured of getting up-to-date promotional mailings from only those marketers with products and services relevant to their personal needs and interests.

- Try for an *Utne Reader* for Matures. *UR*, as it's often called, is a *Reader's Digest*–style collection from the alternative media. Each bimonthly issue compiles the latest articles on a variety of topics. The biggest difference, though, is that each issue of *UR* focuses on a topical theme. In this way, each issue of *UR* becomes a valuable reference because it provides an overview of a specific topic—you can shelve it and pull it down later when you need it.

BOOMERS: ORGANIZE IT

Boomers are the transistor-to-chip generation, although they often get called the TV generation. It's true that Matures brought TV into the home and then Boomers cut their teeth on it. Boomers and TV took over America's suburbs at the same time. But Boomers experienced something even more fundamental—the ever-expanding miniaturization of things around them. Full-sized items were replaced with those that were smaller—but more powerful. Transistors started it; chips do it now.

The transistor came out of Bell Labs in 1947, but it was Sony that developed the first transistor radio, mass produced for a full-scale launch in Japan in 1955. Four years later, Sony followed up with the first portable transistorized television. Two decades later, in 1979, Sony introduced the Walkman, originally named the Stowaway, and in 1991, the Sony Discman became the latest addition to its family of products.

Miniaturization has affected every medium. LPs and 45s gave way to eight-tracks, which gave way to cassettes, which gave way to CDs. Movies went from big screens to network showings to videotapes to laser disks, and now to DVD. TVs fit in the palm of your hand. Even *Life* magazine finally gave up its oversized edition and squared itself into a less costly size.

In much the same way, computers played an important role in the media. Machines that once filled rooms upon rooms in the basements of university and military buildings rapidly became obsolete. In 1975 the first personal computer, the Altair 8800, sold with 256 bytes of memory. By 1976 Tandy and Apple were mass-marketing PCs. In 1977 the Apple sold the first assembled personal computer. IBM entered the market in 1981 with the IBM PC. Just a year later Compaq brought out the first IBM clone. In 1983 Apple's Lisa, later to become the Macintosh, introduced the mouse and pull-down windows. Not to be outdone, IBM introduced the IBM PC-XT in the same year, the first personal computer with a built-in hard disk drive. The revolution had begun, and today laptops and notebooks and palmtops have carried this even further.

The recent history of computers has been driven by the chip, a technology first introduced by Intel in 1971. Intel itself aptly summed up this phenomenon by naming the chip it brought out in February 1989 the "million-transistor microchip." It had a surface area half as big as a postage stamp covered with a million transistors. For Boomers, it has indeed been a transistor-to-chip experience.

This steady boost in computing power packed into smaller and smaller units has made it possible for the media to share in the information revolution. From computerized graphics and special effects to satellite transmissions to the portability of viewing and reading, the media marketplace boomed right alongside the chip.

This not only defines Boomer media experiences, it's also the Boomer media style. More and more information packed into ever more compact spaces is what they want. Boomers value knowledge and information, as much as they can get, and in a format they can control.

Boomers look for a more efficient *organization* of information and entertainment. Pack it in, but make it easily available; indeed, make it more available by packing it in. Let Boomers browse, store it, recall it when they need to, and apply it productively. They don't want to spend a lot of time searching for what they want, but summaries aren't the answer. Boomers like details. Media that make information and entertainment stackable, portable, hierarchical, browsable, and procurable are preferred.

In our MPA study, Boomers described themselves as interested in many subjects. They want to be mini-experts on everything, often browsing through lots of information just for fun. They prefer text to charts and graphs. They feel comfortable with information, and they know how to use it. No surprise, then, that they are by far the least likely to report ever having a problem finding the information they need.

Boomers watch and read the widest range of things. They share with Matures an interest in the news; and with Xers, a penchant for comedies, reality-based shows, sports, alternative dramas, and late-night fare. Boomers pay close attention to consumer watchdog media, and are attuned to special interest shows and publications that relate to home, family, and money management.

- Remember what's worked for Boomers before, usually a good model for doing something new. *People* magazine and *USA TODAY* are two good examples. Both magazines organize lots of information into digestible snippets that make data easy to remember and use.

- Rework Boomer icons. They're familiar shorthand Boomers can understand and enjoy. Like *Star Trek*. Xers, of course, like all the new versions—*The Next Generation, Deep Space Nine, Voyager*—but Boomers watch them just as much.

CHART 7.2: MEDIA MEMORIES

MATURES	BOOMERS	Xers
Peyton Place	*Dallas*	*Melrose Place*
Fibber McGee and Molly	*The Mary Tyler Moore Show*	*Roseanne*
This Is Your Life	*Candid Camera*	*America's Funniest Home Videos*
War of the Worlds	*Close Encounters of the Third Kind*	*Independence Day*
Tarzan movies	*Star Wars* trilogy	*Die Hard* sequels
Bridge over the River Kwai	*Bridge over Troubled Water*	*The Bridges of Madison County*

- Frame it as news. Boomers like news shows and news magazines. The investigative style and emphasis on information appeal directly to their core generational values. They respond to quick-hitting headlines based on in-depth investigation. Entertainment as news has succeeded with this, as has the Internet. Go look, for example, at the Time Online web site.

XERS: UNDRESS IT

Xers are the participatory generation. TV and PCs were already on the scene when they arrived. These were never any big to-do; the question for Xers has always been, instead, what to do.

Xers have never been a passive audience because their media always demanded participation. For them the TV was a platform for various video entertainments. You didn't just turn it on and "veg out." You made choices. You made the video screen do what you wanted—play videotapes or video games, show a Pay-Per-View selection, or record programs to watch later. Even something as simple as the number of available channels demands more participation and decision-making than was ever required of Boomers or Matures. The growth of cable and multiset households meant they always had a TV set to lord over.

Music on CDs means more participation—programming selections or equalizing the mix or choosing what goes in the changer. And now there's CD-i, a format borrowed from video games, used to facilitate listener participation (illustrating the blurring of the lines between leisure and media). Some CDs even contain videos that you can watch if you have the right kind of player. Laser disks require the same kinds of user participation. Virtual reality games straddle the boundary of media and leisure entertainments, but again, make similar demands.

Video and computer games, close media cousins, further reinforce what's going on. These games are highly involved participatory leisure experiences. Atari's tele-game Pong was the first popular hit, introduced in 1975 at a retail cost of $98.50. Video arcades brought us Space Invaders in 1978, Pac-Man in 1981, and Ms. Pac-Man the following year. These eventually made it into versions designed for TVs.

In 1984 the video game market collapsed. Computer games stole all the customers. But Nintendo's NES release in 1985 restored a high level of quality to video game products and saved the market. Nintendo continues to expand its offerings, but competitors have been active, too. Sega introduced Master System in 1986, Genesis in 1989, and Saturn in 1995. The Sony Playstation hit the market in 1995.

The Nintendo Game Boy took this experience off the TV and put it in our hands. And computer games have provided another screen-based, medialike experience with highly popular products like Doom and Myst.

It's all interactive and highly participatory. And it's taught Xers sophisticated ways to convert media devices to other uses. For Xers, media and leisure do not mean just being entertained, but being involved in the entertaining. We now see the same behavior with the Internet.

Xers take raw media resources and create their own world. This defines Xer chic—control over how to combine individual elements to create unique experiences. Xers want it stripped down so they can dress it up in an individual style. They want to partici-pate.

TV writers already know this. Xers are less interested in "packaged" TV storylines, so stories in shows targeted to Xers, unlike those targeted to Matures or Boomers, don't always have happy or conclusive endings and don't always move linearly through a single plot line. Xers can handle, and prefer to get, their information and media unembellished and unadorned.

The personal connection Xers want from the media market-place is built around the freedom to mold their experience in what-ever way they see fit. To do this, they need to see their media *undressed.* This way they can reconfigure and rearrange it. Style is what's important here, but it can't be imposed from the outside.

Our work for the MPA has shown that Xers clearly think of themselves as part of a new information age, one driven by new media and new technologies. They want to keep up with the latest trends, and they want the media to help them do this. They want to get only the information they're interested in, and if possible, from just a few sources, a preference they share with Matures.

Xers prefer nontextual information. They also share with Matures the sense that to truly understand something, they need to experience it themselves—63 percent of Xers and Matures versus 43 percent of Boomers. Boomers mostly believe you can know what you need to just by reading about it.

Though Xers and Matures share these two attitudes, they do so for different reasons. Matures find it increasingly difficult to keep up with a media marketplace that outdistances their skills and experiences. They prefer graphic summaries and personal experiences. Xers aren't worried about being left behind, they're worried about staying on the leading edge of the wave. They want to frolic in all of this, not just read about the cutting edge. It's a postlinear vernacular—more visual, where text itself, as in cyberspace, is an icon of participation and self-direction.

Their behaviors are consistent with these attitudes. Xers are disproportionately more involved with TV, radio, and the Internet, and less involved with magazines and newspapers. This is typical—younger people watch more TV and read fewer newspapers. But even more than previous generations, Xers are a lot less likely to ever connect with print media. Music is a big part of their lives, particularly as a way to pass time. And with the advent of MTV and VH-1, music has become as much a visual as an aural experience.

- Make it participatory. Xers want to interact and to create something new in the process. Let them help, if only by reacting on-line. Watch the credits for any TV shows hot with Xers. They all roll a web address across the screen. The NBA has theirs emblazoned on the scorer's table. Every new rock band has a site for fans to go to. Even magazines publish independently on the Internet.

- Make it visual. This is the video generation, more interested in graphs than text. Apply video concepts to print media. Even better, use new technologies to deliver the video: virtual reality books, where the story is delivered visually. Or plug-in books that you read and watch on TV at the same time. Looking instead of reading, though, does not imply turning everything into pabulum. Xers want sophistication, they just want it in a contemporary style. If you want a flavor of this, go check out any "avant-pop" fictional anthology published in the last five years.

- Don't try to style it yourself, but do get rid of the warts. Let viewers or readers put the wrinkle on. Don't scare them off before they can get to it. This is what *Reader's Digest* discovered. Just because it's an old magazine doesn't mean Xers don't read it. Indeed, our tracking shows it's the number one magazine for all three generational groups; *TV Guide* comes in at number two. Stories with suspense, high drama, and a moral at the end, that are also a fast read, have universal appeal. But the publishers recently realized that while Xers read *Reader's Digest*, they are embarrassed to be caught with it. Like Boomer teenage boys with a *Playboy*, Xers hide it inside other magazines. *Reader's Digest* is now making itself less stodgy.

- Take the edge off diversity. Make diversity into something celebratory, not something that conjures ideological debates. *Wired* magazine is a good example. It's barbed and prickly, like the on-line cutting edge it reports. But it produces this feel with features on offbeat personalities and ideas as well as with bright, bold colors mixed together into all kinds of patterns and icons. Diversity is the magazine's sensibility, but it's created in a noncontroversial way.

MEDIA MODELS

Every medium is managed according to some model of how consumers use it. For example, magazines calculate readership based on how consumers pass copies to friends and where they read them. The traditional magazine readership model, developed in the fifties, wouldn't count someone as a reader unless they read at home. Many of today's publications would undercount their readerships using this model because readers on planes, in doctors' offices, or in the reception areas of media research firms would not appear in the final count. Reading habits obviously have changed.

The same is true for television. For years, advertising agencies and media research companies struggled with how to calculate viewership. The traditional model assumed that people watched when the TV was on. Advertising rates were set based on audience sizes calculated in this way. But we all know this assumption isn't true anymore.

As media and advertising clutter continue to worsen, old models based on the relative efficiencies of different vehicles will need to be updated. If you want to know the payback on your initiatives, you have to have models that accurately reflect consumer responses. This will be a growing issue. Marketers will find new ways to deliver their messages. One such opportunity is point-of-sale. As message retention drops, getting the attention of consumers at the moment when they are buying will become a lot more important.

Browsing will increasingly characterize the way consumers of all generations use media. It's a summary style for Matures, a way of sorting for Boomers, and a means of sampling for Xers. It is already everywhere and takes many different forms. Zipping. Zapping. Thumbing. Surfing. Listening stations. Previewing. In fact, for many consumers, browsing itself, *not* watching or reading, is their single most common media behavior! Yet, our marketing strategies and models are based upon watching and reading.

For many, browsing is not a way of deciding what to watch or read. It is what these consumers do instead of watching or reading. Guys with remotes aren't always channel surfing to find just the right thing. A lot of times they're *just* channel surfing. This is their primary behavior. Advertising that's created and placed to be watched or read won't adequately reach consumers rapidly flipping through pages or channels.

Too many media will make browsing more of a necessity for consumers. The only high-profile efforts to capitalize on this so far are Headline News and the Weather Channel. But there are many more possibilities: minute mysteries. Sprint sports. TV billboards.

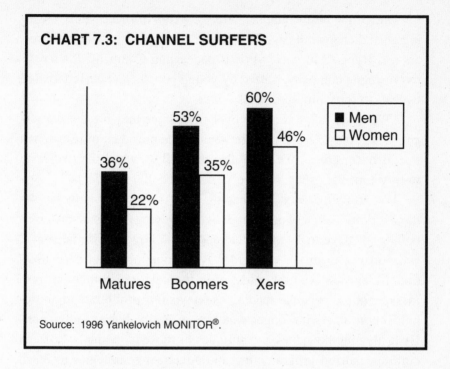

CHART 7.3: CHANNEL SURFERS

Source: 1996 Yankelovich MONITOR®.

Regular replays. Dramatic shorts. One-liner comedies. Even, perhaps, a channel or a magazine that offers nothing but jump-cuts from one image or subject to another.

To picture this, think of the recent ad campaign for Tasters Choice—a serial romance that ran in thirty-second snippets. It captivated millions of viewers, who looked forward to each new installment. This campaign, of course, isn't the final answer, but it does show that there are many untapped possibilities awaiting the canny marketer who can offer entertainment and advertising that's styled for browsing.

FROM SPECIALIZATION TO SPECIAL AGENTS

The standard way of personalizing consumer connections with a medium has been to specialize its content, the presumption being that this will facilitate consumer self-selection. Advertising can then be better directed through highly targeted placement.

One of the best examples in recent years of successfully target-ing an audience in the age of multiple channels and media prolifer-ation is Rupert Murdoch's Fox Broadcasting Company. It's a rela-tively young company, staffed by young people, and geared toward twelve- to forty-nine-year-olds.

"We never talk to anyone over fifty, since they are not our tar-get," said Andy Fessel, then the senior vice president of research at Fox Broadcasting. "We have also carefully tracked the twelve to twenty-four age group, and we've tracked college students."

Fox has succeeded by shaping itself as an alternative to the three traditional networks, and by conveying a clear and com-pelling message to its target audience. The Fox premise is simple, and borrows from the standard way of thinking about specializa-tion: Television is in the midst of a dramatic transformation from mass media to personal media. As televisions proliferate in house-holds, consumers no longer watch as a family, but as individuals. By analyzing the values and attitudes of those individuals, Fox can craft specialized programming and advertising strategies to reach them, and only them.

But along the way, Fox discovered that even its hippest televi-sion shows appeal to more than one generation. For example, explained Fessel, the company's focus groups show that grand-mothers watch "Beverly Hills 90210" because they want to know what their grandchildren are going through. In much the same way, parents watch the show to educate themselves about contemporary high school angst about things like date rape, underage drinking, and fraternity hazing.

The network that began by targeting young people continues its efforts for that generation, while expanding its efforts with an older audience. More than expected, its content cuts across age groups, so Fox's next priority is to find ways to refine further the specificity of its appeal to various segments within this broad audience.

The step beyond content is personalization. Specialized content only takes you so far. Consumers seek both *what* they want to see and *how* they want to see it. This is the marketing opportunity of the future. The technology is coming. In a content-prohibitive way, parents now have it with the V-chip—they can say what they don't want. Their personal preferences prevail over media proliferation.

The next stage will move beyond the V-chip to the "me-chip." It will seek the content you want and give it to you in the personalized style you prefer. Already, smart cards with embedded chips abound, carrying stored data about personal information, cash amounts, medical needs, and the like. Popping one into a card reader at a newsstand or a cable box on your TV is the obvious next step. The system would instantly match your personal preferences for information and media to what's available, a form of specialization that remakes self-selection into a more personalized selected-for-self.

The coming media moguls will be the middlemen who broker this for consumers. These intermediaries will offer services—like me-chips or other approaches—that provide individual consumers with their own personalized filters. Instead of having to sort through the media glut on their own, consumers will hire these proxies or agents to put it in order for them, and then to put in their orders for them. Consumers can spend more time with what they get and less time getting it. Media formats in the future will themselves benefit from consumers having more time to spend interacting with them.

BACK TO HOT

Marshall McLuhan once described TV as the "cool fire" because it's a highly involving medium that requires nothing of the viewer beyond passive attention. Not so for all media, McLuhan argued. Listening to the radio or reading a magazine is hot. We actively engage our minds to get what they have to offer.

Boomers were the only generation weaned on a cool medium. Matures grew up on radio, magazines, and newspapers; Xers on interactive formats, in which TV was more of a platform than a broadcaster. Boomer cool has left us with the media forms we have today. A TV news magazine show like *60 Minutes*, for example, was the perfect Boomer program—information and the inside story, coolly delivered.

But this is being completely overhauled. All media in the foreseeable future will be hot.

Advertising is already moving this way. Direct response ads are the hottest trend in the business—commercials with 800 numbers; long-form advertising (aka: infomercials); ads with web addresses for more information about, or promotions for, the product; pharmaceutical ads that tell you to ask your doctor; ads that say mention this ad for a discount; and shopping channels where you can interact with the people on the screen, even bargain for a better deal.

Content too has changed. It started with call-ins on talk shows and unscientific 900-number polls, and it continues today with shows like CNN's *TalkBack Live*, on which a discussion with the studio audience is augmented with viewer participation through faxes, e-mail, or phone calls, all in real time.

Future TV shows, under development right now, will contain interactive participation via e-mail or call-in voting as an integral

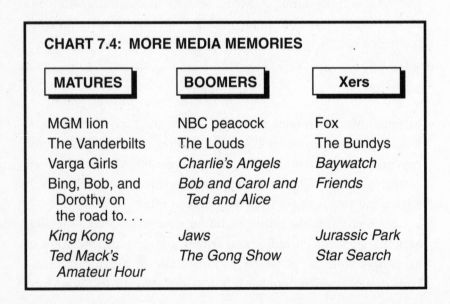

CHART 7.4: MORE MEDIA MEMORIES

MATURES	BOOMERS	Xers
MGM lion	NBC peacock	Fox
The Vanderbilts	The Louds	The Bundys
Varga Girls	*Charlie's Angels*	*Baywatch*
Bing, Bob, and Dorothy on the road to. . .	*Bob and Carol and Ted and Alice*	*Friends*
King Kong	*Jaws*	*Jurassic Park*
Ted Mack's Amateur Hour	*The Gong Show*	*Star Search*

part of the action. Decidedly this is the character of the Internet—hot, involving, and inherently participatory. Interactive cable systems will carry this even further. Over the past several years, business travelers at major hotel chains have used early versions of these, like Spectravision, to order movies, arrange for room service, review their bills, or check out.

This increased interaction will provide an unexpected boon to advertisers. The hotter the medium, the more effective the advertising. Even for something as simple as capturing viewer attention, the hot media of the future will be better for advertisers. We completed some experimental work years ago on the relationship between the power of a TV program to capture attention and the impact of TV ads on recall and persuasion. The same ad had dramatically different effects, depending on the TV show during which it was aired. Not only did a more powerful show bring more eyes to the ad, it made the message more compelling.

Going hot will help build media credibility and trust. As active participants, consumers will no longer merely receive information. They will participate in the making of the message, and thus have more confidence in it. Inviting consumers to participate in the creation of marketing campaigns is something media organizations should pursue more aggressively, especially given that the level of public trust in the media continues to be low.

Lest you jump headlong into all of this, remember that the proliferation of hotter media is a big part of what turns consumers off. To make it actually work for your brands, you must build in the kinds of hooks that establish the personal connections each generation needs and wants.

And it doesn't have to be high-tech. Howard Stern remade talk radio with nothing but bawdy banter and an amen chorus of Manhattan misfits. Push limits. Use the medium to your advantage—press people to become involved. It works for Don Imus and Rush Limbaugh too. Pizzazz can sometimes put people off. Smart and simple is in, and one way that media are getting back to hot. Get personal, like Howard, and hook 'em.

TIME-SHIFTING

Our daily schedules no longer need to accommodate what we want to watch or read. Media can move around to fit our schedules. First we had cable channels showing the same movie at different times during a month. VCRs pushed this further, becoming household fixtures during the eighties (though many of us still are programming-challenged). CNN and Headline News were built around this concept. Even remote controls made their contribution by reinforcing the sense that you're not stuck watching whatever's on after you sit back down. You can always switch channels.

A colleague of ours was the first person we heard of doing this. He turns in every night by 10 P.M. But he hates missing Letterman. So for years he's been setting his VCR and then watching Letterman over breakfast. The morning paper got moved to early evening. He has time-shifted his day.

The days when we built our daily schedules around radio or TV lineups are gone. Now we've fit media in around everything else. So far, only content has adapted to our schedule. But advertising and direct response soon will be designed so that these too are moveable.

Time-use studies have shown that we don't really give up our old media habits to take up new ones. If we like something, we stick with it. When we find something else we like, we just add it. So our total time with media has increased. What we give up is sleep—we are a sleep-deprived society, not a media-deprived one. This will intensify with time-shifting.

And Xers will lead the way. They are already the most likely to time-shift, even when doing so costs money, like watching Pay-Per-View. But other generations will also work it out. Boomers will take it up as a means of simplifying overload and reducing stress. Matures will find it a useful way to control the pace of their lives.

Time-shifting will have far-reaching effects.

- Access to many things will open up as conflicts in scheduling go away. Indeed, potentially conflicting events could offer time-shifting services, in the same way that many places now offer child care services to enable people to get there.

- People will start negotiating for more time instead of more money. As time is needed for new kinds of schedules, it will be more precious in many cases than money.

- We will have to address the challenge to our circadian rhythms. Products to help us manage and regulate new sleep patterns will become essential. This may even extend to changes in work schedules that better fit our new timetables.

- Service providers will need to extend and adjust their hours of operation. All-night hours will become the norm, for everything—couriers, barbers, doctors. Overnight services may need a 10 P.M. delivery guarantee in addition to the one for 10 A.M. Schools and leisure activities may have to run alternate hours.

In this environment, consumers will take charge, as they now are beginning to, no longer servants to the media. Indeed, consumers could become partners with media marketers in dramatic new ways. But only if marketers make generationally appropriate personal connections.

An Economy Built on Dreams

The traditional American Dream is being dusted off by Generation X, which is reinvigorating it with new energy and a new style. Virtually all Xers—92 percent, more than any other generation—say that the American Dream is something they really want to achieve. Xers are taking ownership of this Dream, and in doing so setting the agenda for the American Dream in the twenty-first century.

The American Dream is far from dead, despite what the pundits say, many of whom describe our situation as hopeless. *U.S. News & World Report* writes despairingly about the attack on the middle class. *Newsweek*, reflecting on growing disparities between rich and poor, has announced the ascendancy of a new elite, the so-called overclass. *The New York Times* published a remarkable series on downsizing that terrified most of white collar America, about the insecurity of their jobs and the potential for personal financial disaster.

All of this hand-wringing, say others, is needlessly pessimistic. Consumers, they claim, worry about problems that don't exist. Michael Elliott and Robert Samuelson, two experienced journalists and students of the American scene, have each set out separate indictments of the American mood, but arrive at the very same conclusion. Our old expectations were just too high. Things today are bad, but not nearly as bad as most Americans think.

Either way—hard times for real or just in our minds—consumers still have hopes and dreams for the future. The important story beyond these bleak headlines often escapes notice. The challenge is tough but consumers have not given up, particularly not Xers, the generation so often pitied in these accounts. Consumers remain hopeful dreamers. Indeed, there is an aspirational revival afoot, led by this new generation. Marketers must attune themselves to the more relevant question of exactly *what aspirations are now guiding consumer purchasing*.

The post–World War II American Dream was a shared vision of the good life. You aspired to personal fulfillment through a material success achieved because you had the opportunities to go as far as you cared to. What's really different today is only that consumers take many divergent paths on the road to the good life. Todd Gitlin has called this, in his most recent book, "the twilight of common dreams"—the disappearance of a universal commitment to fall into the melting pot. This, not headlines about diminished prospects, is the focus marketers must take. Consumers still dream, still wish for the things that the marketplace can satisfy, doing so in many different ways.

It is this very diversity in which Xers revel, so the absence of a shared vision does not cause them to conclude that the American Dream is dead. Instead, they are demonstrating that a community of values can be found amid a diversity of styles. They accept the plurality of styles, all of which are united in a common focus on success. Xers will restyle the traditional American Dream with this in mind, becoming in the process a generation of entrepreneurs, and reshaping national aspirations.

Knowing these dreams sharpens your competitive marketing edge. The marketplace is an economy built on dreams. These dreams of consumers have their own vernacular, and signal various badges and connections. They are reaffirmed through daily rituals and celebrations, and achieved through the purchase and use of a variety of products and services. These dreams are the aspirations that open up opportunities for savvy marketers, and generation is a big part of understanding these aspirations.

ASPIRATIONS

The American Dream is not just about what you buy; it's more about how you earn it. In a MONITOR-based study on the new American Dream done in collaboration with TBWA Chiat/Day, 90 percent of every generation agreed that the "opportunity to go as far as talents and ambitions will take you," defined the Dream, while only 55 percent thought the American Dream is expressed "just by the ways [people] spend and save their money."

This attitude does differ by generation. Matures, as we would expect, more often tie the American Dream to how people spend and save their money—63 percent, compared with 49 percent of

---

CHART 8.1: CORE ELEMENTS OF AMERICAN DREAM

	Matures %	Boomers %	Xers %
"Very much a part" of American Dream:			
Freedom of choice in how to live life	81	86	82
Being happy	80	83	81
High school education	79	81	81
Financially comfortable retirement	81	78	78
Owning your own home	74	79	81

Source: Yankelovich MONITOR® OmniPlus, 1996.

Xers and 54 percent of Boomers. Similarly, half of all Matures say the Dream is more about "the things I have than the ways I live my life." The generational need to signal conformity underlies this. The aspirations of Matures were a very basic *economic material-ism* that is still expressed today. But while still connecting to the Dream, Matures now see themselves on the home stretch and want the leisure they feel they've earned.

Boomers grew up taking material success for granted, so their aspirations for personal fulfillment have been different. Boomers never strongly connected with the traditional American Dream because of this. The Dream skipped a generation. Boomers have not wanted tangible goods any less than Matures but the American Dream has not been the centerpiece of their goals and ambitions. Their aspirations were tied more to a *fulfillment materialism* with which they continue to struggle. Early retirement is an idea that captures much of what Boomers feel—financial freedom from things that tie them down and a relaxed chance to complete their search for self.

Xers have taken up the Dream and reinvigorated it as a force that defines buying motivations in the marketplace. Partly, of course, this is because more Matures and Boomers feel they've already achieved the Dream—64 percent of Matures and 34 percent of Boomers, versus only 14 percent of Xers. Xers are looking forward to getting started on the American Dream. They sound serious, and they are, with aspirations that reflect a *competitive materialism*. But they pursue personalized visions of this; they do not hew to a common Dream.

MATURES: A LEISURELY PACE

When they came of age, married, and settled down, Matures moved to the suburbs to make better lives for their kids. But that was then. Today they are living out the endgame of the American Dream. A desire continues to create a simple life, but a life focused on rest and relaxation. They've paid their dues. Now it's time to reap the rewards.

CHART 8.2: SPECIAL EMPHASIS OF AMERICAN DREAM FOR MATURES

	Matures %	Boomers %	Xers %
"Very much a part" of American Dream:			
Having a happy marriage	77	74	70
Having children	64	59	51

Source: Yankelovich MONITOR® OmniPlus, 1996.

Comfortable Living. Two-thirds of all Matures want "enough to be comfortable [because] more than that is just not worth the effort," contrasting sharply with most Boomers and Xers who don't think comfortable is nearly enough.

Of course, for Matures, comfortable is a lot more than what previous generations had to retire on. Matures are rare in that regard. Much of their standard of living has been made possible for them by the government, although deriding these benefits as "hand-outs" seems an unfair disparagement to Matures. After all, they feel they put all the money into those programs. So what they're getting now is something they've earned. Taking some out in their advancing years is fair, not foul. And they believe they're only asking for enough to be comfortable. They don't dream of more than that.

Simple Living. All generational groups, but especially Matures, agree that a "simpler life is a better life"—85 percent, versus 79 percent of Boomers and 66 percent of Xers. Now is not the time to complicate their days. Simpler choices work better and are more consistent with how Matures always behave.

Fewer Matures report they would change the products and brands they buy if their standard of living altered—only 50 percent, versus 60 percent of Boomers and 63 percent of Xers. What was good enough before, they reason, is still just fine. Stepping up the product ladder no longer fits their style.

Easy Living. At this point in their lives, Matures don't get too cranked up about setting goals and accomplishing them. Over 60 percent of Matures say they don't live life according to goals, they just take things one day at a time, whereas the majority of Boomers and Xers believe the opposite.

Focusing on Others. A little over 90 percent of Matures say the success of their children is more important than their own success. Only 80 percent of Boomers agree. That's still a lot of Boomers, but it's a notable difference, because it's Boomers who are rearing children these days.

This attitude helps explain some of the generational interactions that make tabloid and talk show headlines: Matures turning their houses over to their Boomer children; Matures making down payments on bigger homes for their children; Matures parenting in their children's places; Matures funding their grandchildren's college savings accounts; Matures buying the frills that enrich the lives of their grandchildren.

BOOMERS: WORRY ON MY MIND

In contrast to the leisurely, worry-free lifestyle Matures aspire to, Boomers fret that the march of time has walked them down the gangplank. They worry about disappointments and ongoing responsibilities, and notwithstanding their material successes, they still feel unfulfilled.

A Fresh Start. People of all ages feel if they had another chance, they could do things better, but Boomers feel this most. Boomers see not just missed opportunities, but imprudent behavior. Nearly three-quarters of Boomers agree that "if I had the chance to start over in life, I would do things much differently," versus just 59 percent among both Xers and Matures.

Indeed, Boomers were careless with their fortunes because they always got second and third chances. They saw life as a series of new

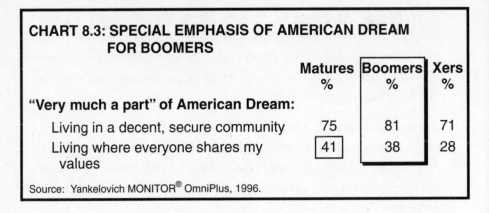

CHART 8.3: SPECIAL EMPHASIS OF AMERICAN DREAM
FOR BOOMERS

	Matures %	Boomers %	Xers %
"Very much a part" of American Dream:			
Living in a decent, secure community	75	81	71
Living where everyone shares my values	41	38	28

Source: Yankelovich MONITOR® OmniPlus, 1996.

experiences, each to be enjoyed to the fullest. Today they are being penalized for their past indulgences. They hope for one more chance to set things right, to undo the damage caused by their profligacy.

More Than Money. Make no mistake, Boomers haven't changed stripes. They still remain focused on experiences, intangibles, fulfillment, and spirituality. Almost two-thirds of Xers and Matures agree that "material things like what I drive and the house I live in are really important to me." Not so for Boomers; only half agree. While material goods have their place, they don't get at the core of what makes life meaningful. While Boomers always have bought lots, and will continue to do so, possessions never will satisfy their quest for meaning.

It'll Take a Miracle. Boomers are no longer copacetic about being able to reach their goals. They are much *less* likely than Matures or Xers to feel that they *won't* "have to do anything extraordinary" to reach their goals because "eventually [they'll] just get there." To be a winner, it seems, takes long odds. This realization, set hard against youthful expectations, makes this a serious concern.

XERS: GETTING AHEAD

Despite their tough start, Xers have an aggressive set of aspirations reflecting their pioneering sensibilities. Xers reject the paths they

CHART 8.4: SPECIAL EMPHASIS OF AMERICAN DREAM FOR Xers

	Matures %	Boomers %	Xers %
"Very much a part" of American Dream:			
Unlimited opportunity to pursue dreams	63	71	70
College education for self	50	56	63
Being a winner	45	40	50
Becoming wealthy	33	37	46

Source: Yankelovich MONITOR® OmniPlus, 1996.

have been directed to. They see these as dead ends, and this is not a dead-end generation. Their aspirations are part of their resolve to write their own life scripts.

My Way or the Highway. Xers want to steer their own course. Ninety percent of them agree that "however much I succeed in the future, it will be more than enough as long as I've done it on my own." They are also slightly more likely to say they'd rather "fail at something completely new than be the very best at something that's just the same old thing"—64 percent, versus 58 percent of Boomers and 60 percent of Matures. More Xers prefer working on their own than for somebody else.

A Little Help. This preference for doing it on one's own does not preclude getting help. Two-thirds of all Xers admit they need help from others to accomplish their aims.

Many Xers have simply not finished studying. So, while 70 percent of Boomers and 78 percent of Matures think they've "pretty much got the background and training" they need "in order to get where [they] want to go in life," only 58 percent of Xers think this.

Put an Edge on It. Everybody likes to compete. Xers thrive on it. They get pictured as slackers, but beneath their diffident exterior is

a real fire in the belly. Eighty-two percent of Xers agree that competition makes them perform better. Eighty percent think that they'll
have to "take some big risks and chances" to get what they want, and
more Xers agree that they can't be "too nice in [their] dealings with
other people."

Make a Plan. Xers want a plan, unlike Matures, who tend to leave
things to their own devices. Hedging and betting against the
unknown takes planning. Having resources means making lists.
Avoiding risks means anticipating, then preparing for them.

Worry. A plan also helps relieve the anxiety 61 percent of Xers say
they get "worrying about the future." Seventy-eight percent agree
that, no matter what they plan, the future "is always different" when
they get there, compared with 66 percent of Boomers and 60 percent
of Matures.

Tell Me I'm There. Xers need more signposts and reassurances than
other generations about their progress. This opens the door for marketers to position their products in ways that send positive signals.

ASPIRATIONAL FIT

A good way to picture these different aspirations is to put yourself
in Silicon Valley. Imagine who you would see there. Matures have
already retired from places like the big aerospace firms that no
longer offer new workers the same kinds of opportunities as in the
past. They relax on their pensions with family and hobbies.
Boomers have broken the mold, started new technology firms,
which later laid them off in waves of five and ten thousand at a
time. They are harassed with financial concerns and family obligations. Xers all work eighteen-hour days at small Internet firms that
are waiting to go public. They are obsessed with cyber-this and
cyber-that, bright, intensely driven, and highly competitive about
everything from computers to cars. These descriptions exaggerate,
to be sure, but they give some idea of the aspirational styles that
motivate buying in today's marketplace.

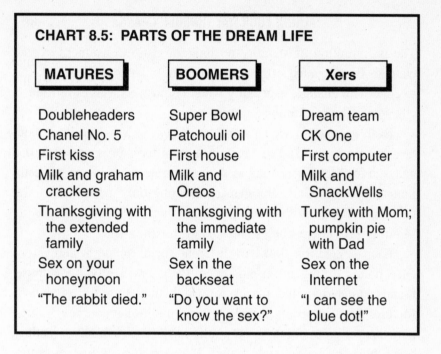

CHART 8.5: PARTS OF THE DREAM LIFE

MATURES	BOOMERS	Xers
Doubleheaders	Super Bowl	Dream team
Chanel No. 5	Patchouli oil	CK One
First kiss	First house	First computer
Milk and graham crackers	Milk and Oreos	Milk and SnackWells
Thanksgiving with the extended family	Thanksgiving with the immediate family	Turkey with Mom; pumpkin pie with Dad
Sex on your honeymoon	Sex in the backseat	Sex on the Internet
"The rabbit died."	"Do you want to know the sex?"	"I can see the blue dot!"

Dreams and aspirations are the roots of the consumer economy. They determine its shape. The aspiration for suburban living among the young Matures, for example, meant there were suddenly markets for refrigerators, romper room furniture, no-wax floors, all-purpose spray cleaners, sandboxes, garage door openers, lawn sprinklers, power mowers, deck furniture, plate glass for bay windows, dining room suites, backyard fencing, exterior lights, driveway basketball hoops, and so on—all the accouterments necessary for a satisfying suburban lifestyle. Advertisers could speak to people in these terms, media companies could use these settings in their programming, and retailers could locate their stores nearby.

Similarly, today's dreams will be tomorrow's realities. And it's Xers whose dreams are leading us towards tomorrow. Matures have retired from the game. Boomers are playing a slightly different game. Thus, it's Xers who have taken over setting the rules of the game—and this will define it for us all. As the marketplace changes in response to this, each generation will adapt in its own unique way.

TALKING YOUR WAY THROUGH CHANGE

The presumption of stability no longer exists. Consumers expect change. Brands must offer consumers the resources they look for to cope with change, especially when brands themselves introduce changes in the marketplace.

Each generation views change differently. Xers see it as their best bet for some kind of breakthrough in their prospects. It's not an issue for Matures as long as they can protect what they've accumulated. It confounds Boomers, presenting only greater risks. So celebrate change with Xers, focus on continuity and safety with Matures, provide resources and support for Boomers.

Each generation looks to different social supports and reference points during uncertain times. People will rely upon those brands situated in the places to which they turn for guidance. Matures have generally relied more on traditional sources of support like religion, community, public leaders, and family—institutions they considered time-tested. Boomers have relied more on their own resources and families. Family for Boomers usually means the one in which they grew up rather than the ones they head, which have been more fragile and unstable. Xers fall back on themselves, their friends, and peers. Traditional institutions, especially family, haven't proven effective or trustworthy.

WHAT "NEW" MEANS

Much marketing is about what's new—new products, new and improved, new look, next generation, never seen before, new release, new sound. For all this to resonate with consumers, though, the new must offer them what they expect. But what they expect differs across generations.

For Matures, new meant revolutionary. Things that reshaped our world and our homes. For Boomers, new meant novel. Things that were different and out of the ordinary. For Xers, new has meant interesting. Things that are intriguing and stimulating.

Matures have tended to spend conservatively on new things, not least because they don't see value in that which isn't truly revolutionary. Boomers have looked for products that reflected a change from the status quo. They would try anything as long as it wasn't the same. Xers discovered that surprise is not necessarily good—they suspect all novelty until it's proven. Their satisfaction stems from putting a sharper, more clever edge on things they already know.

TALKING TO MY GENERATION

Consumers look forward to the future again. Since the nadir of hope in the early nineties, our MONITOR tracking has shown a steady, year-to-year revival. Fewer consumers now feel that they will be forced to accept limits in the future, a trend reflecting an ongoing rejection of the paralyzing aspirational pessimism that prevailed for a brief time. But it is a qualified optimism. Today's dreams fit a more limited set of expectations. An understanding of the emotional side of these more moderate yearnings will enable brands to successfully connect with the ways each generation is looking towards the future. Brands should recognize this and refrain from asking buyers to overreach their means. People still want to create better lives for themselves and their children, but their dreams now reflect a more sober temperance about what they are willing and able to do to get there.

This is most pronounced among Boomers—they reached far and failed to grasp the brass ring, creating a visceral despair that gave rise to an ugly period of denial and victimization. Boomers recovered by retreating to moderate ambitions. Sympathize with this struggle, but don't pander to it. Boomers want reinforcement, so make your brands part of their smart new approach to success. Remember too that Boomers still carry many obligations—mortgage, college, parents, retirement. Perhaps even more than moral support, Boomers need real help with these commitments. They'd love a panacea, but they've given up that sort of wishful thinking.

Xers see limits as givens, a part of life that must be faced, but not something that will constrain their potential. Their expectations and lifestyles account for these restrictions, so, unlike Boomers, the impact of these limits does not represent some sort of loss. Also, they believe they can succeed through their own entrepreneurial efforts. Xers need help, feedback, resources, training, and empowerment. Brands should offer remedies and encouragement.

But it's more than this. In their aspirations, GenXers seek to be in command—forging a future on their own terms. Over the next decade, as Boomers look for escape and relief, Xers will step in to lead the way in defining our vision of success. They will remake the traditional American Dream according to their pioneering spirit and *reshape the market from one in which entrepreneurs are respected into one in which everybody is an entrepreneur.*

Matures feel the closest connection with tradition. A modest future is not a threat to most of them, unless it's so modest that it's meager. They fear impoverishment if times get too hard. They want a safety net against unexpected problems or shortfalls in their own plans and savings. Brands should give them both insurance and reassurance.

SUCCESS AMERICAN STYLE

Freedom to choose how we live. Happiness. A good marriage. Unlimited opportunities to pursue dreams. Living in a decent, secure community. These are not the kinds of things you can buy. Rather, they come from the sense of well-being that flows from lives that are under control and on track. These are fast becoming the new symbols of status and prestige.

Through MONITOR we have maintained an ongoing ranking of those things consumers most associate with success and accomplishment. For years, traveling for pleasure topped the list, an experience tied to materialism. Indeed, material things came first.

Today tangible luxuries like high-end cars and designer jewelry no longer enjoy this cachet. They are no longer the most exclusive things to have. People see them everywhere, and as a result no longer view them as symbols of privilege and prosperity. Additionally, many consumers who finally have acquired these possessions soon take them for granted. And in their search for novelty, they look around for other things to covet.

Today it's the intangibles that are scarce. These are the rarities in life. The people who have these things are the more accomplished among us. A good marriage is harder to find than a designer outfit. We know more Mercedes owners than happy people. Big houses stare back at us block after block down any suburban street, but we almost never see a pleasant, smiling face stare back at us on the subway.

Our most recent MONITOR research shows the top four determinants of success and accomplishment as: being satisfied, being in control, having the respect of other people, and having a good marriage. This is a big turnaround from fifteen years ago. It's the intangibles that consumers want to accumulate nowadays.

Expensive cars, luxury hotels, travel, gold credit cards, investment portfolios, prestige stores, and high technology no longer connote status. This is not to say that consumers no longer want these things. It's just that they are no longer most associated with accomplishment.

Young people have always been more focused on tangibles, and that remains true today. However, in a big change from the historical pattern, even among Xers the status of luxury items has dropped. Xers want them, of course, but they don't signify premier status. A Lexus is a good car, but just wheels. A Seiko looks good, but it just keeps time. Air Nikes wear well, but they walk the same pavement as a pair of K-Swiss. Xer achievers will, like all consumers, find status in other things.

All this indicates a shift from what looks good to what feels good. From what others think to what I think. Consistent with an emerging reliance on the self and a distrust of external sources of information, consumers see their own opinions as the ones that matter. No explanations, no apologies, no shame. An entrepreneur's sense of what's best.

When status is driven by whatever I say it is, it could just as easily be tangibles that I choose. So certain tangibles are making a

CHART 8.6: TANGIBLES DOWN FOR ALL

	1985 %	1995 %
Signs of success and accomplishment:		
❖ Owning an expensive car		
◆ Matures	38	12
◆ Boomers	46	18
◆ Xers	54	28

Source: Yankelovich MONITOR®.

comeback, particularly indulgences like cigars and martinis and the Wonderbra. Tangibles can still be signs of status, and some are now coming back. Outside of these few, though, tangibles have been displaced.

What can be worn on the sleeve nowadays, in a time when "sublime status" has replaced "show-off status," is expertise. Money can't buy being in the know. But smarts offer the proof intangibles can't provide that you're on the cutting edge.

For many years, we have tracked the things that people say are "really important." In the ten years from 1985 to 1995, all tangibles went down—designer names, credit cards, cars. Firsthand knowledge went up—knowing the "in" places to eat, being aware of the latest exercise trends, being recognized as someone "in the know." Having the inside scoop and being best informed are the new ways to grandstand in a time when grand possessions no longer stand out. Which is why bumper stickers now carry this message: "Too bad ignorance isn't painful."

SHARING OUR VISIONS OF THE GOOD LIFE

We celebrate the moments in our lives with the products that ornament them. General Foods International Coffees tell us exactly this. But it's important for us to do more than just that. We want to

CHART 8.7: WHAT YOU KNOW

	1985 %	1995 %	
Things "really important" to most people:			
Knowing the "in" places to eat	28	53	
Being aware of the latest exrecise/ fitness trends	27	45	↑
Being recognized as someone "in the know"	19	39	
Wearing designer names	34	29	
Using prestige credit cards	29	24	↓
Having an expensive foreign car	28	13	

Source: Yankelovich MONITOR®.

make connections with others. A celebration alone is no celebration at all. Separate dreams may disunite us, but we will still seek other ways of coming together.

Our MONITOR research shows a continuing need for association. Across generations, over three-quarters of consumers admit to "a growing need to share and observe important occasions with others." Sixty-nine percent wish for "the opportunity to participate in activities and rituals that remind me of the values I share with others."

Differences can be and should be celebrated even as we unite. The new self-reliant, entrepreneurial spirit is itself the new basis for community. A recent wedding announcement in *The New York Times* summed it up nicely: "They were married at Trinity Episcopal Church in Portland, with a reception at the nearby home of the bride's family . . . The house, filled with Northwest art, is so large the bride's mother calls the hallways 'avenues' . . . While some couples see their wedding as the moment when everything, from their bank accounts to their taste in foods, must merge, [they] chose to marry over the Independence Day weekend to celebrate their separateness."

MAKING IT

In an ad for the rollout of Windows 95, Microsoft related a simple yet telling tale about making it today. A Boomer dad at home phones people to schedule an important meeting. As he makes these calls, we see his young son peeking around the door jamb, playing in the hall, creeping up to the edge of daddy's desk. The meeting gets arranged and as dad prepares to leave, his son utters one of those plaintive, small-fry whys: "Why can't they come here?" The only good answer is the one shown in the next scene, where dad meets with his colleagues via videoconference, courtesy of Microsoft software. His son plays contentedly by his side, and dad himself looks on top the world.

Making it means little anymore without balance. The struggle today is to develop a work style that accommodates a lifestyle. Without some perspective, success at work is a hollow achievement. This doesn't mean taking work less seriously. Rather, it means creating an environment in which work gets done without compromising other aspects of one's life. This is all about balance, the new ingredient for success.

Through the end of the nineties, perhaps no issue will dominate the workplace more than this one. After years of making work the central focus of their lives, Boomers now tell us this just makes them unhappy. For their part, Xers say they have never contemplated defining themselves by their work in the ways their Boomer parents did. And Matures, after careers spent in service to the Puritan work ethic, now make plans to enjoy their leisure time in the coming years.

Balancing work and leisure will pose stiff challenges to both employers and marketers. Complex and sometimes competing demands will swirl around the workplace and the marketplace. Marketers, in particular, will have to develop products and services that satisfy new styles of work and play, in everything from work clothes to telecommunications services to vacation packages. Consumer expectations about work and leisure are deeply rooted in generational experiences.

WORK AND LEISURE

Pre–World War II, people spoke of a "leisure" class, rarefied elites whose wealth and social status enabled them to avoid the daily grind of earning a living so familiar to most Americans. As depicted by popular stories and characters, from Edith Wharton's tragic heroine Lily Bart to F. Scott Fitzgerald's Gatsby to the screwball comedies of the thirties like *Bringing up Baby* and *It Happened One Night*, the leisure class stood apart, fascinating yet peculiar in a world where everybody else worked. Their misadventures were outlandish, headline-grabbing public spectacles. To the average person, these frolics, while entertaining, confirmed their suspicions that, in truth, the idle rich were morally bankrupt.

Only work redeemed. It was about more than just economics or survival. Hard, honest work defined how most Americans saw themselves. The Puritan work ethic decreed that hard work made decent human beings. Having too good a time was suspect, if not downright sinful.

For Matures, the challenge of balancing work and leisure was straightforward. The two pursuits remained distinct—work was one thing, leisure another. Work was what you did at the office; leisure, at home. Men worked fifty weeks a year and took two weeks vacation in the summer as their well-earned reward. Weekends were spent in productive, home-centered activities like fixing up the house or keeping up the car. Women were told that activities outside the home, like jobs, would compromise their success as wives and mothers, so they focused on taking care of their families.

Men and women applied persistent effort to every task, work and leisure. No matter how long it took or how hard it was, pleasant or not, once you started something, you stuck with and finished it. Duty and obligation were the guiding principles that committed Matures to the needs of others over their own wants—a set of commitments, however, that they took great pleasure in fulfilling.

So after they paid for the necessities, they took time off to participate in family activities and family vacations. Indeed, there was no better way than a vacation to reaffirm the value of family and to reinforce togetherness. No thought of selfish getaways as they dutifully piled the kids into the car and headed for the Grand Canyon or Old Faithful or Myrtle Beach. It was fun and it was educational. Learn to swim. Visit battlefields and other national historic sites. Learn about geology at Carlsbad Caverns. Catch up on science and technology at the Smithsonian. At the very least, expand your horizons by traveling the new interstate highway system.

Holiday Inn played a big part in transforming the experience of the overnight motor car excursion from a Marco Polo fantasy to a common-man car trip. In doing so, it built a business as "The Nation's Innkeeper." Between ritzy upscale hotels and seedy, overpriced roadhouse inns, there were few tolerable options for overnight lodging. In 1951, Kemmons Wilson, a real estate developer from Memphis, finally got fed up with the unsatisfactory motels he and his family had to stay in every time they took a trip. Things came to a boil after a night spent in a particularly unpleasant motel outside Washington, D.C. The next day he got a tape measure and a notepad to carry with him for the rest of their trip. Each night he would measure the room in which they stayed, and work from that on a design for the ideal overnight space. He developed a motel with moderately sized rooms, each complete with a TV, a telephone, an in-room "coffee host," and a Bible, opened each day by the housekeeper to a different page. He named his motel chain after the Bing Crosby movie of the same name. He located the motels next to highway exits, and built them all with swimming pools and playgrounds for the kids. It was an instant success, followed just a few years later by Howard Johnson, then Marriott, then Ramada.

The pleasures of leisure pursuits like family trips made all the hard work worthwhile for Matures. The compartmentalization of work and leisure made sense to them. Leisure was the reward of work, and involved family. It provided a solid, supportive framework for the Boomer children of Matures, creating among them a sense of stability and expectation that eventually led to a change in the relationship between work and leisure.

LEISURE NOT WORK

As Boomers came of age, their sense of entitlement replaced the Mature's sense of obligation. This shift, from self-sacrifice to self-fulfillment that Dan Yankelovich wrote of in his 1981 book, *New Rules*, was "nothing less than the search for a new American philosophy of life." Boomers embarked on this search, and early on came to view leisure as their primary source of fulfillment. This would change, of course, but the move back to work in the eighties was a shift in the *sources* of fulfillment, not an abandonment of the search itself. As Yankelovich noted, "The search for self-fulfillment is not a yo-yo riding up and down the string of the economy: it is a powerful force that once unleashed works its way irreversibly into society."

Conformity and sacrifice were not part of the Boomer game plan. Experiences held the key to self-discovery—the more varied, the more exciting, the richer they were, the better. Indeed, our MONITOR data showed that for a time in the seventies Boomers coveted experiences much more than possessions.

In our 1975 tracking we identified a plurality of consumers— 44 percent—with an orientation toward the kind of leisure we called "active." These consumers, largely upscale, young, single men, saw leisure as a means of satisfying psychic needs not adequately fulfilled at work. They rejected the Puritan work ethic, a philosophy that had largely guided Matures, and pursued leisure activities as the primary vehicle in their quest for self. This group represented an important target for marketers because they actively bought many kinds of value-added leisure products and services. The leisure market boomed.

Boomers believed that time for one's self was a "right," not a privilege, and that shutting out dull, unpleasant obligations in favor of more fulfilling pursuits was their birthright. Not every Boomer trekked to an ashram in Tibet, but their boots were made for walkin'. Many donned backpacks, and clutching copies of *Europe on $5 a Day*, set out across the Atlantic. Others put a mattress in the van and headed across the country to find themselves.

The more instant the gratification, the better. This meant growth for leisure activities that were easier to master. Tennis too tough? Try racquetball. Golf too expensive? Try Frisbee golf. Running too hard? Slow down a step; take up jogging. Surfing too far away? Get a skateboard. Arthur Murray too tricky? Just twist.

It wasn't that any of these activities had transcendental powers. The point was to have the freedom to play around and experiment with novel things in life. The more unconventional the better, particularly if these leisure pursuits taught the steps to inner tranquillity and self-improvement. Hence, *Zen and the Art of Motorcycle Maintenance* topped the bestseller lists.

Some of this attitude even rubbed off on Matures. While they never threw out their old values, they did become more tolerant of those who looked for the new. Over time they even moved closer to what Boomers believed—the fitness boom touched them, their sexual attitudes loosened up a bit, and they started to live less for the future and a little more for today.

Particularly resonant with Matures was the idea that leisure did not always have to be productive or character-building. Along with this came the lessening of many social stigmas. Boomers accepted much that previously had been considered taboo. For instance, in his recent book on postwar America, journalist Michael Elliott quotes sociologist Christopher Jencks on the change in views about out-of-wedlock births. Jencks notes that from the late sixties to the early seventies, the moral high ground shifted from those looking down on single mothers to those looking down on those who looked down on unwed mothers. This was true in the workplace as well, as commitment to company or union, for example, yielded to a commitment to the self.

A new elitism took hold, and had a dramatic impact on life. Certain segments of the population, traditionally outside the marketing scope for particular activities, now included themselves. Access to the best things was opened up by individual interests or expertise, irrespective of education or socioeconomic status. The market for upscale or exclusive services and experiences expanded. Everyone played tennis. Everyone snorkeled. Tiffany opened branch stores. Travel abroad became everyone's prerogative. Blue collar workers began signing up for package tours to Paris.

LEISURE AS WORK

The leisure ethic was well on its way to becoming standard operating procedure when it pulled up short. As the seventies gave way to the eighties, Boomers tempered the pace and intensity of their trip to self-discovery. A combination of factors was at work, chief among them the perception that prosperity and growth could no longer be taken for granted. Boomers were forced back to the grind. In addition, they had found it tougher to attain fulfillment than anticipated. Work was the new path they hoped would provide a shortcut to fulfillment.

Work, which had sat on the sidelines for much of the "me decade," took center stage. Just as Boomers obsessed about leisure, they now obsessed about their work. And just as the emphasis on leisure spilled into the workplace, so the new focus on work affected leisure.

The yuppie style of the eighties put a premium on working hard. Everybody bragged about the long hours they put in. Weekend leisure was supplanted by billable hours at the office. Employees at one New York ad agency sported T-shirts on the weekends that read, "If you don't come in on Sunday, don't bother coming in on Monday." It was "no pain, no gain," so squash at lunch gave way to lunchtime boxing on Wall Street.

Not everybody worked on Wall Street, of course, but this yuppie style set the tone. You worked and worked, and when you played, you worked. You worked hard and you played hard. Leisure, in fact, became an important way of competing. A great vacation said, "I win. You lose." If two people took the same vacation, one could still win by having a better time. And you made sure you worked hard at having a good time. For Matures, productive leisure was a virtue. Boomers in the eighties worked at leisure because that meant winning.

This new chic showed up everywhere: Cell phones by the pool. Memos dictated from planes on the way to Hawaii. One colleague of ours came back from a vacation during the height of this frenzy and told us what a great time he had lying on the beach for two days in Puerto Rico . . . programming phone numbers into his new electronic organizer!

Savvy marketers understood that this sensibility meant leisure needed to be remolded to fit the constraints of work. Many businesses did things to make leisure activities more accessible—closing later or relocating closer to the office or implementing ways to accommodate rather than penalize last-minute planning. Other marketers made it easier to keep in touch while out having a good time—voice mail in hotel rooms or charge-card phone booths at the top of ski lifts or pagers that worked anywhere, anytime.

In an economy that demanded it, consumers gave up play to work overtime. Consumers, Boomers especially, made every moment count, with no idle time. Work was a necessity, but self-fulfillment was still the goal for Boomers, so worklike styles infused everything. Perhaps nowhere was this more evident than among women, particularly the young Boomer women who made their mark in the eighties.

POST-FRIEDAN

Betty Friedan, a Mature, threw down the gauntlet in 1963 with the publication of her landmark book, *The Feminine Mystique*. In her analysis of circumscribed roles for women in American society, she wrote of "a strange stirring, a sense of dissatisfaction, a yearning that women suffered in the middle of the twentieth century in the United States. Each suburban housewife struggled with it alone," quietly wondering, "is this all[?]" What troubled Friedan most was that while the older women with whom she spoke could recall giving up personal hopes and dreams to accomplish what was expected of them, many younger women she interviewed "no longer even thought about them. A thousand expert voices applauded their femininity, their adjustment, their new maturity. All they had to do was to devote their lives from earliest girlhood to finding a husband and bearing children . . . [I]n the fifteen years after World War II this mystique of feminine fulfillment became the cherished and self-perpetuating core of contemporary American culture." Many women heard Friedan's clarion call to move beyond this definition of womanhood, but it was Boomer women who really answered her by striking out on a new path, one that led them into the workforce.

The acceptance of women in the workplace is the single biggest shift in American social values since the end of World War II. Twenty or more years ago it was Boomers who most readily accepted women in the workforce, and they passed this value on to their children. Therefore, Xer women have entered the workforce amid the strongest-ever acceptance of this value.

CHART 9.1: MONITOR Trend: *Female Careerism—"Acceptance of Women in the Workplace"*

% "strong" on trend	Xers today*	Boomers then**	Boomers today*	Matures then**	Matures today*
	61	47	60	36	50

 * Today: 1995.
** Then: 1973.

Source: Yankelovich MONITOR®.

Women became independent operators in the marketplace, and undermined the long-standing marketing assumption that women aspired chiefly to building a family. This notion showed up even in commercials for personal products like cosmetics. With new views about femininity, many married women kept their maiden names or opted for hyphenated versions. Others took off their wedding rings. Still others stopped wearing makeup. Unisex fashions flourished, as did access to traditionally male-only institutions. Military academies finally admitted them, and banks for women found a market niche.

With great eagerness, in the belief that their time had finally come, many women went to work thinking that almost any job was better than staying at home. Other women who opted to stay home, or who had no options at all, were affected by this, too. They became more forthright and experimental, looking for fulfillment and personal creativity in ways unconnected with homemaking.

Women began to reexamine their roles, turning introspective. They read self-help books, evaluated their psychic needs, participated in consciousness-raising sessions, and formed their own political groups. More and more they began to link their physical health to their emotional well-being, recognizing that looking good was not only about hair and makeup, but also about feeling good.

While not all women agreed on every issue, the differences of opinion we measured were largely confined to the more extreme tenets of the women's movement. But even as early as 1974, all women were, in the words of Dan Yankelovich from his book, *The New Morality*, "solidly behind equal pay for equal work, prepared to believe that it is as important for a 'real man' to be concerned about the sexual satisfaction of his partner as it is for him to be a good provider and 'family man,' [and] no longer committed to the idea that the man must be the main decision-maker in the family."

By the end of the seventies, work for women, just as much as for men, emerged as the primary vehicle for self-expression and self-fulfillment. The eighties saw working women throwing themselves into their jobs just as much as working men. They had emancipated themselves from the societal expectations Betty Friedan excoriated. Of course, not all women welcomed this. But even the so-called total woman, by rejecting it, was exercising the freedom to make her own decisions, independent of societal pressures to conform, that constituted the fundamental development of this era. It was, as Florence Skelly used to say, the ability to choose without penalties.

POST-FREEDOM

Today's headlines make much of women rethinking the role of work in their lives. But as early as 1979, MONITOR detected the first murmurings of discontent. Even before their next big push into the workplace—over 50 percent of all women were already working by 1980—many women who embraced these new freedoms in the early seventies questioned them less than a decade later. While few women wanted to relinquish the psychological and financial rewards of work, we saw signs that the sense of self-worth provided by work was decreasing. Women expressed more reasonable expectations about their jobs, having seen firsthand some of the trade-offs required. The thrills of work had started to dull, the everyday stress and routine had taken some of the bloom off the rose.

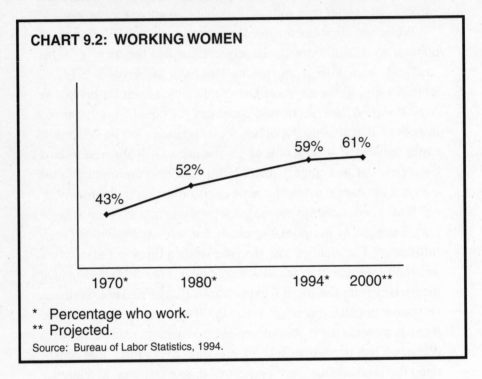

CHART 9.2: WORKING WOMEN

* Percentage who work.
** Projected.
Source: Bureau of Labor Statistics, 1994.

While the appeal of work diminished, the impact on femininity became increasingly disconcerting to many women. Women did not bemoan the demise of the feminine mystique and its one-dimensional emphasis on marriage and motherhood, but they did regret certain losses. Early on, many women had attempted to minimize the emotional and physical differences between themselves and men. By the mid-seventies, a growing chorus of authors was warning against looking too feminine at work—it distracted men and it kept women from being taken seriously, they said. Attempting sameness, many women decided they had to act and look tough. They donned suits, white blouses, scarves, bow ties, dark hose, and pumps.

As women entered graduate and professional schools in greater numbers and filled middle management ranks in many fields, they

gained a self-confidence that gave them a new freedom—the freedom to reintroduce femininity into their look and style without
paying a price. At first they wore frilly underclothes beneath their
power suits, but soon the suits themselves became a memory.
Women realized that they did not have to be the same to be equal.
They could be different and equal too.

In the midst of all of this, Revlon looked to MONITOR in an
effort to keep young women interested in their best-selling fragrance Charlie. When introduced, Charlie ads had captured the
mood and temperament of young, independent, "with-it" women.
With the revival of femininity, Revlon realized that it had to consider softening the image of Charlie without undermining the independent point of view it celebrated. So the pantsuit-clad model
swapped her signature look for a dress.

By the mid-eighties, women were under pressure. With freedom
had come isolation. Economic pressures, relationships, divorce jarred
them. Self-fulfillment seemed more elusive than ever before. One
enterprising soul started selling T-shirts that read, "Oh my God, I for-
got to have children!"

Redbook popularized this image with an ad campaign about the
"Juggler," the new woman who did it all. She had mastered how to
shop, how to manage her time and her money, how to raise kids,
how to be competitive at work, indeed, how to win at all costs.
And, of course, she read *Redbook*.

Unfortunately it didn't quite work this way. Frustration, disappointment, and stress were often the only fruits of her labors. As the
atmosphere of the eighties collapsed into a mood of denial and victimization, women had their own specific complaints and heartaches.
Little wonder that Calvin Klein, who brought out Obsession in the
eighties, offered her Escape in the early nineties.

FINDING HER WAY OUT

None of these misgivings and frustrations undermined the confidence women felt. Rather, their concerns were about the price they

had to pay to exercise their talents. They weren't trying to abandon careers, *only balance them.*

In partnership with *McCall's*, we completed a MONITOR-based survey in 1993 of adult women titled "The New Female Confidence Report." And confidence was what it showed. Three-quarters of women in every generation saw themselves in control, knowing what they wanted most out of life. Nearly all women surveyed, Boomer women in particular, saw themselves as willing "to fight hard for the things" they believed in, and nearly as many said that "a single woman can lead a full life." There was little they felt they "couldn't handle on their own."

But this research also uncovered signs of disquietude. Far fewer than half the Boomer women surveyed described themselves as happier or luckier than their mothers at the same age. Even more striking, 43 percent of Xer women saw themselves as more conflicted about choices than their mothers. Seventy-six percent of all women believe that "life today has become much too complicated," versus 62 percent a little over a decade ago.

We looked into this in more detail for a cover story in *Fortune* that appeared in September 1995, concerning the midcareer crises of Boomer women and their approaches to handling them. The willingness to make changes to fix whatever they felt wasn't working was well summarized by one woman interviewed for the article: "The message of the day is that change is possible. You don't have to get it right the first time." The article concluded that women would go forward, but in some very new ways: "[T]hese mid-life crises are ultimately not about retreat but about redefinition. In great numbers, women executives emerge from this period making decisive mid-course corrections."

These women are in the vanguard of what's happening in the marketplace as a whole. Consumers have wearied of being dominated by work. So consumers are striking a new balance, and women, Boomer women in particular, having most intensely felt the demands of the workplace over the last few decades, are leading the way.

In this research for *Fortune*, all but 13 percent of the women we interviewed said they had made or were seriously considering major changes in their lives: 45 percent cited starting their own business; 44 percent cited changing jobs in the same field; 38 percent cited going back to school; 37 percent, taking a sabbatical; 35 percent, changing careers; 33 percent, making a major personal change; and 31 percent, leaving their jobs and not working.

Most women we have interviewed in our MONITOR tracking, career and noncareer women alike, have discovered that less is actually more. As women took on more and more in the seventies and eighties, they increasingly saw diminishing returns. In their search for balance, many women have tossed out some of their juggling balls for the few that genuinely matter.

Women feel freer to construct the kinds of lives they want, but they don't want to do it all. Marketers trying to reach out to women, particularly Boomer women, should note: They need fewer reminders of their complex lives and more kudos for their know-how and accomplishments. Fewer portraits of the juggler and more laurels for her talents.

LEISURE INTO WORK

The work-intensive eighties burned us all out, and we didn't turn into the winners we thought we would be. For several years following the 1987 stock market crash, we pulled back and hunkered down, hoping the storm would soon pass us by. We retreated into our homes to minimize our exposure to risks—it seemed we always got burned when circulating in the world at large. We felt sorry for ourselves. And often, sorry about what we found at home—more "mommie dearest" than mommy. For a while we couldn't stop ourselves when Oprah or Geraldo or Sally Jesse came calling, only too ready to whine and wheedle for the sympathy and pity of all who watched. It was good TV.

But now we have wearied of all that. We have come to terms with our disappointments and are looking to the future with renewed enthusiasm. It's not like us as a nation of engineers to spend as much time and energy as we did in recent years on endless, introspective analyses of our problems. Americans fix things and move on. We're back to that again.

Leisure reemerges as a key element in this mending. Not that work has fallen out of favor. Boomers in particular continue to express a strong commitment to their careers. Rather, people want to make work more gratifying. Adding a bit of fun is key.

During the recent period of denial and victimization, leisure was more about time off and time out than time well spent. But the call for fun has rebounded dramatically in the last few years. Today "having more fun" tops the list of things consumers tell us they plan to do in the coming year.

Snapple captured this new way of thinking in ads featuring "two guys and a van." Their sole mission is to bring good cheer to everyone they see by giving them a Snapple. They drive their Snapple-painted van across fields, or stop in the middle of streets, just to make people happier. These guys salute the ordinary things that fill our days, from the moment we wake up until the time we go to bed. You toast these with a Snapple, taking the edge off by putting a smile back into the everyday.

The workplace will be affected by this resurgence of leisure. Already manifest in our data is a dramatic rise in the percentage of consumers who see "being able to take a day off when you want to" as a sign of success and accomplishment. This is clear evidence of leisure taking precedence more and more over work.

We recently completed a MONITOR-based study for "Family Re-Union V: Family and Work," the annual family conference that Vice President Al Gore chairs in coordination with The Children, Youth and Family Consortium at the University of Minnesota and the Tennessee Select Committee on Children and Youth. We studied the impact of workplace changes on families and children. The results showed clearly that stress accounted for many of the ways the workplace affected parent-child relationships. The more the workplace exacerbates stress, the more detrimental its effects on families.

We classified working parents into six groups according to the types of workplace changes they experienced over the last two to three years. One noteworthy younger group of Xers and Trailing Boomers consisted of those who had recently quit a job and moved on to something new. This particular group was remarkably free of stress.

The highest-stress group, of course, consisted of those workers who had been laid off. The second-highest group, and not lower by much, consisted of their colleagues, the downsizing survivors. The workplace changes these two groups had experienced were involuntary and painful, whereas those who had simply moved on their own felt more in control of their lives.

There were two big reasons why these workers had moved on. One, to simplify their lives; two, to spend more time with their children. They felt they had succeeded at both, even though most were now making less money. These workers made leisure decisions first, then established a work style that fit, a 180-degree turn from the eighties, and a clear indication that the workplace is being reshaped. For many consumers, there is no life without leisure, and they have recast their own lives to strike the balance they seek.

CASUAL FRIDAYS

Consumers look to take the hard edge off work. Work itself is stressful enough, so cut away some of the ragged edges that rub us raw. Why add the worry each day of matching shoes and dress or tie and braces? So first there were casual days. Now there are casual companies. Why add the stress of a commute, jockeying each morning with a big rig for the inside lane on the interstate? More and more people work from home, telecommuting with technology. Why not make the office itself more flexible? Virtual offices have taken hold. IBM has them. Most days, employees work at client sites, but when they do show up at the office they "check out" a space for the time they're there. TBWA Chiat/Day has them, too. Same idea, with some technological flair. Each employee carries a cell phone on his or her belt. That way each person has a direct line even if they don't have an assigned desk. A centralized computer system ties everybody into a common company site, and makes it possible to work from anywhere while being just as linked to the company as anybody else.

It's all about opening up work to the requirements of employees, and allowing those needs to drive work arrangements rather than the other way around. Deloitte & Touche has developed a consulting practice that helps companies organize these new work environments. On the back cover of a report they published, about a study on women and work we did for them in partnership with *Fortune*, they ran an ad with this headline: "Work day and night. Hike at noon." The ad shows a picture of Patricia Gallup, chairman and CEO of PC Connection, Inc., sitting on a boulder in a glade next to a stream. She is quoted saying many positive things about how Deloitte & Touche helped her firm, especially in achieving the balance she seeks for herself and her employees: "It makes for a nice balance to walk out the door after a fast-paced day and realize, hey, I'm in New Hampshire."

Workers have become less and less confident that their personal goals match management objectives. They no longer wholeheartedly give themselves to companies to the exclusion of everything else. This shows up in our research as a generational phenomenon. Matures still in the workforce are more likely to believe their companies can "retain high-quality employees"—76 percent versus 68 percent of Xers and 66 percent of Boomers. Matures continue to feel that loyalty and conformity prevail. The impact of this is most pronounced among Xers. Far fewer (75 percent) say they "are committed to the growth and success" of the companies for which they work than Boomers (85 percent) and Matures (87 percent).

Xers understand that they will have to adapt more than generations before them. Matures learned a trade or entered a career and then put in thirty years. Boomers skipped from job to job in a competitive hustle to be on top and to keep the job interesting. Xers see neither the stability that Matures enjoyed nor the opportunities

Boomers had. Xers realize they will have to train and retrain themselves to stay on top of opportunities.

Amidst the uncertainties and risks they see, Xers apply a multitude of approaches to the workplace of the future. For instance, not long ago four eighteen-year-old high school senior girls sat around a kitchen table with us in Connecticut discussing their futures. They were bound for top-notch universities—Berkeley, Columbia, Northwestern, and George Washington—and perhaps destined to become part of the next generation of American leaders. But not one of them was willing to devote her life to a career. Each said she would not be willing to delay getting married and having a family simply to advance her career. This younger generation watched Boomers utterly commit themselves to their work, sacrificing their families and personal lives in the process. They believe, as do many of these Boomers now, that the price was too high.

One of our clients, a large management services company, came to us a few years ago wanting to know why their young employees seemed unwilling to make the sacrifices traditionally part of a career climb. Why wouldn't a promising young New York assistant be willing to transfer to Cleveland for a stint there on the way up the corporate ladder? A Boomer of the eighties would have been on the next flight. Our client wondered if they were recruiting the wrong people or if their incentive plans were insufficient or if the company just wasn't communicating its goals and requirements well enough with new employees. So we set about surveying their young employees.

We found it was generational myopia all over again. Boomer managers simply did not understand Xer career perspectives. To these young employees life isn't about sacrificing for the job. They want success, and want it badly, but they want it with balance. They will not give up a life for a career. To many Boomers this is just more proof that Xers are a bunch of slackers. But they're wrong.

Indeed, if Boomer bosses don't wake up, they will soon find themselves unable to attract high-quality employees. As the labor pool shrinks because of the smaller size of the up-and-coming Xer cohort, Xers will be in a stronger position to negotiate the kind of balance they seek. After all, Xers do have an alternative—they can just do it themselves.

Xers will lead the way as entrepreneurs. Don't laugh—twenty-year-old multimillionaire entrepreneurs are already doing this in Internet businesses, and they have the full attention of Wall Street. This phenomenon will become more and more commonplace. Xers have concluded that being The Man beats working for The Man. The things they want as a generation are just hard to find in traditional corporate settings. They are the most likely to say in our MONITOR tracking, for example, that their companies "need more cultural diversity."

According to an IBM study, one in five small businesses today is owned by someone under the age of thirty-five. Thirty-eight percent of college students in another national survey said that owning a business is the best route to a successful career. In comparison, only 24 percent said they would prefer working for a large corporation. The number of universities that offer entrepreneurial programs has grown from 16 in 1970 to more than 400 today.

"We are in the midst of a huge economic expansion driven by the Information Revolution," said Paul Zane Pilzer, economist and author. "It will make the Industrial Revolution pale by comparison. Advances in technology and communication, now as never before, have made it possible to run an entire global business from a single mind seated before a solitary personal computer."

A decade ago one of the authors of this book, J. Walker Smith, introduced an audience at a meeting of the Advertising Research Foundation to the concept of "real-time marketing": A marketing manager of the twenty-first century sits in his or her darkened *Starship Enterprise*–like office, surrounded by monitors and computer screens humming faintly as they receive and process sales information from around the world. As stores and shops complete transactions, they are instantly scanned and computerized, then transmitted at the speed of light via satellite. From moment to moment, brand managers watch sales and make instantaneous corrections or adjustments to counter a competitive threat or to take advantage of a sudden market opportunity. Competitive advantage in this marketing environment accrues to those companies with better decision-making software and faster, more secure reporting technologies.

Though it seemed like a fantasy at the time, real-time marketing is now here. Coca-Cola, for example, recently announced Project Infinity, a five- to seven-year, multimillion-dollar initiative to provide Coca-Cola brand managers with daily sales information in specific global markets. Coke already does this to a limited extent with things like radio devices in vending machines that transmit information about how many soft drinks sell each day.

A decade ago, when we first thought about real-time marketing, we envisioned it as something big companies would move towards to more closely manage their sales. But we see now that perhaps the biggest impact of these technologies will be to give, as Pilzer notes, young entrepreneurs the opportunity to create their own businesses free of the constraints and demands of large corporations.

LABOR-LESS LEISURE

Consumers want leisure that comes easy. Fun for the fun of it. Consumers don't want to have to work at leisure. They don't want to go far to find it. They don't want to have to make big plans to get it. They feel leisure that adds worry, energy, or effort is not worth it.

Not long ago *Time* reported a story on outdoor activities. They observed that many people who go camping today choose less rugged paths. These "smooth-experience" campers opt for tents with gear lofts, sleeping bags with temperature controls, and portable kitchens complete with paper towel racks. This trend toward leisure without labor will create new demands for convenience and labor-saving products across all types of recreational activities: Armchair entertainments. Virtual excitements. Passive participation. Imagination games instead of mind games for a change. Just-bring-yourself vacations, picnics, excursions, parties, events. Even, we'll-bring-you-too services that not only provide it all, but get you there and back as well.

Just having fun is particularly important to Xers. They aren't as consumed as Boomers were by a passion for introspection and self-enlightenment. In our MONITOR surveys of the early seventies, nearly half of all Boomers, then at the age Xers are today, were "strongly" committed to a pursuit of self-understanding,

---

CHART 9.3: MONITOR Trend: *Introspection—"Focus Internal Cues"*

% "strong" on trend	Xers today*	Boomers then**	Boomers today*	Matures then**	Matures today*
	26	46	24	27	16

* Today: 1995.
** Then: 1973.

Source: Yankelovich MONITOR®.

CHART 9.4: MONITOR Trend: *Personal Creativity—"Creativity Comes from Within"*

% "strong" on trend	Xers today*	Boomers then**	Boomers today*	Matures then**	Matures today*
	18	30	14	19	11

* Today: 1995.
** Then: 1973.

Source: Yankelovich MONITOR®.

compared with only a quarter of all Xers today. In a similar vein, Xers today are half as likely as Boomers were in the early seventies to feel that anyone can be creative just by looking hard enough deep down inside.

The interest of Boomers in enrichment, understanding, and fulfillment fueled the constant trial of new things, especially leisure activities. But marketers can no longer take this for granted. Talking to Xers about creativity or building products to facilitate the expression of their inner creativity won't register.

There will still be market opportunities. Extreme sports are one of these. In our MONITOR tracking, Xers are a lot more likely than Boomers or Matures to cite interest in doing things that other people think are dangerous, to watch extreme sports on TV or read about them in magazines, and to actually participate in them. The risk is the thrill; the extremity is the attitude. Extreme sports are a way for Xers to throw themselves into life and be totally absorbed by the fun of it. Xers want the thrill of something edgy to do, where Boomers had hoped that their leisure time would help them come to terms with things, perhaps even lead them to some sort of enlightenment.

FUN TO DO

As we look ahead to the leisure marketplace of tomorrow, we see other broad trends with various implications for each generation.

Fun Without Peril. True, Matures are more adventuresome than previous fifty-plus generations, Boomers wrote the book on experimentation, and Xers don't even blink at the thought of parachuting out of a plane for sport. Nonetheless, no one wants their survival imperiled by their leisure activities. There are many risk-management issues that marketers should consider.

For Matures, this means physical and psychological *safety*. Malls understood this many years ago and opened early so that older consumers could walk for exercise year-round in a relatively risk-free environment.

For Boomers, it means *predictability*. They want control, as we know, and are stressed without it. Boomers still want to expand their cultural sensibilities and experiences, but they don't want to fret about something so unfamiliar that they worry whether things will turn out as planned.

Nostalgia travel is a big market for Boomers. They will enjoy leisure opportunities that allow them to relive their youth. Old times appeal to them, with places and themes they remember fondly providing more predictable kinds of experiences.

And you must deliver what you promise. No fine print is too small for Boomers to read, and if they don't read it and are penalized, they will do as they've always done—punish the marketer. Extra charges. Extra hassles. Extra steps. Boomers don't want it, so consider integrated, all-in-one, money-back-guarantee packages. Especially options that include kids.

For Xers, this means a *safety net*. They like the high wire, but they don't want the fall to kill them. Xers know all about high-tech devices and services that guard against and treat trauma. They just don't want to be so encumbered by them that they can't have any fun. But they do want these devices and services there to get them out of jams when they're in trouble.

Boomers and Xers can get the kinds of risk management they're looking for with electronic leisure technologies. Boomers can get an enriched experience over which they have more control. Xers can get simulated thrills without any of the spills.

Off-Peak. Matures are particularly flexible about time. They already fill movie theaters for early afternoon matinees, and restaurants for early bird specials. But remember not to talk about this as something especially for "seniors." Appeal to their generational sense of competence, reward, and victory. Matures who can afford it will travel to France in June to see Monet's garden at the height of its glory or go whale watching when kids are in school and parents at work.

Flextime options are becoming more important as Boomers age. Flextime will allow them to be more in control, and they will be more receptive to your leisure offerings. Mini-vacations that can be built into busy schedules and taken at a moment's notice are what they need.

Pragmatic Xers look at it from their eat-dessert-first perspective. When they see what they think they might like, they want to sample it sooner rather than later. Xers make up another part of the growing market for mini-vacations. Can't afford a week in Cancún or Steamboat? Don't save for a year; take the four-day special now.

Home Too. Traditionally, as people age, their need for excitement outside the home goes down. Matures today are more on the go than ever before, yet they spend a considerable amount of their leisure time at home. While Boomers will undoubtedly invalidate this rule of thumb, we do see them being more home-centered in recent years, spending more time, money, and emotional resources. Xer interest in home and homeowning is on the rise. A lot of the ways they relax are home-based, like napping or soaking in the tub.

There is an opportunity here to help all generations redefine at-home leisure, in particular by making it possible to enjoy leisure activities from a home base. A simple example illustrates this. In the summer of 1995 a news reporter told the story of sitting at home while joining several others at a California vineyard and a New York City office in a virtual wine tasting over the Internet. No reason others across the country couldn't also have sampled the pinot noirs and cabernets.

New Rituals. Much leisure celebrates or commemorates. As our work and leisure styles change, we will need to rethink the things we do to end the workday, to start the weekend, to welcome a new colleague to the office, or to congratulate someone on a business success or the birth of a child.

This is particularly true as the workplace is overturned and reconfigured. We ask people in our MONITOR tracking to check off all the ways they meet new people and expand their circle of friends. Number one was "socializing with coworkers," cited by over 60 percent of all consumers, and the *only* way mentioned by more than half. As the workplace we know today changes, we will have to invent new ways of developing communities.

We also will need new leisure connections. Matures still can remember the old industrial leagues of baseball, basketball, and softball teams. Boomers still participate in company bowling and softball leagues, not to mention carpooling and nights out with coworkers. Facilitating new connections to sustain old pastimes or provide new pursuits will become a key priority.

Our MONITOR data show declines in the commitment people have to traditional forms of community, neighborhood, and volunteerism. But new forms have replaced these—kids' soccer leagues, Internet chat lines, neighborhood watch groups, talk radio, walks and marches against everything from AIDS to homelessness, twelve-step programs, parent support groups. Some coalesce around happy things, others around unhappy events, but they all provide new sources for personal connection and community.

Many of these new sources of connection will combine two or more old sources. Consider orientation programs at colleges. No longer relying on just the campus tour and Greek rush, many colleges, from Stanford to Yale to the University of California at Santa Cruz, have started using wilderness programs like Outward Bound. The stated objective is to put students in an environment that facilitates bonding without temptation from the traditional vices, alcohol in particular. The genius of these programs is in their use of old ways of coming together to create new sources of connection.

Beyond the Booster Seat. Children are back. Boomers are having them late, while Xers are having them early. Now is the time to build child-friendly elements into all leisure pursuits, from diaper-changing facilities in restrooms to restaurant tables without sharp corners to movie previews that really are okay for kids to see. Let Xers and Boomers know that their kids are welcome and valued; celebrated, not merely accommodated. Fly British Airways, for example, and you will see parents in bulkhead seats with their babies settled peacefully in a roomy crib that specially attaches to that row.

AFFORDING IT

Needless to say, a large part of this move to lighten the work environment depends on the financial ability to do so. Only Matures describe their financial situation in our MONITOR research as "comfortable." The majority of Xers and Boomers say they have "just enough to get by." On the other hand, Xers and Boomers do say they are a little better off today. Consumers are reasonably confident about getting by, so the issue for most has become how to relish life, not how to skirt bankruptcy. Doom and gloom fill the press about the debt of Boomers and the prospect of Xers. Both groups, while recognizing challenges, want to press ahead.

The financial issue for Boomers is not debt per se, but the ability to service that debt. They need help finding ways to restructure their finances to prevent debt from dampening their historical willingness to spend. Their angst about the future, particularly the future they'll be able to provide for their children, and their disappointment with the recent past both suggest they want more help than what's available now: Information on the Internet. Seminars. Software. Call-in services. Special TV channels. Newsletters. Walk-up advisers in places like Nordstrom or REI. Brochures about saving for college at Toys "R" Us.

Focus on income-oriented strategies. Saving sounds like sacrifice and deprivation. Selling this idea to Boomers, even with scare tactics about impoverished retirements, will be much harder than talking to them about earning money. Boomers have largely thought that if they needed something they could just earn more to get it rather than save for it. They don't think in terms of long-term savings. In a recent article, *Fortune* cited a study of Boomers by Putnam Investments, a money management firm, in which 54 percent admitted they had no idea what their retirement would look like. Maybe that's why some of Aetna's recent ads bear the headline "Forget retirement." They're talking to Boomers in terms that Boomers understand.

A good financial product for Boomers would be one that gives something back even as it socks something away. Boomers like immediate rewards. They want the inside track on good deals. Say those things to them. Give them those kinds of products. Don't demand that they save or else. Show them how putting their money in your instrument will allow them to keep spending even when they're retired, or show them how your plan grows their capital while also paying back a dividend they can use to splurge on themselves.

LEAVING WORK BEHIND FOR GOOD

Income issues will continue to worry Boomers for a long time to come. As we discussed when introducing Boomers, they are unlikely to retire in the way Matures did. Indeed, historically, the prospects faced by Boomers should not come as a surprise. Matures have had an exceptional retirement, made possible by Social Security and the postwar economic expansion that steadily drove their wages up year after year. Several years ago a survey of retired people for the National Taxpayers Foundation reported in *American Demographics* that many retirees depend upon Social Security to support their retirement. Over half said Social Security was their single most important source of retirement income, well ahead of pensions and savings. Part-time work was barely mentioned at all.

Matures feel relatively secure, but they are concerned about keeping their share of the pie. Many worry about outliving their savings or entitlements. Others fear that hard times in the future could turn their financial situation upside down. Matures look for financial products that can help them enhance their standard of living without depleting their savings. Saving is much of what their lives have been all about. Don't ask them to give this up. Offer, instead, products that trade some other asset or equity for the income they need today.

They want reassurances about stability and growth. That's what products and communications should stress. Of course, this is exactly what investment experts counsel for older consumers, but the continued dependence on entitlements will make these considerations even more important if the market turns sour in the years ahead.

Boomers, though, will respond less to messages about stability and consistent growth, even when they get to the age Matures are now. To start with, Social Security won't be as important, mainly because, if the experts are right, it won't have enough funds for all the Boomers who'll be asking for support. Their savings will be poorer. Boomers will have obligations that continue far beyond the age at which they ended for Matures. Boomers put off getting married and starting families, and they're going to live longer than any generation before them. Finally, many Boomers will have poorer pensions because of corporate consolidations, downsizings, and cost cuttings.

The *Fortune* article made some dramatic predictions about the future income of people over the age of 65. Contrasting actual figures for 1992 and projected figures for 2029, some key changes appear in the offing: Traditional pensions as a source of income will drop from 8 percent to 4 percent of total income. Federal income like Social Security from 19 percent to 7 percent. Investment income will just about hold steady, going up slightly from 46 percent to 48 percent. Salary income, however, will jump from 27 percent to 41 percent. Clearly a lot more Boomers will continue working.

WORKIN' IS ALRIGHT BY ME

Boomers will retread, not retire. And this is okay by Boomers because even with a shift in balance between work and leisure, Boomers retain a strong connection to work. They'll have many options: Consultants. Franchisees. Temps, both with an agency and independently. Designers and engineers. Writers. Turning avocations into vocations, sidelines into specialties. Teachers. And of course, entrepreneurs. Indeed, Boomers have already discovered the benefits of starting up their own businesses. According to a study by Challenger, Gray and Christmas, an outplacement firm, 12 percent of those laid off have launched their own companies, twice the rate from just three years ago.

Three elements of this trend will be important to watch. First, Boomers will end up responsible for their own health care. They clearly will need a greater variety of affordable products than what's available today.

Second, Boomers will need training, help, and continuing education. Adult students aged 25 and older are the fastest-growing segment of the student population. With new career interests, this group will only get bigger. And they'll need books and services to walk them through their new start in life.

Software products are a good way to provide this assistance. For example, Kemper Financial Services rewrote its financial planning software to take into account people who will continue to work past retirement, or who will work part-time during retirement.

Third, Boomers will continue to try to satisfy the need for fulfillment they carried into the workforce two and three decades ago. For the most part, they haven't found it in the workplace yet, so their next career choices will be guided by this unsatisfied aspiration. Work will be balanced on their terms when they do so, not, as before, on those of a large corporation.

X-RETIREES

Xers don't worry about retirement yet, but they do think about it. Sixteen percent of all Xers report in our MONITOR tracking that they are already saving money for retirement. While this is definitely a minority, many more, 68 percent, say they would like to.

Those who haven't figured out how to start saving are probably open to advice. Xers in general would welcome this, in fact. Our MONITOR data show Xers as the most likely to say they are "confused" about what they should be doing with their money.

But you don't want to talk to Xers about saving. That's passé. Xers want to invest. They are anxious to move forward and willing to take some chances. Establishing your business with them now is a good long-term strategy. Xers are still settling upon their preferences for things like financial services, so brand building will help you both today and tomorrow.

A few special characteristics are worth remembering: more diversity, so a greater variety of needs. A willingness to mix and match, so an openness to new, innovative financial combinations. Savvy about marketing, so not keen on hype or stereotypical sales-people. More women, so gender-specific and gender-sensitive products and communications are a must.

Perhaps most important, though, is their technological sophistication. Distribution is one of the biggest issues facing financial services companies today. While technological options should be made available to all generations, Xers will have the greatest facility for them over the long run. Indeed, they will be far less responsive to more traditional forms of distribution. Computer software is one option, but the Internet is probably the best, one requiring that financial services companies adopt a new idiom to use in their selling.

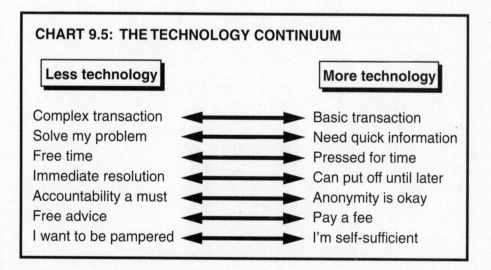

CHART 9.5: THE TECHNOLOGY CONTINUUM

Less technology	More technology
Complex transaction	Basic transaction
Solve my problem	Need quick information
Free time	Pressed for time
Immediate resolution	Can put off until later
Accountability a must	Anonymity is okay
Free advice	Pay a fee
I want to be pampered	I'm self-sufficient

Technology is not always a simple answer, though, even for Xers. Concerns about privacy must be allayed. Xers expect the worst from marketers, and any breach in privacy would only confirm their suspicions. Moreover, there remain lots of situations where the human touch is preferred to the high-tech system. So be sure to carefully match distribution options to consumer needs.

WORK AS LEISURE

The quest for balance will continue to grow in years to come. Innovative lifestyles will proliferate, designed to reconcile work and leisure. Work, though, will undergo the biggest metamorphosis. Just as work shaped the leisure styles of the eighties, leisure will shape the work styles of the future.

This creates an opportunity to do some leading edge marketing. New Balance athletic shoes has already captured the essence of this transformation in its positioning. In a recent print ad that ran in *Outside* magazine, a nondescript Boomer or Xer man is shown running above this copy: "Monday: Father. Husband. Banker. Friend. Runner. / Tuesday: Husband. Banker. Father. Runner. Friend. / Wednesday: Banker. Banker. Banker. Banker. Banker. / Thursday: Runner. Husband. Father. Friend. Banker. / Friday: ? / Achieve New Balance."

For consumers today, that is, indeed, the answer to Friday's question.

GOOD HEALTH IS A GOOD DAY AT THE OFFICE

Today thinness is giving way to wellness. Food and fitness, which for the past few decades have been the ol' one-two of good health, don't pack much of a punch anymore. To be well, you have to do more than just eat right and get the right amount of exercise.

We're told now that diets only go so far; our bodies are genetically programmed to seek a certain weight. Happiness too, perhaps. A *New York Times* headline recently announced: "Study Finds a Three-Decade Gain in American Eating Habits, but a Long Way to Go." We're eating better, but not sufficiently better. Exercise hurts even as it helps. Runner's high comes from hormones released to mask the pain of the damage done during exercise. Bad knees and bad backs are becoming less and less acceptable as trade-offs for aerobic conditioning. We give it up and give it up, and then give up more, but the better we try to feel, the worse we wind up feeling. With all of our sacrifice we still come up short.

Diet and exercise can't make up for an otherwise unwell lifestyle. On the other hand, good diet and good exercise can be completely shot by a bad day at the office. To truly be well, you have to live a healthy lifestyle. That's why we say it's all about a good day at the office. If the way you work and play and live your life makes you feel better, then you are better. Much of this has to do with relieving *stress*.

The path to wellness is the path of no stress. Vigilance against exposure to risks and disease is good in and of itself, and it also minimizes stress. But reducing stress requires more than defensive measures; it takes proactive measures—doing things to soothe the body and the mind. Running gave way to power walking, which is being replaced by foot massages and pedicures, even just a night now and then with the feet up.

In many ways this focus on wellness through lifestyle brings us full circle with the generations. We're back to where we started.

MATURES: HIDE, THEN CONQUER

As children, Matures learned that being healthy meant avoiding getting sick. Good health was preventative—decisive counter-actions to stop disease from reaching you. You didn't want to catch anything in the pre-penicillin world. Cures were few and the slightest cold could lead to something fatal. The imperative was to live a lifestyle that kept infection away.

The great flu pandemic of 1918–1919 swept through the entire world in five months, leaving perhaps 25 million people dead. Over 500,000 of these victims were Americans, and 10 percent of the American workforce was bedridden. Whole villages in Alaska were wiped out. In Western Samoa the entire population contracted the flu, and one in five people died from it.

Every disease threatened serious illness and death. Worldwide, smallpox killed 2 million a year during the forties and fifties. Syphilis took the lives of 9,000 Americans a year in the twenties, as many as 13,000 in 1940. So it went for all diseases, particularly those like staph, strep, whooping cough, measles, and polio, which hit children especially hard.

No one, it seemed, was immune. Even FDR, as strong and as powerful as he was, was a victim of polio. He survived his affliction, but, still, it crippled him. The best protections were sometimes no better than old-world remedies and reminders to eat right and dress warmly. An apple a day was often your best advice to ward off disease.

Maybe an apple a day wasn't enough, but better food was thought to help. The seventy-year-old father of one of the authors of this book, Jack Smith, Sr., had this to say about why he still prefers white bread, a taste he retains in the face of his wife's conversion to "healthy" foods like yogurt and multigrain cereals: "When I was growing up, white bread was what rich people ate. It was more expensive because it was more refined. We always thought of it as 'better' food, and that's how I still think of it."

Diets high in fats and low in legumes were the foods of the rich. Indeed, even as recently as thirty years ago, the middle-age heyday of Matures, this held true. A recent study at the University of North Carolina found that in 1965 the diets of lower-income consumers were actually nutritionally superior to those of higher-income consumers because poorer people couldn't afford meats and other foods rich in saturated fats.

Exercise was emphasized less. Calisthenics were the rule, but that was about as far as it went. Good, healthy outdoor activity was something relaxing, like getting some sun, a tanning revolution started by Coco Chanel in the twenties. The very best athletes of the day were not necessarily in the very best shape, certainly not by today's standards. Hard physical exertion was not something Matures avoided, but it was something they did for work, not for leisure.

When you got sick, though, and you needed them, doctors

would come see you. House calls were commonplace. Many women gave birth at home. Medicines were dispensed more directly. Doctors were respected figures in most communities— men, largely, who braved the elements to visit those needing care.

Matures knew disease as a threat from which they had to hide. While doctors weren't all-powerful in the fight to beat back infections, they were authorities there to help with the very best medical science had to offer. Unfortunately, quite often this was not enough.

So in the same spirit in which Matures faced every challenge, they set out to conquer disease. And their successes gave their children a respite from worry about disease and illness.

BOOMERS: WHAT, ME SICK?

Boomers grew up in a world of antibiotics and inoculations. Penicillin, available for widespread use in 1944, became a catchword for the easy fix. Its impact on the quality of people's lives was astonishing. Many serious diseases became distant memories overnight. Staph, strep, VD, TB . . . gone. And penicillin was just the start. Other antibiotics quickly followed. Streptomycin. Gramicydin. Tyrocidin. Aureomycin. Get sick? No problem. There's an antibiotic for you; 25,000 different products by 1965.

But why get sick? You could now take something to build an immunity to disease. After the start of the first vaccine trials in the mid-fifties, polio nearly vanished—76,000 cases in 1955, only 1,000 in 1967. Early and middle Boomers, at least, can all remember the massive community public health programs to get people vaccinated—those Saturday morning walks with their parents to the local high school to take a sugar cube.

The pattern was set. Nearly all life-threatening childhood diseases were reined in with massive inoculation programs. Widespread use of the measles vaccine began in 1965. Smallpox was wiped off the face of the earth by the end of the seventies, but had disappeared as a major problem years before. And with Grand Rapids, Michigan, taking the lead on January 25, 1945, even dental decay was brought under control through programs to fluoridate public water supplies during the forties, fifties, and sixties.

Boomers never knew disease as the threat their parents experienced. Boomers only knew that the shots hurt or that there were too many pills to take or that the syrup tasted awful. That got fixed, too, with one-a-day vitamins and cherry-flavored cough syrup.

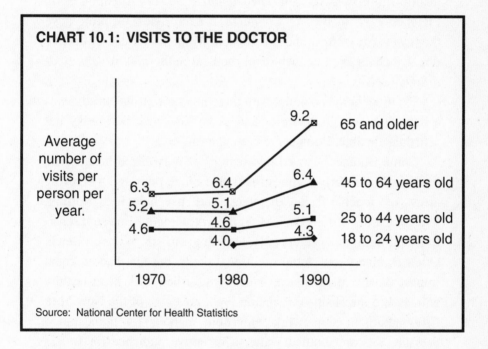

CHART 10.1: VISITS TO THE DOCTOR

Average number of visits per person per year.

65 and older
9.2

45 to 64 years old
6.3 6.4 6.4

25 to 44 years old
5.2 5.1 5.1

18 to 24 years old
4.6 4.6 4.3
4.0

1970   1980   1990

Source: National Center for Health Statistics

Boomers could take good health for granted. They didn't have to worry about survival, so they focused instead on enhancement. They expanded the notion of good health. No longer did it mean not being sick, now it meant being in shape. As Boomers saw it, you could be completely free of disease, yet still be in poor health because you weren't in shape.

Achieving this meant better nutrition—yogurt, bran, brown rice, vitamins. It also meant better exercise—jogging, running, biking, hiking. It meant, quite simply, undertaking deliberate efforts to optimize your health. Out of this came the fitness craze of the late seventies and eighties. Health clubs boomed—from 7,500 nation-wide in 1980 (not counting places like YMCAs) to almost 21,000 in 1988. Good health was an obsession, something you had to work at and make sacrifices for if you were really going to have it.

And Boomers accomplished this on their own initiative. Respect for authority figures declined, doctors included. Boomers decided that they knew better, and looked for new arbiters of health. Jim Fixx gave them *The Complete Book of Running*, Colin Fletcher gave them *The Complete Walker*, Alex Comfort gave them *The Joy of Sex*, and the Boston Women's Health Collective directly challenged conventional medical authorities in *Our Bodies, Our Selves*.

No more home cooking, with three hearty, well-balanced meals a day. Thin was in. Calories had to be low. Nutrition-savvy but schedule-flexible, Boomers rewrote the rules.

Some Boomers carried this search for maximized health even further. By the early eighties many had blitzed through a dizzying array of touchie-feelie therapies and psychologies: Rolfing; Esalen; Carlos Casteneda; TM; Tao; tarot; Gregory Bateson; sensitivity training; bioenergetics; R. D. Laing; sufism; Wilhelm Reich. Other Boomers took more traditional paths, but that had an equal impact on the marketplace, with menus filled with heart-healthy entrees and the Heart Association logo; coverage of the New York City marathon on network television; markets for home blood pressure kits and bottled water; a receptive audience for fitness gurus like Richard Simmons and Jane Fonda. Through it all a presumption of basic health and a determination to "fix" oneself through diet, exercise, and mental discipline guided them.

Matures also began to feel more assured about their own health, and benefiting from programs like Medicare and Social Security, began to look for ways to optimize their well-being. Matures felt they had earned this, and they learned from their Boomer children what it meant to be free of worry about serious diseases.

XERS: DON'T TOUCH

From Boomers to Xers, the good health handoff didn't work. The change was abrupt and fundamental. In the same year the world's last case of smallpox was discovered in Somalia, the first two homosexual men in New York City were diagnosed with Kaposi's sarcoma. Only a few short years later, the supreme confidence that Boomers felt about health had vanished.

CHART 10.2: GETTING TO KNOW YOU

Current age	Average number of sex partners since age 18
18-29	5.7
30-39	8.0
40-49	9.0
50-59	9.0
60-69	5.3
75+	3.7

Source: National Opinion Research Center, 1993.

That infamous year, 1979, was the pivot point for the transition—the final year after the introduction of penicillin in which we could feel unplagued and complacent because of our medical armamentarium. As preparations were made for the May 8, 1980 announcement by the World Health Assembly that "the World and all its peoples have won freedom from smallpox," a flurry of reports started to appear about a strange new ailment among gay men. On June 5, 1981, the Centers for Disease Control (CDC) published a report about the cases that had been seen over the previous two years by Drs. Michael Gottlieb at the UCLA Medical Center and Joel Weisman in his private Southern California practice—the first official recognition of AIDS.

The medical successes of the forties, fifties, and sixties broke down in the eighties. Many illnesses were simply too resilient for our puny medications. And our lifestyles had become too reckless and indulgent to keep these diseases at bay, not just sexually, but environmentally and socially as well. As a result serious diseases made a comeback, eliminating for Xers, in their perceptions if not in actual fact, the presupposition of good health that Boomers had enjoyed.

Xers, growing up in the shadow of the super-virus, have returned to the recognition that good health means avoiding getting sick. Don't get AIDS, for example, because there's no wonder drug to give you a miracle cure. And since you can't get inoculated for AIDS, you have to avoid it in the way you live your life.

AIDS was the big news of the eighties, and with it came a variety of diseases no one had heard of before. Even worse, AIDS, drug use, and homelessness were contributing to the emergence of more virulent strains of diseases like pneumonia and TB, strains that now pose health risks to the general population. Other immune diseases like Epstein-Barr or chronic fatigue syndrome appeared. Staph infections were now resistant to most forms of antibiotics, posing serious risks for any stay in hospitals. Strep had developed resistance, too. Measles started making a comeback in 1985.

Even cancer, the focus of much research and medical technology by Matures and Boomers, remained out of control. From 1973 to 1987, we learned, the incidence of cancer was up 14 percent. Increases were even more pronounced for lung cancer, melanoma, prostate cancer, breast cancer, and colorectal cancer.

Toxic shock syndrome showed up in the seventies and continued to quietly grow throughout the eighties. Hantaviruses started to spread, and received public notice during the Four Corners outbreak of the early nineties. The world over, it seemed, diseases

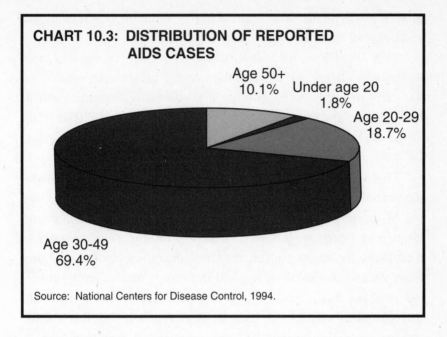

CHART 10.3: DISTRIBUTION OF REPORTED AIDS CASES

Age 50+
10.1%

Under age 20
1.8%

Age 20-29
18.7%

Age 30-49
69.4%

Source: National Centers for Disease Control, 1994.

were running wild. The names themselves were fearful: Lassa. Marburg. Ebola.

The virus fighters became minor pop heroes. Celebrated in books and movies, the scientists of the CDC and World Health Organization (WHO) have been portrayed as bigger than life. But unlike the Salks and the Sabins of yesteryear, these hardworking scientists don't believe they can eradicate diseases with miracle cures. The problems are more complicated, and the solutions start with better decisions about the way we live our lives.

Obsessive habits, though, are at least one legacy of Boomers that Xers can use to their advantage. Xers grew up in households that jogged and counted calories and shopped for healthful kids' cereals. Xers' homes were littered with the detritus of health-conscious living: empty Evian bottles, used water filters, granola bar wrappers, sweaty Danskins waiting for laundry day, diet soda cans in the recycling bin, old model Lifecycles waiting for a yard sale, sprung ab crunchers no longer offering much resistance, crushed skim milk cartons, scattered vials emptied of vitamins and protein supplements. Xers learned to pay attention to what they ate and did, and how they organized their day.

Xers also know that, while we have not been victorious in our battles with illness and disease, the average lifespan for Americans has crept upwards. Even as other diseases proved hard to control, heart attacks and strokes dropped substantially from 1950 to 1992. To get the good, though, Xers see that you have to have a vigilant lifestyle and take nothing for granted.

This means taking care to minimize exposure to risk—know the sexual history of your partner, avoid secondhand smoke, stay out of the sun, minimize the risk factors for heart disease, get an air bag in your car. It means detecting health problems early— treatments for breast cancer, prostate cancer, melanoma, and any other disease work only if applied in time. It means getting medical attention fast if you suffer a trauma—survival rates are better and complications less severe if heart attacks, shootings, falls, strokes, head injuries, and so forth are attended to immediately. It means diligent attention to getting well—misuse of an antibiotic only makes the infection worse; controlling something like AIDS involves a complicated regimen of drugs. It all comes down to managing lifestyle.

IT'S ALL ABOUT LIFESTYLE

The cycle here is not complicated: The fix-it philosophy, applied in different ways by Matures and Boomers, no longer works. All magic bullets have been spent, yet serious health threats remain. The power of medicine offers the greatest benefits to those who are more watchful. Good health comes back to lifestyle.

Something new has to be taken into account today, however— stress. Protecting yourself from disease while living a stressful life is not, as consumers see it, protecting yourself from disease. So in meeting today's challenge to live in a healthy way, consumers must face up to stress as the single biggest lifestyle issue of the day. This is the key difference from before.

STRESS-LESS

The nineties can be summed up in this one word—stress. Stress avoidance now shows up in our MONITOR research as the number-one force in the consumer marketplace. Which is to say that consumers prefer products that entail the least stress. This will continue to be the leading influence in the marketplace for the foreseeable future.

This is what good health means to people today. You must be stress-free. There is no other way to good health. Indeed, all the nutrition and exercise that went along with the fix-it craze of the seventies and eighties have become unhealthy in and of themselves because they have added so much extra worry to our lives.

The topic of coping with stress has given rise to a whirlwind cottage industry. It's swept through bookstores, where health sections bulge with titles peppered with the word stress and book indexes have copious entries under the word.

The Internet has been affected as well. Go to any search engine and enter the word stress. Thousands upon thousands of entries appear, many cross-indexed against sister topics like massage, spas, holistic medicine, biofeedback, happiness, violence, burnout, finances, angels, relaxation, grief, downsizing, time management, vitamins, aromatherapy, hypertension, insomnia, asthma, immuno-suppression, meditation, humor, and longevity.

There seem to be as many folk remedies for stress as there are for hiccups. We've run across dozens. One company we heard about, Tripod, ran a contest for people to send in original tips about managing stress. It published the thirty best submissions on its home page and awarded one of its Home Massager products to the winners. The top suggestions included deep breathing, working out (to get "that so-called 'runner's high' that makes you feel like a Maharishi who just received communion with the eternal"), sex, ice cream cones, tea, techno-rock at high volume, visualization, running nude at midnight, long drives, singing the Sesame Street theme song at the top of your lungs, imagining bossy people in your life without their clothes on, and smashing yard sale china against the walls in your basement. One winner, identified only as Tony, suggested passing it along: "In my place of employment, I am in charge of an intern. When I'm stressed I take my carpal-tunnel-preventing wrist pad, which is made of thick rubber, and proceed to beat the intern senseless. I feel much better after that. After he gets out of the hospital, I usually take him out for a beer to show him that it wasn't personal."

Many companies sell stress-relief products along this line. Sunrise Multimedia markets pieces of molded polyurethane shaped like hammers. The PC Hammer remedies computer-induced stress; specifically, "[I]t can be used to threaten the computer and keep it in line." It provides the user with "an icon of empowerment."

These examples are just a sideshow to what stress avoidance means for the marketplace as a whole. In growing numbers and with increasing fervor, consumers have reshaped the ways they live and shop in order to sidestep stress.

STRESS IN THE NINETIES

Every decade has a certain character to it, a personality that defines the ways people think of it and react to it. So far people think of the nineties in terms of stress. We have seen this in MONITOR, and confirmed it in a special CnXn study we fielded by recontacting our MONITOR respondents for a follow-up interview. Using a list of thirty-five adjectives, we asked people to think about each decade from 1940 to 1990 and to tell us which adjective they felt described each "extremely well." Every one of these decades had a distinctive profile.

Fifty-nine percent described the nineties as "stressful." The only other decades with any notable mentions were the forties and the eighties—33 percent and 39 percent, respectively, saying so. Stress sets the nineties apart in people's minds.

The meaning of this hits home even harder when we ask people about their own lives. In our ongoing MONITOR tracking, we see clearly that the percentage of people citing a need to find ways to reduce stress in their lives has hovered around 80 percent, peaking in 1994 at 85 percent. In our most recent MONITOR research, 84 percent of all Boomers, 75 percent of Xers and 71 percent of Matures cite the need to reduce stress.

TOO MUCH IS NO GOOD

It all starts with the little things. A few at a time, slowly accumulating, adding up, becoming lots and lots of little things. Soon there's a proliferation of little things. And suddenly they turn into one big problem. People aren't living stress-filled lives nowadays because of bad things in their lives. People are living stress-filled lives because they're overloaded. It's the surfeit of things, good and bad, big and small. Too many responsibilities. Too many decisions. Too many choices. Too many to-dos. Today's stress triggers are not only the awful things like grief and loss; they are mostly the ordinary, everyday things that give us grief and make us lose it.

With too much to deal with, we find ourselves overstretched, unable to maintain control, so we feel uncertain of our ability to handle an increasingly complicated array of choices and decisions. It is exactly this feeling that we see increasing. In 1985, a little over a decade ago, 58 percent of consumers agreed that life was too complicated. In our latest MONITOR tracking, 73 percent of all consumers say this.

Consumers helped bring this on themselves. The makeup of the marketplace today largely reflects the demands made on marketers during the eighties. Consumers, Boomers especially, wanted total control of marketplace transactions, so marketers obliged. Now, deluged with details, people are crying uncle.

Eighty percent of consumers say they are looking for "more and more" ways to simplify their lives. This figure has steadily crept upward. Eighty-four percent of Boomers and 77 percent of Matures express this desire, up from 79 percent and 71 percent, respectively, just four years ago.

CHART 10.4: GEN-O-GRAM—TALKING STRESS WITH A BOOMER WORKING MOM

Born:	1960
Education:	High school plus two years of college
Occupation:	Supervisor
Household:	Divorced; living with two preteen children in an apartment
On finances:	"I try to save, but it always seems like I have to dig into it for unforeseen things. For a while it was a car. I have a 401K for my retirement and I'm saving for my kids' education at our credit union."
On the times:	"I worry that the fun has gone out of growing up, with issues like crime and health. This AIDS thing is really scary. Just watch sports on TV or police shows and you see people putting on rubber gloves just to do their jobs. We can't trust our babies out there anymore. My kids want to ride their bikes in the neighborhood, but I have to set boundaries. Everything is much more serious than when we were kids. The consequences. The only danger in premarital sex when I was a kid was pregnancy. Today, with AIDS, it is death."
On the generations:	"My parents' generation was hardworking with a good sense of values. In the 1920's, there were a lot of things going on. There was a chance for a lot of change. But instead of taking advantage of it, we just let a lot of that lie there and die."
On future plans:	"I'm not really satisfied with my current job. I'm looking forward to a second career now. I want to go back to school and then go back into counseling. My mother tells me that I'm not too old to do it. "

Simplification does different things for different people. It gives some just a chance to breathe. For others it restores a sense of control. For still others it's a way of taking a second look at their priorities and getting them back in proper order. As a popular T-shirt says: "Rule #1—Don't sweat the small stuff. Rule #2—It's all small stuff."

Simplification makes people feel healthy. No surprise—stress is bad for you. We get worked up, which makes us tired, brings on headaches, and gives us ulcers. It's not unlikely that, by the close of this decade, stress will be viewed as *the* disease of the nineties.

Simplification to the point of superficiality, however, will have the opposite effect. At the same time that they want simplification, two-thirds also report they want more control. These often don't go together. Control may mean more complexity; simplification may mean less control. Getting too simple only adds stress because it undermines control. Successful marketers will simplify in ways that don't exacerbate concerns about control. Offering this balance is one of the keys to success over the next five to ten years.

GETTING TOO MUCH OF WHAT'S GOOD FOR ME IS BAD FOR ME

Wellness means feeling good about oneself. Consumers want to create lifestyles that keep them feeling well, which makes the "no pain, no gain" approach seem a lot less appropriate than one based on moderation and periodic pampering. Such healthy lifestyles will have little to do with the high-maintenance diet and exercise regimens that pervaded the seventies and eighties. Indeed, obsessing about what we eat and how we exercise can be pretty stressful.

Worrying about working a vigorous fitness program into a busy schedule each day builds stress. Keeping up with miles run and crunches done provides a little more to fret over. Fighting traffic, shopping for equipment, paying the health club, keeping up with the new styles of clothes and workouts, waiting in line for your turn on the machines . . . all of a sudden it's no fun anymore. It's just another hassle to haggle over.

The same is true of diet and nutrition. Not only is it a lot of bother to manage carefully what one eats, the whole subject is too much of a jumble to figure out. Sorting through the facts and figures is unproductive, so people abandon the effort. Three-quarters of all consumers agree, there's so much information about nutrition today, "it's confusing" to know what to eat and what not to eat. Even if they want to eat more healthfully, consumers find it difficult to puzzle through the information at hand. The worry about what to know and who to trust leaves people feeling almost as unhealthy as if they'd done nothing at all.

HEALTH AS A SIMPLE IDEA

Through MONITOR, we tracked a turnaround in attitudes about health at the end of the eighties and the start of the nineties, exactly the period when consumers began to reassess and refashion their approach to the marketplace. We keep up with a long list of health issues, and every year ask consumers whether or not they remain concerned about each of them. If respondents tell us they are not concerned about something, we follow up and ask if this is because they are taking care of it or because they just don't care. Between 1988 and 1993, attitudes shifted 180 degrees.

Over the years, as medical knowledge about diet and nutrition have advanced, consumers have become more sensitized to various health issues like smoking, drinking, blood pressure, cholesterol, sugar, salt, fiber, and fat. Indeed, it's almost a problem-of-the-year phenomenon. In our MONITOR tracking we typically see the amount of concern about any particular issue mirror the level of press coverage.

There has been a gradual sea change, however. The level of overall concern has risen, but this shift masks what's really going on.

At most, only half of all consumers express concern about any particular health issue. It's in our follow-up questions with those consumers expressing no concern where we get a clue that attitudes have actually become less obsessive, *not* more.

In our 1988 MONITOR study the majority of consumers who didn't care about a particular health issue felt that way because they were taking care of the problem. This was true of alcohol (58 percent), calcium (56 percent), blood pressure (55 percent), sugar (54 percent), salt (54 percent). By 1993 the majority of consumers who ignored a particular health issue did so because they just didn't care—alcohol (66 percent), calcium (60 percent), blood pressure (64 percent), sugar (63 percent), salt (59 percent). This is a big reversal, which continues to be seen in our latest MONITOR results.

No more worrying about nutritional panaceas. If they're easy to figure out and use, fine. Otherwise forget it. Enjoy yourself and feel good. There's only one thing that consumers continue to take into explicit account in their nutritional and health decision-making. That's fat. Otherwise, consumers have new habits.

DON'T BE SICK WITH WORRY

Consumers have adopted new habits. All point to a new fix on stress-free lifestyles as the way to good health.

Consumers report new snacking preferences. "Good" snacks are mentioned less often by consumers as something they eat frequently. Fruit is now cited by 55 percent of all consumers, versus 71 percent as recently as 1992. Raisins are down to 19 percent from 25 percent in 1992. Frozen yogurt is down from 24 percent to 15 percent.

On the other hand, mentions of "bad" snacks hold steady. Cookies, crackers, chips, popcorn, and ice cream maintain their position, while nachos and candy are up. Little indulgences provide small rewards that relieve some stress.

Consumers also report new exercise preferences. Only 16 percent of all consumers report that they participate in some sort of planned physical exercise once a week, and nearly one-third report that they never engage in any planned exercise. Fewer consumers report worrying about their weight, down year to year from 37 percent to 32 percent.

Many vigorous activities have lost favor, now mentioned less frequently as something consumers do at least twice a week. Outside work is down from 46 percent in 1992 to 29 percent; long, vigorous walks, from 38 percent to 29 percent; aerobics, 17 percent to 12 percent; bicycling, 16 percent to 11 percent.

Consumers are increasingly willing to make nutritional trade-offs. Our MONITOR tracking shows a year-to-year decline in the percentage of consumers willing to give up taste for nutrition in the foods they eat—43 percent now versus 48 percent in 1995.

Sixty-one percent agree that "when I eat out, I eat what I want and don't worry about nutrition." This level has gone down steadily since 1992, when 67 percent agreed. But it's not just taste that overrides nutrition. Speed and ease of preparation are often important, too, 54 percent of consumers agree, especially Xers. Cost is another factor, also relatively more important to GenXers.

Boomers appear unwilling to pinch off the rewards of home and family in order to meet the demands of nutrition. Only 43 percent of all Boomers report concerns about "making sure my family eats healthy and nutritional foods," down from 51 percent just a few years ago. Obsessing about eating may take away some of the enjoyment and pleasure Boomers want from family interactions.

Half of all consumers report interest in "seeking medical help from practitioners of alternative medicine." This includes acupuncture, chiropractic, herbalism, and homeopathy. Interest is expressed by 55 percent of Xers, though only by 46 percent of Matures. The focus seems to be on practices that can help people live more relaxed, comfortable lives.

Along these lines, we see several high-potential marketing opportunities to help consumers address the stress in their lifestyles.

STRESS-APPROPRIATE COMMUNICATIONS

Matures look for *continued reassurance*. They face not only the resurgent threat of disease, but also the potential loss of care due to the political scrutiny of Social Security and Medicare. Their longer life spans, partly a result of their successes in battling disease and illness, raise the possibility that they will outlive their savings. Matures, who fought so hard to bring good health to everybody, are now potentially at risk again.

Boomers will need to *come to terms* with the new health realities they face. They grew up with few worries, concerned only about achieving optimum health. Now they are looking at a future filled with problems. This is especially true when they think about how their children will cope. Help with family health will take a high priority. Reinforcing their sense of smarts and control will provide them with positive, stress-relieving support about the decisions they make.

Xers will face the future with more *resilience* than either of the other generational cohorts. They see the challenges before them as simply the way things are, and have no illusions that massive social programs will wipe out today's major diseases. Indeed, they've already seen high-profile efforts to find a cure for AIDS come to nothing. Xers don't want to feel constricted, and will look for ways to empower themselves and develop their own solutions. Sensory stimulation will contribute to their self-empowerment— relaxing aromatherapy, soothing flavors, celebratory fizzes.

Abstinence will be a more important survival requirement in Xer lifestyles than it was for Boomers or Matures. Just contrast the quintessential Boomer movie, *The Big Chill*, with the Xers' *Reality Bites*. In *The Big Chill*, fear of herpes is the reason one character's husband never strays. In contrast, one character in *Reality Bites*, who secretly keeps a log of all of her sexual liaisons, goes through the terror of learning the results of her AIDS test. A different experience altogether.

Abstinence isn't just about sex, though, it's a broader phenomenon for Xers. Avoiding risks. Hiding from danger. Not being exposed. The marketing opportunity here is to provide support and substitute satisfactions. It demands a recognition of the self-denial consumers have to practice, and of just how hard this is. And it will, perhaps, even open up markets for new kinds of safer indulgences, or for the information and lifestyle alternatives needed to facilitate abstinence.

SHORTCUTS

In our MONITOR tracking, fat has defied the usual up-one-year-down-the-next pattern of most food ingredients and additives. It continues to worry consumers. The huge, growing success of Nabisco's Snackwells is testament to this. Experts predict that low-fat foods will grow from an $18 billion category in 1994 to a $30 billion category in 1997.

Fat, though, is of most concern to older consumers—Boomers and, especially, Matures. It provides a shortcut through the nutritional information clutter, one that works particularly well for Matures. Fifty-two percent of Matures say that "low in fat" strongly influences their purchasing, compared with 47 percent of Boomers and only 36 percent of Xers. Snack preferences for fat-free foods like pretzels have risen the most among Matures, while not rising at all among Xers.

Another nutritional shortcut is *fresh*. Food stores and food service operations both recognize the importance of freshness in consumer decisions about what is healthful. It's a cue intuitively linked to the notion that something is good for you. This will be particularly important for Boomers as they look for ways to meet the demands of their schedules and their families without sacrificing the goodness of what they eat and serve.

A final nutritional shortcut is *ethnic*. Many positive elements come together with ethnic foods—variety, good taste, balanced diet, good nourishment, vitamins, proteins, avoidance of bad alternatives. Despite the attention given them since the early eighties, ethnic foods have by no means tapped out their potential. More traditional ethnic styles like Mexican and Italian continue to see growth, and many more new styles stand ready in the wings— Thai, Caribbean, Polynesian, Vietnamese, Cuban. Xers are already predisposed to cultural diversity, and consider these kinds of alternative ideas superior. Indeed, combinations of ethnic styles present the long-term growth opportunity of tomorrow. Trendy new restaurants now feature dishes offering this—for example, an Eastern European meat entree, a South American vegetable, a Polynesian sauce, and a Middle Eastern bread . . . all on the same plate.

THINK "AWAY"

Twenty years ago over 60 percent of all our spending on food took place in food stores. Now the majority of our spending goes to food service establishments. The reasons for this are clear: Matures need the convenience. Boomers need to save time. Xers are out and about. But the pattern of food service spending is not confined simply to restaurants.

We order take-out or have food delivered. Caring for our health in the ways we eat at home means thinking more broadly than just about what we cook at home. Many good marketing opportunities exist here.

One is to put together convenience with nutrition. Much take-out now is an afterthought, and where it's not, the food is usually of lesser quality.

Also remember that just because people don't cook at home doesn't mean they don't want to be involved in some way in the preparation of the meal. They worry about doing the right thing for their families. Preparing it for the table, instead of cooking it from scratch, becomes the new way in which people add TLC. Sensitive marketers will find ways to make preparation more than just scraping food from a paper carton onto a plate.

Finding new approaches involves rethinking relationships to consumer lifestyles, indeed, breaking down the walls of our business concepts and categories. A grocery store can be a restaurant, and vice versa. A sit-down restaurant can have a gourmet-style take-out business. Convenience stores can serve fast food. Fast food restaurants can offer gourmet coffees and desserts.

Kroger has just opened a store in downtown Atlanta with gourmet food and five chefs. It's a small store with a heavy emphasis on take-home meals. It also serves as a test-bed for new recipes that can be offered in its other, bigger locations. It's a radical attempt to move beyond traditional business categories to offer more stress-free, lifestyle-supportive options. And because this particular store is near the Georgia Capitol, it sells newspapers from around the country. Every wall is going down—it's a newsstand, too!

THE FOCUS IS ON LIFESTYLE

Simplification is not just about fewer shopping decisions. It isn't simply about cutting down on variety. Indeed, if you offer only one brand or just one flavor, you may actually wind up complicating the shopping process. Think of simplification not just in terms of shopping decision-making; think of it in terms of lifestyle integration. That's how you get control at the same time.

It's about making your product or service fit the ways people live so they can buy or use it *without going out of their way.* Think about how to minimize the need to make special trips or special arrangements to buy or use what you have to offer. The idea is not to make it simple once they're there; it's integrating it seamlessly into their lifestyles.

Matures want it to fit where they are, which is usually at home. Boomers want it to fit wherever they are at the time, which is driven by their daily schedule. Xers want it to move with them. A simpler lifestyle is one where consumers don't have to add hassle to get a product or service they need.

In their lifestyles, consumers look for moderation, for new, meaningful alternatives that aren't totally out of the mainstream. Gardening fits all of these criteria, and it's a new Boomer craze. Spirituality also flows out of these priorities—angels are the rage; *The Celestine Prophecy* and *The Bridges of Madison County* have been huge bestsellers.

Consumers want to feel good, and thus feel healthy. They want to make indulgence a part of living, not something reserved for special occasions. They want to be celebrated, not accommodated. They want relaxation, not sacrifices. Weight Watchers understands this. Over the Christmas season of 1995 Weight Watchers shifted its emphasis from the sacrifice of fixing it to the relaxation of feeling good. Being well is not doing it for looks, but doing it to feel good. The right weight is the one that feels good to your body, not one that looks good to the rest of the crowd.

EMPOWERMENT

Simple does not mean dictated. Consumers want it to be simpler, but they don't want to be told how to do it. Make options available and give consumers tools to use them, like software or on-line sites that track and store data, particularly for things like exercise routines or insurance submissions. New, alternative approaches will attract more customers, especially Boomers and Xers.

Spas are booming because they offer self-directed, healthful stress relief. They restore energy and vitality, they don't repair damage. Massages. Loofah scrubs. Mud baths. Facials. Steam baths. Pedicures. Herbal wraps. Hydrotherapy. Reflexology. No more making time for workouts. Now it's reserving time for a makeover or a workover. Spas are satisfying a broad need that can be applied elsewhere. Consumers want to be massaged and revitalized. Products that do so will be sought. Services that treat them this way will be preferred.

FOREVER AND NOW

People want the long-term benefits of better health. Nine out of ten consumers in every generation express the need to do something now "to make sure my health will be good when I get older." This health concern has not changed since we began measuring it.

What we have seen change is the willingness of people to trade off their long-term health for short-term pleasures. Just a few years ago 68 percent of consumers agreed that "I am concerned about doing what I can in order to ensure good health today; I'll let the future take care of itself." In our latest tracking only 59 percent agreed with that. This willingness has dropped most among Boomers and Matures— down from 63 percent to 56 percent, and from 74 percent to 58 percent, respectively.

The long term will be compromised by stress. Short-term gains that take a toll on the long term because they add stress are less and less acceptable. This preference defines the terms by which consumers participate in the marketplace—terms that say no stress or no go.

GENERATIONS AT HOME

Mitchell Hochberg, a developer in affluent Westchester County north of New York City, first noticed the trend in the early nineties. Traditionally, couples buy a smaller home when their children leave the nest for college or for jobs. But a few years ago a new breed of empty-nesters started asking for something else: luxurious, maintenance-free living in a house comparable in size to their family home. Big kitchens. Palladian windows. Amenities like tennis courts and bike trails.

"It's kind of like the Club Med approach to a house," Hochberg explained. "They want to feel like they're living at a resort. They can have Saturday morning tennis games, glitzy bathrooms with two sinks, a steam bath. These people get so excited by the new house, it's amazing."

Or, perhaps, not so amazing. These customers provide the first glimpse of what will happen as Boomers move into this real estate market. These customers, just now showing up in realtors' offices, represent the transition from Mature empty-nesters to Boomer empty-nesters. Their buying reflects the different values that motivate their generation.

As their children start to move on, Boomers will refocus on themselves while insulating their psyches from stress and worry. For Matures, home and family were closely linked. When the family grew up, the house could get smaller. The tasks ahead weren't as big, so the need for space diminished.

For Boomers, life does not become more intimate when the kids leave; it becomes more expansive. Vast new horizons open. It's time to find new excitements, fresh pleasures. They want homes to inaugurate their new lives, not be a retreat following old triumphs.

These Boomers are reaching the point where they will have fewer of the big responsibilities that made their lives hectic and stressful. Spacious, well-appointed houses will let them breathe, relax, and recharge as they prepare for their next adventure.

Boomers won't trade down once their children leave home. They will sell their family homes, but also will break all the old rules while doing so. Though they may have less interest in more bedrooms, a sturdy playroom, and a big backyard, they will pay for kitchen upgrades, extra conveniences, quality, and, especially, more space.

This is an important generational development in real estate. These empty-nesters, now with fewer financial obligations, will find their resources freed up, available to buy new furniture, new fixtures, even new additions. These buyers are wealthier than other households in their age bracket, with a median net worth 50 percent more than married couples with kids. They will make up a big part of the high end of the housing market for many years. As a result, these new buyers will have a profound effect on the type of housing built over the next ten to twenty years. *USA Today* reported some initial signs of this coming trend in mid-1996. The vice president of research for Chicago Title and Trust noted that buyers trading up to bigger homes, not first-time home buyers, were driving the home market during the first half of 1996. William Apgar, executive director of the Joint Center for Housing Studies at Harvard University, said that this "trade-up segment will be an important anchor" in the home-buying market through the end of the nineties. Clearly we have come a long way from the early tract houses of Levittown, New York.

UNCLE SAM WANTS YOUR AMERICAN DREAM TO COME TRUE

"No cash down for veterans." For veterans of World War II, the GI Bill made single-family housing affordable. It fueled the housing boom that led to the creation of suburbs and the modern housing industry.

Home ownership was the ultimate symbol of arrival, a signal to others that you were now part of the middle class. This was an important goal in the postwar pursuit of the good life. And if, from Levittown to countless other suburbs and subdivisions across America, these starter homes looked pretty much alike, it didn't matter. For up-and-coming Matures, conformity was okay— exactly the sort of tangible possession that proved you, too, had a piece of the American Dream.

As America rebuilt itself after the war, Matures thrived in the pursuit, and for many the acquisition, of middle-class status. Home was the place to demonstrate and reaffirm your commitment to the spirit of the times. Spending money on the home—adding rooms over the garage, setting up backyard swing sets, or installing a dishwasher—signified reaching another step on the upward-mobility ladder as well as an understanding of the "virtue" of spending on tangibles. Spending time on the home—devoting weekends to finishing basements, installing flagstone patios, or pruning bushes—signaled an understanding of the "virtue" of leisure that was both home-based and productive.

Soon Mature homeowners discovered that by periodically selling their homes they could almost automatically increase their capital stake and continually buy a bigger and better house, until at some point in the future, usually around retirement time, they could cash out of the market with a sizable investment gain. The emotional dream was an economic anchor as well—as we have noted, for Matures, the emotional and the material were linked together as one.

From Cape Cods to split-levels, the homes Matures bought were symbolic not only of the good life, but also of the sanctity of the American family. Norman Rockwell magazine covers came to life, with Dad mowing the lawn, Mom cooing over her new refrigerator, and teenage daughters chastely kissing their dates goodnight on the front porch. Much of the time the kids' needs came first. Boomer children each got their own bedroom before their Mature parents would even daydream about having their own bathroom.

Matures succeeded. They largely realized their goals, going further than they might have dared to dream growing up. No wonder that today, in our MONITOR tracking, 83 percent of Matures, far and away the largest among generations, agree that "my current home is nicer than the one I grew up in."

Matures still live this dream. They remain actively involved with their homes. Free weekend time is often spent reading, gardening, working in the yard—conventional pastimes for older people. Less typically however, many Matures stand ready to upgrade their environment, planning changes that go beyond necessary maintenance. In our MONITOR research, 41 percent say they plan to redecorate, 31 percent say they will put in a new garden, and 19 percent say they are going to buy new furniture. As New York City interior designer Robert Bray puts it, these people are busy creating their "final resting place."

WELCOME TO MY BIRTHRIGHT

Peanuts character Charlie Brown once said, "Security is coming home and hearing your mother in the kitchen," words that could easily have come out of many a school-age Baby Boomer. Millions of Boomers could count on seeing their Mature mom at home when they got there. While suburban America wasn't always tidy and cheerful, Boomers did see the home as generally comforting. It validated the middle-class family norm and reinforced the sense that home was a safe place where kids' problems were quickly resolved.

Television. Patios. Dens. Barbecues. Croquet sets. Princess phones. Pajama parties. Jungle gyms. For this new generation, the good life that home provided was no remote dream fulfilled or a symbol of success and achievement. That's what home ownership was for their parents. Home life was just a fact of life, and eventually, another expectation. Realtors, contractors, designers, architects, furniture manufacturers, landscapers, and more all eagerly anticipated future profits as these Boomers, soaked in the good life, came of age.

CHART 11.1: HOME STUFF, THEN AND NOW

MATURES	BOOMERS	Xers
Chevrolet	Toyota	Saturn
Timex	Casio	Swatch
Life	*USA Today*	*Wired*
Cadillac	BMW	Lexus
Tonic water	Perrier	Evian

But Boomers threw everyone a curveball. As the leading edge left their neighborhoods for jobs or college, they didn't follow the plan. Instead of marrying and having children, Boomers settled into interim lifestyles. And they did so in rentals. They were sure there was plenty of time to figure out permanent plans. Meanwhile, they explored new things and got in touch with their inner selves.

In 1975 we asked Boomers which decisions they believed were better postponed "until after the age of thirty." Their top answers included buying homes and starting families. They weren't ready to settle down for a "real" home. If and when they did decide to buy a house, financing would hardly be a problem.

For many Boomers these first rented residences were mere pit stops between experiences. There were few intrinsic rewards at home that could compare to the experiences they could have away from home. Time and money were spent elsewhere. Apartments and walk-ups were stocked with only the important essentials: Roommates. Big speakers. Other stereo components. Plants galore. A mood enhancer or two, like lava lamps or black lights or incense burners. Beanbag chairs. A wok hanging on the kitchen wall. And one or two pieces of do-it-yourself furniture.

Magazines and retailers were quick to jump on this new approach to living. Meredith Publishing started *Apartment Life*. Door Store and The Workbench sold accessories and trappings that furnished these interim living spaces.

Modest and spare, these households were stocked with what Boomers could afford. Not being able to afford too much was alright; indeed, it was morally superior. Their lifestyles reflected an ongoing rejection of material possessions. Boomers didn't want any of it. Along with Cadillacs and twelve-year-old scotch, a house in the 'burbs represented all they didn't want to be.

By the end of the seventies, Boomers started thinking about settling down. As the seventies ended, they sought more settled approaches to living, lifestyles providing a home base for success-fully competing. Even single Boomers put down roots. All hit the stores for china and crystal, furniture and lamps, washers and dry-ers, rugs and artwork, even houses. To stay on top of this, in 1981 *Apartment Life*, as we noted earlier, became *Metropolitan Home*.

Boomers also recognized the financial benefits of owning real estate—tax deductions and wealth creation. Those with the early edge reaped the greatest rewards. Even as mortgage rates skyrock-eted, a get-in-while-you-can mentality, combined with the size of the cohort and the sheer competition for what was available, drove real estate prices through the roof.

Homes themselves became showplaces, trophy rooms filled with the material goods that proved success. Even the sizes of homes grew sharply. In 1964 the average house had 1,470 square feet of living space; only 15 percent of new houses had 2.5 baths. By the time the real estate frenzy subsided in the late eighties, the typical new house had almost 2,100 square feet, a two-car garage, and 2.5 baths. Bathrooms became mini-spas, as comfort-conscious Boomers installed Jacuzzis and Shower Massages. Kitchens were designed or remodeled to accommodate stove-top ranges, indoor grills, and other gourmet gadgets.

Return on investment was the reigning notion. Sell one at a profit. Buy another. Sell that one at a profit. Renovate one to boost its value. Homes were first and foremost a good investment. The typical Levittown tract house that sold for about $7,000 in 1947 cost $15,000 in 1967—a good, solid return but nothing spectacular. In 1980 that house would cost $60,000. A mere six years later, $125,000. All of a sudden, prices were exorbitant and Boomers were scrambling to get their share.

Having to trade off emotional satisfactions for windfall profits eventually wore thin, however. As the eighties turned the corner into the nineties, Boomers, feeling frustrated, disenchanted, and victimized, began to take a second look at the role of home in their lives. Faced with an increasingly hostile and unpredictable world, home was one of the few places where Boomers could find some protection from outside pressures and demands.

This trend has continued to grow, until today it has become a new emotional commitment to home. Now, as they build and buy, Boomers are more concerned about heart and soul than about profit and loss. The reigning notion is "return on enjoyment." Home has to be a safe, stress-free haven, more like "fulfillment central" than "asset optimizer."

For many Boomers this has meant rediscovering home-centered divertissements, such as gardening, decorating, or just puttering around the house. In our most recent MONITOR research, 46 percent of Boomers expected to redecorate or paint in the coming year, while 42 percent planned to landscape or put in a new garden. Retailers like Home Depot have made a connection with this return to enjoyment. They offer what's needed and they hire knowledgeable salespeople who can ensure that the home improvement experience of consumers is not frustrating or unproductive. If it's fun, it gives consumers what they are seeking and provides them with the respite they want.

This must be working because we see an increase in the percentage of Boomers agreeing that all or most of their satisfaction comes from home and family—65 percent saying so in our most recent MONITOR tracking compared with just 54 percent in 1992. Additionally, 46 percent of Boomers report that, compared with a year ago, they are spending more time with their children.

Picking up on this theme, IKEA, a furniture and home furnishings retailer, developed a TV commercial centered on a forty-something couple with two young boys, who have recently adopted another youngster, Sam. Combining emotional tugs with practical considerations, the ad salutes adoption while promoting IKEA's reasonable prices. This commercial communicates the idea that this choice is praiseworthy, but also entails tough financial realities associated with having another child in the household. IKEA is the place to go to deal with these challenges. The ad also allays any concerns about quality by showing Sam arriving at his new home where, to his amazement, he and his new brothers are even allowed to jump on the bed; it's sturdy enough to take it.

DOWN, BUT NOT OUT

Xers are just now beginning to contemplate buying a home and establishing a household. One-third of Xers tell us in our MONITOR research they are "currently" looking for a new place to live. Almost as many Xers as Boomers, 29 percent and 33 percent respectively, say that they expect to buy new furniture in the coming year. The desire to move up is natural at this stage in their lives, and 45 percent of Xers agree that their current residence is not as nice as the one in which they grew up. Our most recent data show an increase in recent years in the proportion of Xers who say they are saving for a home—from just 16 percent in 1992 to 23 percent today.

Home ownership is a dream to Xers too, but also one of their biggest worries. Unlike Boomers, they can't presume success. In one of the thirty-plus public issue polls we do each year for *Time* magazine cover stories, in 1990 we asked Xers to compare themselves with the young adults of the seventies. In general, Xers felt they were better off. The one notable exception was in their prospects for buying a house. While three-quarters believed they would wind up with a high-paying job, 69 percent believed they would have more difficulty buying a house than young Boomers did in the seventies. Less than one-quarter of these Xers reported that they actually expected to be able to buy a house one day. This is tough for a generation in which one-third see an expensive home as a sign of success and accomplishment.

These attitudes reflect real circumstances. For households headed by people twenty-five to thirty-four years old, median real income dropped 11 percent from 1973 to 1992. And, notes economist Michael Carliner of the National Association of Home Builders, it's likely that this drop in income was even steeper than the statistics indicate. Young adults living with parents probably experienced more of a decline in real income, and they are not counted in these calculations. Today's new home buyers are forced to look at more expensive houses on less sizable incomes. The prospects for owning a home come close to being the impossible dream for Xers.

Xers seek something different anyway. They never developed the sort of emotional attachment to home that Boomers did. While Xers today are forced to put off home ownership or rethink it for financial reasons, they will not return to previous notions of home. Boomers put off moving to the suburbs for reasons other than finances, even if finances weren't available, but they did eventually return to that life because it held meaning for them.

CHART 11.2: GEN-O-GRAM—TALKING WITH A LIVE-AT-HOME Xer

Born:	1975
Education:	High school and ongoing
Occupation:	Works for Dad
Household:	Living at home with parents
On finances:	"I'm saving for an apartment to live on my own. It's expensive out there. My parents let me live here, rent free, as long as I go to school."
Plans:	"I'm not really one for education. I'm a doer, not a thinker. The only thing I've ever planned for is just to get a job, get married, and have kids. I don't want to be an old fuddy-duddy father, in my fifties, having kids. As a younger parent, it seems like more fun. Some of my friends, their dads are too old to do anything with them and it kind of bums them out. Sometimes, they borrow my dad because he is only 42. My father and I do a lot together."
Concerns:	"The only thing that really bothers me is not being able to accomplish my goals in the time I set. Here I am at 23 and I'm still living at home. All my friends do, too. I only know one guy who just got married and doesn't. As far as the rest of the world goes, it worries me, but I don't lose sleep over it. To me, it's just the way the world is. It's never going to be perfect. I guess I try to help out sometimes. When I am going to San Francisco, I make an extra sandwich to give to someone on the street. That sort of thing. I like to help individuals. "

Far fewer Xers know about stay-at-home moms or carpools, family meals or family vacations, safe parks or open neighborhoods. Dislocation in their lives has diminished the role of home as an emotional centerpiece. They do remember happy times, but these recollections are a lot less likely to bring lumps to the throat. Xers will build something new rather than re-create something old. They will find something *to* remember rather than try to recall something *that* they remember.

Finances and feelings may have them down, but that's not going to keep them from settling down. Indeed, they are eager to move ahead. Xers are less restrained than were Boomers at the same age. For example, in contrast to what we found among Boomers in 1975, fewer Xers today express a desire to wait until after age thirty to have children. This will accelerate their decisions to make homes. At the same time, Xers are more likely to wait until after age thirty to decide where in America they want to live—a reflection, we suspect, of their sense that moving around will never be easy again.

THE MATURING HOME

Generational perspectives and goals do overlap. For example, Matures will be selling older homes that, at first glance, may seem outdated to many younger buyers. These houses, though, are more than just old. They are vintage homes—bungalows from the twenties, ranches from the sixties, colonial revivals. Today's first-time buyers are of a generation for whom retro-eclectic is chic. These homes will attract. Matures will search for ways to sell at a profit that also afford new buyers a chance to renovate and repair. Marketers should look for ways to dovetail these generational perspectives.

In their new homes, Matures will need easy access to medical care. In-home medical services that include technologies for long-distance checkups would significantly ease hardships, particularly for older consumers in rural areas. Emergency needs can be monitored, and assistance dispatched when required. Home security systems could tie into this as well. Computer- and telecommunications-driven medical services could be extended to include Internet hookups with software shortcuts to key web sites.

Don't stock up on rocking chairs, though. Matures worked hard and earned their way. Now, they feel, is the time to enjoy life. So enjoy it they will. Matures don't want to be extravagant, but neither do they want to be passive old fogies. Stylish comfort. Creature comforts. Sensible technology, not unnecessary gadgetry. Focus on their age as another of their victories, and fill their houses with the spoils of that triumph.

BOOM AT HOME

Boomers want home like it used to be. Not the house itself so much as that sense of security and well-being they remember fondly. They want homes and home products that appeal to this nostalgia.

While you don't need to pipe in the Donna Reed theme song to make a house resonate with nostalgia, sights and sounds from the fifties and sixties will nevertheless help Boomers recall the best moments of their carefree childhoods. Go beyond simply reviving Boomer-era icons. Update the objects. One company has reissued the once ubiquitous black rotary phone. On this new model, however, the numbers around the dial mask today's requisite push buttons.

Boomers also want to feel in control at home. No Love Canals. No radon. No *E. coli* in the water. No tricky staircases. No nearby power lines. No unsecured crawl spaces. They're all on Boomer watch lists. Explicitly acknowledge these risks and give definitive proof of their absence. Provide products that reduce these risks in existing houses.

Boomer homes have become technological command centers, although often with more technology than command. Remotes lie scattered about the den. VCRs play back static. Cordless phones crackle in various rooms. Garage door openers get lost. Computers sit too far from the phone jacks. Video game players litter the kids' rooms. Everybody has their own TV and CD–clock radio. None of it is integrated, and much time gets wasted trying to figure things out. Homes with built-in systems that organize components will be hot sellers.

Work will be particularly affected by this. Homes must increasingly accommodate the needs of consumers who want to do more of their work there. Over three-quarters of all Boomers want some kind of office environment at home, whether for full- or part-time use. For Boomer families, a dedicated office space will be crucial. Not only will it make work at home more efficient, it will help compartmentalize work-related stress behind closed doors, thus maximizing the possibility of return on enjoyment elsewhere in the house. At-home work space could be built in, or it could be installed as a cubicle in a small room or in a corner of a bigger room.

Flexible floor plans are essential. Boomers have restructured the American family. Marketers must pay attention to all variations. Traditional households—two parents, one earner, and children from a single marriage—are declining. Alternatives abound: Married couples with children and two earners. Married couples with no children, one earner or two earners. Extended families of related adults and children centered around one married couple. Single-headed households, with or without children, with or without other related adults. Married couples with children from previous marriages. The existence of all these variations has an impact on the home buying and home furnishings markets—singles and households of nonrelated adults represented 30 percent of first-time home buyers in 1990.

These various sorts of families have quite different requirements for homes. They operate, relax, interact, and entertain themselves on different schedules. They have different needs for private and shared spaces—bathrooms and bedrooms that split up differently. Yet, they will all look at the same houses when they go to buy one. Flexibility in the ways rooms can be put together and living spaces allocated will make a home more adaptable to the needs of all sorts of potential buyers. And this trend will only grow as Xers get into the market.

Boomers are most likely to be planning to renovate. In our MONITOR tracking, 24 percent of Boomers are planning to remodel or make additions in the near future. Fully half plan to redecorate within a year. No wonder that the Association of Home Builders estimates that by the year 2000, spending on home renovation will increase 56 percent, to $180 billion annually, up from $115 billion in 1995.

Kids' needs will be a priority. Children are an increasingly important part of Boomer households. Sixty-two percent of Boomers say they express themselves through raising their children, and 47 percent relax by spending time with their kids. So when it comes to fixing up, purchasing, or furnishing a home, it's kids above all: Entertainment rooms and big kitchens where the whole family can gather. Large backyards. Proximity to schools. Secured access from the street.

THE X-HOUSE

While Xers appreciate the look of expensive homes, Xer ideas about what to put inside their houses, especially their first homes, will reflect basic needs and financial constraints more than image. But amenities added later will reflect new lifestyle considerations.

- Technology centers tied to entertainment systems. The PC won't stand alone from the TV. Internet video and music will be fed through stereo speakers. Computer software will run the CD player and set the VCR. Vacation photos will be stored on CD-ROMs and displayed on high-resolution TVs. Access will be throughout the house, not centralized in a single family room. The time to catch Xers with this is now. Boomers and Matures have largely bought their systems, but one in four Xers—compared with one in seven Boomers—is actively seeking new home entertainment systems.

- Kitchens will no longer cook food so much as unpack and process it for consumption. Warmers for take-out food. Entertainment corridors equipped with storage for snacks and beverages. Timers that can be set from the cell phone in the car to defrost and cook dinner as you drive home. Refrigerator spaces resized to hold only condiments and sides, no main dishes. More pantry and freezer space for desserts. Built-in calorie counters and fat meters.

- Private areas will be very important. Reserving a space of your own is a hedge, a means of emotional self-protection.

- Xers will want privacy, but they will also want a place for friends. Mature homes were designed around family areas—dining rooms, family rooms, rumpus rooms, dens. Boomer homes were designed around individual spaces—bathrooms, fitness areas, bedrooms. Xer homes will be designed around places for friends. These are the emotional enclaves of this generation, and networks of friends will continue to be an important part of their lives even as they settle into their own family situations. Some of this already exists and can be adapted: Guest rooms. Big common areas. Recreation spaces. Much of it, though, will have to be invented.

- Multiethnic styles should be considered. Xers reflect more diversity, which will show up in their family situations. Not only will marriages and holidays and religious observances be affected, but homes as well. New kinds of spaces will be needed that reflect the tastes and preferences of mixed households.

- Remind Xers that owning a home is a superior form of risk management. For a generation reared on uncertainties, investing in a home provides some measure of security in their lives. Perhaps not as a way to get rich quick, but certainly as a way to simply ensure a roof over their heads. It's back to basics—a place to come home to.

THE NO-WORK HOME

Irrespective of generation, there is one thing that all consumers want in a home—ease and convenience. In our MONITOR tracking over the last fifteen years, we see this as a major turnaround in consumer preferences. In 1981 just under two-thirds of all consumers said they preferred furnishing their homes to make them "easy to take care of," rather than making them "gracious and attractive though more work." In our most recent tracking, agreement was one point shy of 80 percent, consistently high across all generations and equally true of men and women. Home is back, but not the work.

Furnishings, home care products, and homes themselves must reflect this ever-increasing desire for ease over attractiveness. This is not to suggest that consumers want an unattractive house, but they are less and less willing to make big sacrifices to maximize attractiveness. This is particularly noteworthy among women, because they continue to see themselves as the CEOs of the home while also recognizing that they play a big role in generating needed income for the family. This combination of responsibilities makes for a big job.

The importance of home and family for women is on the rise. In just the last few years, women are increasingly likely to cite home and family as a priority. For example, since 1993 the percentage of women agreeing that "most working mothers would rather stay home and be with their children full-time" has risen from 57 percent to 66 percent, and this increase is true of both working and nonworking women. Along with this is an increasing interest in returning to more traditional styles of homemaking.

Women remain conflicted about these choices and responsibilities. Most women, 68 percent, believe it is "harder and harder for a woman to feel she is a successful person if she is a housewife." Increasingly women seek time to themselves as a refuge from home, family, and work conflicts.

We examined the topic of women reclaiming their private lives in a study completed for *Victoria* magazine in 1994. Most of the Xer and Boomer women surveyed expressed the need to regain some control over their lives. Twenty percent of these women told us that not only did they feel entitled to take time for things they wanted to do, they actually took this time for themselves. These women were not retreating or having midlife crises. In fact, these women in the vanguard were generally more satisfied with their lives, knew what they wanted, and felt in control. They made the effort to reset their priorities so they would have the time they needed to satisfy their emotional needs. This is a new home-based need for women. Homes must be designed to support it.

It is not enough anymore for a home simply to be there. Homes shouldn't rile. They should offer, instead, the life of Riley.

BRAND LAND, WHERE RECIPROCITY RULES

Many years ago Prudential coined one of the most memorable lines in the history of advertising: "Own a piece of the rock." A simple statement, compelling in its day and emblematic of what brands used to mean to consumers. Come to Prudential, it beckoned, to get your piece of the good life.

Prudential doesn't say that anymore. Times have changed and so have brands. Today Prudential says, "Be your own rock." Don't come to Prudential; do your own thing. Prudential will come to you.

In the past, brands ruled. No more. Consumers have turned the tables on brands. Now brands have to come knocking. "Be your own rock," Prudential says. Live your own version of the good life, and we'll be there to help you do it, however and whenever you see fit.

This is a new era for brands, one governed by the *reciprocity* model. The old model, a one-way communication from brand to consumer, has yielded to reciprocal exchange. Consumers today have more options and more information so brands can no longer dictate terms. Brands must look, listen, and learn, taking their cues from consumers. And giving something back to consumers in response.

Historically, marketers set the terms of transactional relationships with consumers. Brands determined the when, where, and how of what they offered. This one-way dependency broke down in the sixties and seventies. Experimentation and exploration meant consumers were beginning to use and mold brands according to their individual designs. This evolved into a determination by consumers to win mastery in the marketplace, and by the mid-eighties, consumers had even wrangled away control over price.

Today the situation is nearly the reverse of the fifties, as brands themselves are ruled. Consumers set the terms of their marketplace relationships, and marketers eagerly seek to meet terms set by consumers. It's the rhetoric of business in the nineties: Advertisers talk in terms of direct response. Database marketers talk in terms of relationships. Manufacturers talk in terms of customer satisfaction. Information specialists talk in terms of smart systems.

Reciprocity is about consumers telling marketers what they want and marketers responding in kind ... over and over again. It's about interactive, continuous, real-time dialogue replacing traditional models of advertising and consumer communications.

Reciprocity is a bit of a paradox, because for marketers it means winning by not trying to win, being in control by not trying to be in control, playing a role by not trying to play a role. It means letting consumers rule and being there to facilitate or provide support as consumers seek it out.

Peter Seeley, the former head of marketing for The Coca-Cola Company, sees this as the natural evolution of an information-based economy. Marketers had the initiative when information was stored in unwieldy, high-cost mainframes. As technologies like bar codes and store scanners came along, retailers took the initiative away from manufacturers because they gained control of information. Now, with technology and access to information in the hands of individuals, consumers have the initiative. Seeley sees the Internet as leading to the ultimate triumph of consumers in the struggle for control of the marketplace.

There is much wisdom in Seeley's analysis and we don't dispute any of it. But there's a generational angle that has played a crucial part in this story. Matures were content to let brands control. Fitting in and respect for authority were core values. The good life of the American Dream was tied to big brand names. Quality meant expensive. Brand loyalty was a virtue.

Boomers never bought into this. They were rule breakers from the get-go, and that applied to brands too. They forced brands to extend themselves, to invest in new, not in established, brands, to chop their prices, and to create new promotional campaigns. They punished brands that weren't responsive or responsible. They embraced no-name brands and me-toos.

Xers know nothing of the world of brands that Matures built and that Boomers grew up with. Xers have never known a market in which brands dominated transactional relationships with consumers. They experienced a marketplace in which brands were on the defensive, reeling from the growing and increasingly effective attacks from consumers. In other words, Xers grew up assuming consumers were in control of their transactional relationships.

So we arrive at reciprocity. In a recent MONITOR-based study on consumer responsiveness in the nineties that we completed for *USA Weekend*, 85 percent of all consumers agreed that unless they spoke out and made their views known, "no one else will look out for [their] interests." Consumers are insisting upon a business model based on reciprocity. Just look at what consumers told us they have done in the recent past:

- Fifty-nine percent have called a business to complain about something; 35 percent have called a business to express satisfaction.

- Fifty-four percent have written a letter to a business to complain; 43 percent have written a letter of praise to a business.

- Twenty-seven percent have written a letter to the media to express their views on some issue; 20 percent have called a radio or TV talk show.

- Twenty-two percent have called an 800 or a 900 number to answer a TV poll; 17 percent have called an 800 or a 900 number to answer a poll in a newspaper or magazine.

These are huge percentages. No fewer than 60 percent of all consumers have taken some action to record their opinion—largely unsolicited and without any assurance of a response! Many have taken more than one action.

People don't want to be talked to; they want to do the talking. People want their say, and they expect businesses to listen. Many businesses are. Prudential has. So has Saab—its ads encourage consumers to "find your own road." So has Reebok—its ads no longer tout "Reebok Planet," now they tell consumers to say to themselves, "This is my planet."

I DON'T BELIEVE YOU

One of the core elements of our MONITOR research is an ongoing measurement of the trust people have in public and private institutions—political, religious, economic, educational, media, professional, business. Since the early seventies we have noted a steady decline. It was steepest in the late eighties and early nineties when, for several consecutive years, we saw a drop in confidence in every single institution, every single year, no exceptions.

Consider doctors. When we initiated our tracking over twenty-five years ago, doctors were at the top of the list. More than 80 percent of all consumers reported a great deal of confidence in the advice they got from doctors. By 1994 only 53 percent of consumers said the same; pharmacists scored better. Media institutions have tumbled from percentages in the fifties and sixties to percentages in the teens and low twenties. Religious leaders and educational institutions, from the forties and fifties to the low twenties. Corporations, salespeople, and advertisers sit in single digits.

In such a mood it's no surprise that consumers lost confidence in brands. The economy itself put pressure on brands during the seventies and eighties. Price became more and more important as recession after recession emptied people's pocketbooks. What a brand stood for, and the value it contained, became muddled.

Through this, Matures remained a little more trusting of brands, and a little more reliant on them than Boomers, and later, Xers. For example, Matures are still more likely to agree that, in general, most manufacturers make an effort to create products and services that people really want.

We have seen a sudden turnaround, though. Our MONITOR tracking over the last couple of years no longer shows declines in institutional trust. It's bottomed out—it's stable, though low. And in a few cases—doctors, religious leaders, public schools, newspapers, corporations, government—we see the levels of trust slowly creeping up. These recent results are a notable reversal of a twenty-five-year downward trend.

But consumers are not going back to where things used to be. While confidence in institutions was dropping, self-reliance was picking up. If I can't rely on anyone or anything else, consumers said to themselves, then I'll do it myself. That's the number one thing in which people have a great deal of confidence and trust these days—their own abilities.

While brands are making a comeback, they're doing so in a new marketplace, one in which consumers want to be in charge. Consumers are less distrustful, but *not* to the point of relinquishing control. *They want brands back in their lives, but only to facilitate.* While trust is opening up, suspension of disbelief is not.

Consumers are making sure that they stay in charge. Brands are one of their tools for doing so. The new self-assertion, though, has to be balanced against other lifestyle objectives, like simplified decision-making and less shopping involvement. Generational factors influence how this balance is being struck.

A ROLE FOR BRANDS

Brands enhance a consumer's personal image by signaling status, exclusivity, or cachet to others. Younger consumers have always been keener on this aspect, but lately even this has weakened.

CHART 12.1: WHAT WE BOUGHT, WHERE WE WENT

MATURES	BOOMERS	Xers
Converse	Adidas	Nike
Wayfarer	Vuarnet	Oakley
Coney Island	Disneyland	Disney World
Woolworth's	Wal-Mart	Sam's
Dior	Calvin Klein	Donna Karan
Shopping day	Shopping malls	Internet shopping malls

Xers continue to be the standard-bearers of brand as image. Over half agree that the "brands you buy tell a lot about the type of person you are." Similarly, half of all Xers say they like "to buy brands that make [them] feel like [they've] made it," compared with 30 percent or so of Boomers and Matures. For all generations, though, Xers included, these attitudes have become less common in the last several years.

Xers still use brands to connect with their friends. They are nearly twice as likely as Boomers and Matures to report that they buy the same brands as their peers, and that attitude grows among Xers even while it declines among Boomers and Matures. The importance of enclaving to Xers will make this a continuing role for the brands they prefer.

Brands also offer convenience. It's a decision shortcut. Find your favorite—grab it and go. In a time of overload and stress, this is an important role for brands, and one that is distinctive for Boomers.

"Quick and easy," "near where I live and work," "convenient hours," "reasonable prices most of the time," "no pressure to buy"—Boomers are the most likely of any of the three generations to say these are important factors when deciding where to shop. Efficiency is their focus.

Indeed, for marketers the next big opportunity in convenience is to move beyond "expedited" shopping to "customized shopping." What's convenient is something "just for me," not something that's merely speedier. No matter how fast it comes, it's not completely convenient if it doesn't fit just right. This will suit Boomers particularly well, given the value they place on self and personalization.

Convenience also means being worry-free. During the turmoil of the late eighties and early nineties, consumers in the marketplace were overloaded with worries, yet unable to find brands in which they had sufficient confidence to rely on as decision shortcuts.

Marketers who knew how to provide this confidence had a heyday during this period. For example, Circuit City, a consumers electronics chain, built a retail brand on the assurance that, no matter what, they would stand behind everything they sold. You could buy at Circuit City with complete confidence—no fine print, no-hassle returns, extended warranty coverage, thoroughly trained salespeople. This meant no worry, no stress. And Circuit City doesn't sell any brands of its own, just those of other companies—which Circuit City stands behind. In fact, it's this experience that Circuit City has used to enter the used car business. Its knowledge of how to train the people and put the systems in place has been crucial to the start-up of Carmax, its new retail venture in used cars.

This kind of reassurance is important to all generations, but particularly to Matures. Relying upon a brand to take the risks out of shopping is something that Matures frequently mention in our MONITOR research. Matures have a strong affinity for brands to start with, and they continue to want brands that can be reliable authorities for them in the marketplace.

A NEW ROLE FOR BRANDS

Four basic value-agendas have come and gone over the last fifty years. A fifth agenda, now emerging, will generate yet another shift in the overall consumer climate. Xers have moved away from what they perceive as Boomer overindulgence and self-righteousness. This, combined with the strong desires of Boomers and Matures to leave behind the pervasive anxiety they've created for themselves, has crystallized a new set of social values.

The Possibility Agenda, as we refer to this new, emerging value-agenda, is supplanting the denial and anger of recent years. It will create big new opportunities for brands. Recapturing the future is replacing mere survival. Reasonable expectations are replacing having it all. Strategic control is replacing strategic shopping as a style of marketplace participation. Consumers want straight-shooting out of marketers and are willing to invest trust in those marketers who offer a fair deal.

Brands are the vehicle to reach this future. In just the last few years there has been a dramatic drop in the percentage of consumers agreeing that "it is risky to buy a brand you are not familiar with." This is an important MONITOR measure because in choosing *not* to agree with this idea, consumers are explicitly *rejecting* denial in order to embrace possibility. And doing so in the context of brands.

The marketers of Miller beer suspected this, and found it confirmed in MONITOR. Their current campaign is all about possibility and the use of brands to capture it. "Reach for what's out there," say the TV ads. The ads show consumers of all ages in bright, positive settings, enjoying novel experiences. It's all about brands, the Miller brand specifically, facilitating self-reliance through a commitment to reciprocity.

Coca-Cola knows about this, too. In an *Adweek* profile, Coke's powerhouse global marketing director, Sergio Zyman, was explicit about opening up the Coke brand to consumers. No longer does Coca-Cola have just one ad campaign; it has twenty . . . or more! The company has moved away from forcing consumers to relate to it in just one way through a single ad campaign. Now Coca-Cola offers many different ways for consumers to relate to it. Consumers can pick the one that works best for what they want.

Like Prudential, like Saab, like Reebok, like Miller, Coke wants to facilitate whatever consumers decide for themselves. This is the essence of reciprocity, and a key element in the emerging value-agenda of possibility.

All generations share this desire to seek new possibilities. Under the Possibility Agenda, consumers will increasingly reject sticking with the same old thing. As they search for new solutions for living, they will naturally explore new brands. Xers will want enclave identification that reflects hope and opportunity. Boomers will want decision simplification tied to more reasonable definitions of winning and achieving fulfillment. Matures will want risk reduction that can give them back the chance to get out again, to stop being shut out of activities because of worry over safety.

A good example of a brand demonstrating its fit with customer life experiences was the series of TV ads IBM ran under the slogan, "Solutions for a small planet." Every ad presented a story about how IBM products helped people in their lives. Narratives were set all over the world—in an African village, in a French vineyard, in an Italian piazza, onstage with French runway models, backstage with Japanese actresses. Scenes showed ordinary conversations, often in languages other than English, and reminded viewers that no matter what their needs, IBM could provide solutions. Reciprocity lay beneath the message of these ads.

American Express did the same thing in ads with Jerry Seinfeld, connecting its brand to every possible lifestyle need or crisis. Jerry successfully solved his urgent, immediate, and unexpected problems by using his American Express card. The remedy is the brand. It's there to facilitate whatever is needed, whenever and wherever it's needed.

BRANDS ARE BACK

Consumers of all generations have always been loyal to a brand when they find one that really works. The vast majority, over 70 percent, have said year after year in our MONITOR research that once they find a brand they like, "it is difficult to get [them] to change." The problem, of course, is finding one to like. The opportunity has recently emerged for marketers to offer consumers brands they will like well enough to be loyal to.

Just a few years back it seemed that, at long last, brands had finally been crumpled by price. Marlboro Friday, that infamous day in April 1993 when Philip Morris cut the price of the number-one cigarette brand—many say the number-one brand of any sort—by forty cents a pack, was heralded as the coup de grâce for brand name products. This has continued most recently in breakfast cereals, with both Kellogg and Post advertising across-the-board price reductions. But the death knell was prematurely rung for brands. This sort of devaluation has happened before, and it has nothing to do with the power and role of brands; it's more that, periodically, price paid and value received have to be reset. Headlines about these events don't reflect what we see in MONITOR—brands have resurged in the consumer marketplace.

Brands are back. Fifty-six percent of all consumers say they will decide to purchase something because it is "made by a company I trust"—up significantly from just 43 percent a couple of years ago.

As an influence on purchase decisions, brands now equal price. The cost-of-entry factors are basics like durability, reliability, and guarantees. But given some assurance about these, consumers then look for products that do the best job of delivering extras. Until now, the extras they looked for were largely related to price, but this is no longer the case. Price and brand are both cited by two-thirds of all consumers as a "strong" influence on purchase decision-making.

The generational change in sentiment about the importance of brands is noteworthy. Just a few years ago, only among Matures did a majority report "trusted brand name" as a "strong" influence on purchasing. Now the percentage is no different across generations. The traditional risk aversion of Matures is no longer the only driver of brand relevance. The experimentation of Xers and the efficiency of Boomers create powerful lifestyle opportunities for brands.

Don't forget about price, however. Consumers still believe that the real price of something is the deal price. Two decades of non-stop price dealing have taught consumers there's always a better price to be had—they just have to look around. Ninety percent of consumers today agree it's not necessary to pay full price because things can always be found at a discount or on sale. This, by the way, is a passion, not just a preference—71 percent say they *like* price wars.

While the value attached to brands has gone up in recent years, this expressed preference for price wars also has increased. When we look into our MONITOR data to better understand consumers who express a preference for price wars, we see they tend to be less satisfied with the quality of brands across nearly every category, and more likely to say they are looking for something new. In other words, consumers who focus on the cheapest products are *not* the happiest consumers. It is crucial to see that a low price does not automatically create a good, satisfying value. Indeed, the failure to invest in brand building creates consumer dissatisfaction, which puts even more pressure on reducing prices, which further exacerbates dissatisfaction. Marketers with the right kinds of brands will have a fresh shot in the era of possibility, offering benefits that break the perceptions of parity that allow price to drive consumer decision-making.

THE EXPERIENCE AS MUCH AS ANYTHING ELSE

For consumers it's not only about getting what you want, it's also about the getting of what you want. A good brand is both a good product to have and a good experience to get.

Consider a couple of examples. Saturn is a good car because it's a good product at a good price and because buying it is a satisfying experience. McDonald's is a good restaurant because it has good food at a fair price and because it offers a satisfying experience. Saturn and McDonald's have made the whole experience easier—by keeping car buying from being another source of stress; by locating outlets in places where you might get hungry, like superstores, hospitals, or airports. The lifestyle fit is key.

For brands this means widening the focus from the product itself to all aspects of getting and using it. This is how consumers will approach shopping in the future. Brands will have to fit wherever and whenever consumers need them. Reciprocity will force brands to think in terms of life values, not simply product values, to be facilitators for what consumers want to do and how consumers want to live.

- Cooperative branding will be important. This is more than just co-branding, which simply links two brands together. Cooperative branding means helping brands other than your own succeed because doing so is what consumers need: credit card brands recommending retail outlets or vacation resorts; mall anchor stores helping customers by sending them to other stores in the mall (thus encouraging people to come back); beverage brands and salty snack brands cross-selling one another; kids' toy brands and family restaurants recognizing that both celebrate, entertain, and care for children. Consumers want brands to help them with their lifestyles, not just with their shopping.

- Retail convenience will supplement retail service to provide fully the simplification consumers want. Brands that create greater convenience in packaging, promotion, or cooperative efforts with retailers will be more satisfying to buy. Variety packs of related products are a good example. They put together everything needed for a meal or a football game get-together in a single package. Consumers can take all of it as a single item to an express checkout aisle.

- Don't forget about retail service. Over 60 percent of consumers in each generation agree that "most of the time, service people [they] deal with for the products and services [they] buy don't care much about [their] needs." Even though nine out of ten consumers believe that the prices they pay entitle them to the highest level of service, half or more of every generation still would be willing to pay at least 10 percent more with a guarantee of better service. Marketers could take a portion of this and pay to have their own representatives on the floor at retail locations to provide better service. Of course, not every sale requires a high level of service, so offering varied levels of service, priced accordingly, will be the best sort of facilitation in a marketplace driven by reciprocity.

- Handling dissatisfactions after the fact is an equally important part of marketing. Half of all consumers feel it's a "waste of time" to complain about something that has made them unhappy. This is an area where brands have even better opportunities to complement what happens at the retail level.

In terms of generational priorities, we see two things. First, focus on elements at-the-sale for Boomers and Matures. They see shopping as such an unpleasant experience that they try to get in and out as quickly as they can. Second, focus on the elements after-the-sale for Xers. They are the most likely to feel that nothing can be done if they have a problem or a complaint.

IT ALL DEPENDS

Much of the experience consumers have with a brand is situational. Our CEO, John Struck, introduces this concept to many of our clients by recalling the blizzardy winter's eve several years ago when he suddenly remembered it was his anniversary and he was headed home without a gift. "As I went careening around the miserably slick streets of Greenwich, Connecticut, that night at about eight o'clock," John narrates, "I didn't care what I had to pay just as long as I went through my front door, gift in hand."

The point is simple. Depending on the situation, the value associated with a brand will vary. In some buying and retail situations, brands are worth more or worth less to consumers. Those products able to facilitate what consumers need will take account of shifting equations. A savvy marketer will charge less when that's the situationally appropriate thing to do.

We've looked at this phenomenon in work we completed in partnership with MasterCard. We examined which sort of retail outlet consumers would choose, depending on the amount of money they had to spend, the amount of knowledge they had about a product category, who the purchase was for, and whether the purpose of the trip was to browse or to buy. The retail outlets consumers chose in these situations varied quite a bit. The implications of this research are that the very same brand looks different at Home Depot or True Value, Marshalls or Nordstrom. Brands have to be flexible and accommodating if they are going to facilitate what consumers are looking for in different situations.

Sometimes consumers want sales advice; other times, just

stock to sort through. In some situations, consumers want pretty packaging; in others, a pretty cheap price. In some situations, consumers want a specific item; in others, lots of items to choose from. Different generations will approach each of these situations differently. Indeed, generation itself is one of the factors that sets the price a brand can command in a given transaction.

RECIPROCITY FOR REAL

It's easy to give lip service to something like reciprocity. But consumers will catch on if you don't really mean it. This is a potential problem for database and direct marketers for whom talk of building relationships is a standard part of the pitch. For instance, some pretend to learn more about customers to build long-term relationships, while they are actually isolating opportunities to sell them just as much as possible in the short-term. This is not reciprocity for real.

In the long run, customers always figure these things out. For the past few decades consumers have been on the defensive so much they've become cynical and distrustful. It's not customization if the approach leaves consumers feeling they're the targets of exploitation. Failing to be authentic in our dealings with consumers will only hurt our brands.

Consumers know almost every marketing ploy. They hang up in increasing numbers on telemarketers. They register with the Post Office to prevent the delivery of direct mail. They've learned not to shop for groceries on an empty stomach; to bring a list to avoid impulse buying while standing in line at checkout; that the bread aromas and the glistening vegetables only stimulate a biological reaction. They've heard "guarantee" so much that the only thing MCI could do was to turn up the volume and holler, "Proof Positive!" We may still defeat consumers at these games, but because we make it into a competition, that's how they wind up relating to our brands.

The Possibility Agenda is about partnership and fellow feeling.

Consumers know we want to sell them something, but they say, if you want to do that, you'd better bring it to me on my terms because I will not pay attention to you otherwise. In a media- and marketing-saturated society, brands must ask permission and then act like guests if they get invited in.

It is true, too, that consumers want simplification. In the rush to empower consumers, we must not overlook the fact that simplification is sought *as much if not more* than self-empowerment and interactive control. Pushing an overwhelming array of options in front of consumers will shut them down just as much as offering them no choices at all. The key is to empower and simplify at the same time—*to use the dialogue and customization afforded by reciprocity to better match the offerings of marketers to the needs and desires of consumers*. The perspective of generational marketing, as we have seen, provides the key bit of marketing knowledge that it takes to do that.

13

BRINGING GENERATIONS
TO A CLOSE

Is it really this simple? Plot the age, find the markers, then make a beeline for customers with just the right song and dance. Well, yes and no.

It's often this simple because that's a big portion of how we live our lives, as part of our generation. But sometimes it's not this simple because we live our lives as part of many other things too. What we hope we've demonstrated is the value of thinking generationally to understand what's happening in your business.

Other things beside generation certainly make a difference, but we have seen over the years that even when generational influences play a secondary role, they should be taken into account. For instance, marketers of products and services with unique appeal to certain ethnic groups can also find value in generational marketing. Every two years we conduct a special MONITOR study among

African American consumers to track their changing values and attitudes. We see the same generational patterns here, too: Older consumers putting in blood, sweat, and tears to create a better opportunity for their Boomer-age children. These Boomers developing high expectations based upon these new opportunities and the strong economy, but eventually experiencing disappointment. The next generation coming of age amidst breakdown and uncertainty, and responding with a more pragmatic sense of opportunity. In every case these generational experiences have created enduring values and motivations. These experiences, of course, are all very much linked to the complex issues of civil rights, urban reform, and prejudice. But for the consumer marketplace that we study, the impact of different generational formative experiences on generationally unique buying motivations is similar.

Generational factors provide us with a framework for understanding the marketplace. In many cases they explain it all. In others they're only the start. For any particular business or brand, you need a more in-depth look at generations. Transitional groups like Silents or Trailing Boomers, responding to particular symbols or product offerings, sometimes exhibit unique motivations tied more closely to their particular position within the experiences of their generation as a whole. Or symbols and products may sift out within a generation a subgroup with an especially high interest in what's being offered. We saw this happen with cyberspace and Matures.

Discussions of generations in the popular press sometimes sound like alphabet soup—every writer has another way to name them. Furthermore, the reasons for generational groupings often aren't defined well and the resulting generational analyses are based on shaky comparisons. Over the years, we have seen empirically in MONITOR data that our use of the broad groupings—Matures, Boomers, and Xers—consistently provides the most accurate view of developing trends, and the pictures we get of consumers best explain ongoing events in the marketplace. On the other hand, the assignments we take on for clients address specific issues, so we may utilize a more customized look at generations.

With all this in mind, readers should use this book as a framework. This book provides a foundation you can start with and then add to in your efforts to close a sale with a generation for your products or services.

THE NEXT FACE OF GENERATIONS

Duty, individuality, and diversity. These fundamental values define the marketplace perspectives of America's three consumer generations, respectively. And each of these core values unifies a generation, not because consumers of that age are simply resigned to being stuck in a certain generation. They actually prefer them.

In MONITOR-related research, we have asked about the post–World War II decade most preferred by each generation. As it turns out, the decade each cohort most prefers is one that was largely reflective of their fundamental values. The biggest number of Matures prefer the forties and fifties, while for the bulk of Boomers it's the sixties and seventies. The majority of Xers prefer the eighties and nineties. Indeed, the single most preferred decade for Matures is the fifties; for Boomers, the seventies; and for Xers, the nineties.

Change in the marketplace, though, is its one constant feature. This may sound trite, but marketers often forget this simple truth. An item that recently appeared on the news reminded us again of the constancy of change. The report noted that in 1966 the Century Plaza in Los Angeles was the first hotel to offer a color TV in every room. But on the day of that report in 1996, the Century Plaza became the first hotel to provide interactive TV service with access to all commercial on-line services. These technologies are second nature to Xers, but more like a second language to Matures, with Boomers somewhere in between. How will each generation move forward to deal with these changed realities? With their core values, of course, but perhaps by putting a new face on those values in the process. From color TV to interactive TV—it's these future faces that interest us most as marketers.

While we must look back to understand generations, we must look forward to build our businesses in the marketplace. The ways we've seen consumers express their values in the past help us understand what those values *are*, but not the exact ways in which those values will be *expressed* tomorrow. For that, we must apply what we've learned.

The Boomer focus on self and individuality, for example, is a core generational value. But this value has manifested itself in various ways—as hippie, yuppie, and victim. Where it goes next is a key question. We see two potential new faces, neither of which is mutually exclusive.

First, as celebrity. Desktop tools and networks now make it possible for individuals to be their own publicity agents. I can have my very own show with a personal web page or a regular magazine feature in the private newsletter I send to my family and friends. Brands are likely to find they are making pitches to prospect groups filled with self-styled stars. The focus on and celebration of the self will shift from power to renown.

Second, as recluse. Boomers will realize the value of being reclusive, saying to themselves, "The more I give away or let get away, the less special I am." Keeping control over private information will become a way of sustaining the value and position of the self. While they won't completely withdraw their private selves from public or business access, they will make the information available only for a hefty fee. This will change fundamentally the economics of marketing to them.

Both of these Boomer trends portend the rise of *exclusivity* as a key element of status. If money can't buy status anymore and if intangibles can't be shown off, exclusivity combines the best of both. It's nonmaterial and it can signal others. Membership exclusivity zeroes in on the special importance of self.

The Mature focus on duty manifested itself as GI, organization man, and warm-weather retiree. The biggest change we foresee

CHART 13.1: REMEMBER WHEN

MATURES	BOOMERS	Xers
Air raids	Panty raids	Fear of AIDS
Packing the court	*Divorce Court*	*People's Court*
R.F.D.	Suburbs	Exurbs
Yellow brick road	*A Clockwork Orange*	Blue M&M's
Marx Brothers	Smothers Brothers	Menendez brothers
Hobos	Hitchhikers	Homeless
The Grapes of Wrath	Strawberry Fields	Smashing Pumpkins

among Matures is the closing of the circle that has guided their sacrifice and saving. The need to put away for the future is giving way to the recognition that the future is now. The time has come to enjoy the rewards of their hard work. The sacrificing for others, their Boomer children in particular, will be moderated some—although not completely—by an indulgence of themselves.

Xer diversity has yet to show its true face in the marketplace. A number of tentative appearances have captured the attention of the media, but with little lasting value or truth for marketers. This cohort will prove to be the most resistant to marketing stereotypes. We believe Xers will not respond to images formed for them, but will wholeheartedly respond to images they form for themselves. Eclectic images, the hip, the offbeat, that they can reinterpret and recombine, will appeal more than images that attempt to place or define them.

DON'T THINK BY ANALOGY—THINK METAPHORICALLY

We have mentioned this in conjunction with Boomers already, but it is a relevant point for Xers and Matures too. We've cautioned that just because Matures behaved a certain way at age fifty doesn't mean that, by analogy, Boomers will do the same things. Instead, as we've illustrated, Boomers apply their own way of thinking to a new situation, and develop new defining images or metaphors.

Boomers will continue to reject traditional institutions and patterns, usually defined as anything Matures did. So when marketing to Boomers, reasoning by analogy will be, as it has been, dramatically wrong. Boomers will bring the art of spending and consuming to their older years. They will bring more education, and hence more buying sophistication. They will want to be in control, not part of a herd.

Xers will bring a new sense of fun and disbelief to their middle age. They will be much more open to alternative lifestyles. They will tie their lives together around new traditions and networks of friends. They will resist traditional media and sales pitches. Marketers will have to invent completely new ways of establishing brand connections.

Matures will relax and open up a bit in their older years. They have shown a willingness over the years to pick up new attitudes and new styles from Boomers, particularly those that did not present a direct challenge to their basic values. Given the right kind of opportunity, they will continue to do so.

GENERATIONAL ANTAGONISM

Generations have always had disagreements with one another. These conflicts will turn even more strident in the near future, however, as economic issues become their central focus.

The financial squeeze faced by any one generation becomes a burden shared by all. But when all generations face these pressures simultaneously, the potential for discord rises dramatically. Boomers are the source of a lot of this today. Newspapers love to report stories about thirty- and forty-something-year-olds still bumming money from their sixty- and seventy-something parents. And not for essentials. For luxuries that Boomers have come to expect as part of their entitlements: Bigger houses. Wide-screen TVs. New luxury cars. New furniture. The *Wall Street Journal* reported this phenomenon, noting that some economists estimate that money from living parents accounts for about 10 percent of all Boomer wealth. The same article cited the calculations of Boston College economist Donald Cox, showing a tripling of wealth transfers to adult children over the last thirty-five years. Boomers still want. And Matures still sacrifice.

Parents expect a quid pro quo. They want help and support in return for their cash, and their children stay conflicted and tied up by their continuing dependence on their parents' purse strings. Boomers do meet their basic obligations themselves—house payment, car payments, kids' college, household goods and food—but many depend on their parents for the extras. Many Matures give up for themselves some of the very luxuries they give to their Boomer children.

Boomers and Xers have a different set of financial antagonisms. Boomers rode the wave of skyrocketing housing prices and educational costs. Xers are now finding these to be significant hurdles, and they face them without the economic prospects that kept Boomers afloat. Of course, Boomers didn't wind up on easy street. Declining real wages and economic recessions have also hurt their position. As Boomers begin to wake up to these realities, they will start looking around for help. At that point, Xers should beware.

Xers, though, will resist, if for no other reason than they will be unable to handle the needs of aging Boomers. These coming obligations portend a huge burden. In a recent analysis of this problem, *The New York Times* reported some disturbing figures. Between 1990 and 2030, estimates are that the number of Americans over the age of sixty-five will double. At that point, 2.8 million people will be working to provide what's needed to support them, compared with 4.8 million today.

Boomers who continue to work past retirement will compete with Xers—for the same jobs within companies or for the same customers in the marketplace. Thus, the double whammy coming for Xers is the demand for their support combined with competition for the means they will have to provide it, by the very people asking for the support. Of course, Boomers, just like Matures today, may feel Xers owe them something in return for all the extra years they stayed at home or got an allowance.

We see early signs of this in our MONITOR data. For example, we ask respondents whether they feel older workers are more productive than younger workers "because they more than make up in experience what they lack in energy." Sixty-three percent of Xers agree, but it's disturbing that virtually every Mature—92 percent— and 78 percent of Boomers agree with this. These differences in the perspectives of various age groups will remain as Boomers get older. This isn't much of a problem when Xers can still get what they want notwithstanding competition for jobs with older workers. But the marketplace of the future isn't likely to be that generous, so these built-in differences of opinion could become an increasingly sore point.

Two aspects of this potential conflict directly concern marketers. The first is to make sure brands do not become the rallying symbol for a generation, expressive of their frustrations with and complaints about other generations. It's not just the problem of being associated with the wrong crowd. BMWs were known as Boomer-mobiles, but Xers have done little else than make disparaging remarks about them. On the other hand, activist protests against furs and other animal products have forced some marketers out of business.

The focus of these kinds of consumer protests shifts over time. For many years Boomers concentrated their attacks on environmentally unfriendly products. Now most marketers include some kind of "green" piece in their product design. The marketplace was changed by these efforts—efforts driven by a generation and its new values. Don't think that Xers won't have this effect, too, around some new issue like generational inequities. With only aesthetic provocation, they took to scratching "Eat something" on ads featuring the superthin supermodel Kate Moss. Boomers never did that to pictures of Twiggy. The flash point of the future may well be the coming economic conflicts among generational groups.

Second, look for product opportunities within these conflicts. For example, automobile manufacturers see Trailing Boomers and lead Xers facing increasing difficulties in the new-car market. While most Boomers entered the market as first-time buyers when prices were relatively low, cars in that price category are harder to come by today. Designing low-priced cars with just the right features and style will require sensitivity to generational issues.

Trailing Boomers will look at such cars differently than Xers. And both will want something that positions them properly with respect to their own and to other generations. Trailing Boomers will want a closer Boomer fit; Xers will want none of it. Both will look for something with a new face, a new look, and a new affordability.

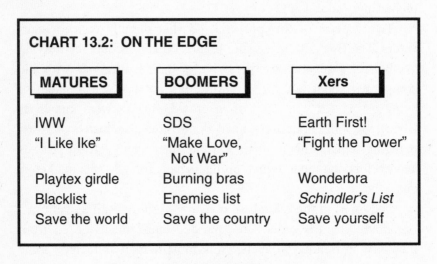

CHART 13.2: ON THE EDGE

MATURES	BOOMERS	Xers
IWW	SDS	Earth First!
"I Like Ike"	"Make Love, Not War"	"Fight the Power"
Playtex girdle	Burning bras	Wonderbra
Blacklist	Enemies list	*Schindler's List*
Save the world	Save the country	Save yourself

GOOD-LOOKING

At the end of World War II, Christian Dior pronounced the end of the era of occupation, rationing, and frugality with the New Look: Ultra-feminine. Extravagant. Romantic. Tight-waisted. Full-skirted.

Strapless. Gloves. Groomed and sophisticated. Young women looked, well, mature.

We are on the verge of another fundamental transformation in the definition of beauty, but one that will occur with much less fanfare. It is driven by two generational factors: One, the aging of Boomers who continue to believe they are the "beautiful people"; two, the emergence of Xers much more influenced by a diversity of cultural factors. We'll see this new standard in several specific ways.

- Age will be beautiful. Youth will be celebrated less as the acme of beauty. This, of course, has been predicted before. But never before have Boomers been older instead of younger. And never before have younger people rejected a celebration of beauty in favor of the stark, ragged extremes of thinness, grunge, piercings, and body art.

- Comfort will be beautiful. Consumers of all ages increasingly reject the trade-offs to achieve beauty. If it takes a lot of work to achieve it, consumers don't want it. Just over the last decade, we have tracked a dramatic turnaround in the attitudes of women about what they are willing to do to measure up to contemporary fashion. Far fewer are willing to do "whatever [they] can to make [themselves] look more attractive." Far fewer want to "add [their] own touch to many of the things [they] buy." Far fewer feel the need to buy "products that express [their] own style and personality." Far fewer, in fact, express any interest in "keep[ing] up with new styles." Women especially, but men too, are more interested in feeling good than looking good.

- Beauty will be polychromatic. The marketplace has moved away from uniformity. No one style rules. Fashions that fit many styles will be the market leaders, not the fashions that try to impose one look or style. Ethnic

styles will represent a new influence, both by themselves and in combinations with other ethnic styles.
Cross-gender styles will also be a big factor, as will
revival of old styles done up in new ways.

The Calvin Klein ads for the CK One fragrance show all these
principles at work. The ads appear in magazines and on billboards,
showing a line of couples all engaged to varying degrees in comfortable, erotic embrace. They show off new elements: Boots.
Piercings. Tatoos. Bare chests. Torn clothes. Jeans. Street wear.
Mixed racial and ethnic couples. All standing. And all worked up
for a fragrance that's androgynous—"for a man or a woman." This
ad campaign taps into all the new aspects of beauty. The ad isn't a
model for every product, but it does show one way of connecting
with emerging perceptions of beauty.

CUTTING ACROSS GENERATIONS

Generational extensions are a good way to revitalize brands.
Marketers often search their existing markets in vain for ways to
jump-start demand, overlooking opportunities from outside the
generational skew of their current customer base.

Cross-generational connections go on all the time. For example, the heroes of one generation often come from the previous
generation. Matures got leadership and guidance from FDR and
Eisenhower. Boomers from Timothy Leary and Eugene McCarthy.
Xers from Bill Gates and Steve Jobs. Ways of speaking across generations are not uncommon.

Indeed, for a brand to survive over time, it must find ways of
introducing itself to new customers as they come along. And it's
not just communications that must change, but the basic value
offered by the brand itself. A straightforward five-step process can
help you outline potential directions for your business:

First, write down the core value that you believe your product
or service satisfies. Second, write down the generation whose

```
┌─────────────────────────────────────────────────────────────┐
│  CHART 13.3:  ICONS OF THE TIMES                              │
│                                                               │
│  ┌──────────────┐   ┌──────────────┐   ┌──────────────┐       │
│  │ MATURES    ▎ │   │ BOOMERS    ▎ │   │    Xers    ▎ │       │
│  └──────────────┘   └──────────────┘   └──────────────┘       │
│                                                               │
│  Ted Williams       Ted Kennedy        Ted Bundy              │
│  Frank Sinatra      The Beatles        REM                    │
│  Joe DiMaggio       Joe Namath         Michael Jordan         │
│  Hitchcock          De Palma           Tarantino              │
│  Tom Harmon         Tom Hayden         Tom Hanks              │
└─────────────────────────────────────────────────────────────┘
```

cohort experiences make this value most relevant. Third, do some primary research to see if the actual makeup of your customer base corresponds to this. If not, your product or service is probably satisfying some other core value, one relevant to the cohort experiences of the dominant generation in your customer base. You may need a little more primary research at this point to determine the dominant generation and values to which your product appeals.

Fourth, once you've gotten this figured out, write down other values your product or service can satisfy—not just those consistent with the core value, but values that reinforce it. As you extend to other generations, you want your current customers to think even more highly of your brand, not just tolerate what you're doing in the marketplace. If you focus on different values that are reinforcing, you'll do this.

Fifth, go after the generation with the reinforcing values that make it most receptive to what you currently deliver and satisfy. Try to stick to one generation at a time as you extend. There's less chance of confusion. And don't ignore other important factors; use generational analysis as just one of many criteria. To do this right, you'll need some more primary research, but having done all this other analysis first, you'll have a good starting point. From this point, you'll find that your investment in additional quantitative information will pay off.

You can't always have a brand with cross-generational appeal. But even maximizing the appeal a brand has with a single generation requires a cross-generational perspective on the marketplace. Smart marketers know as much about why they don't succeed with some customers as why they do succeed with others.

MONITOR-ING THE FUTURE

As we wrap up this book we think about the future. Generational changes have wrought much, and marketers on top of new developments have profited from them. But to keep ahead, the next success has to unfold just as the last success is being enjoyed.

This has been our philosophy from the start. It was perhaps best reiterated by Florence Skelly herself in a conversation she had with Richard M. Clarke, the chairman of Yankelovich Partners, on the occasion of the twenty-fifth anniversary of MONITOR: "MONITOR is not a closed-end system. We started out with thirty-five trends; some were later dropped and added. I think new batteries of questions should always be added. Remember when business was seen as the universal villain in the seventies? Now it is seen as the great hero. But this won't last forever. You have to be looking to see if you are measuring all the new things."

This is the continuing philosophy behind MONITOR and our study of generations. What we know about generations today is valuable, but it's what we know about generations tomorrow that's truly profitable. And that, as we know, is the ultimate worth of generational marketing.

We've learned that if you don't keep changing, you can't keep up. Remember the Playtex girdle? That was all about Matures who hadn't kept up with the marketplace changes coming from the new generation of Boomers. Now, though, the tables are turned. And we'd better not fool ourselves into thinking otherwise.

We were recently at a top ad agency telling that tale to illustrate the importance of understanding generations. It's a story we tell a lot to get the ball rolling on some of our generational consulting assignments. We finished the story, and as always, asked for questions before moving on.

A young AE in the back raised her hand. "What," she earnestly inquired, "is a girdle?" At which point, all of her other young colleagues in the room murmured in assent. They wanted to know, too.

We'd just spent the first ten minutes of the meeting telling a story that well over half the room—including at least one key person on every account of that agency—didn't understand. As Boomers, we'd figured everybody would enjoy the Playtex story as an inside joke on their parents and grandparents. Instead, the joke was on us.

Ann quickly recovered, though. "It's what Madonna wears for shorts," she said.

You could see the recognition register on their faces. Now, at least, they knew our term for it. But we were never quite sure if they'd gotten the punch line about Playtex.

Learn all you can about the generational experiences of your customers. Because you can't "rock the ages" with your marketing until you do.

INDEX